W0035947

BUSINESS INTERESTS
AND THE
ENVIRONMENTAL CRISIS

Thank you for choosing a SAGE product!
If you have any comment, observation or feedback,
I would like to personally hear from you.
Please write to me at **contactceo@sagepub.in**

Vivek Mehra, Managing Director and CEO, SAGE India.

Bulk Sales

SAGE India offers special discounts
for purchase of books in bulk.
We also make available special imprints
and excerpts from our books on demand.

For orders and enquiries, write to us at

Marketing Department
SAGE Publications India Pvt Ltd
B1/I-1, Mohan Cooperative Industrial Area
Mathura Road, Post Bag 7
New Delhi 110044, India

E-mail us at **marketing@sagepub.in**

Get to know more about SAGE

Be invited to SAGE events, get on our mailing list.
Write today to **marketing@sagepub.in**

This book is also available as an e-book.

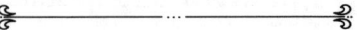

Business Interests
and the
Environmental Crisis

Edited by
Kanchi Kohli
Manju Menon

SAGE www.sagepublishing.com
Los Angeles | London | New Delhi | Singapore | Washington DC | Melbourne

Copyright © Kanchi Kohli and Manju Menon, 2016

All rights reserved. No part of this book may be reproduced or utilized in any form or by any means, electronic or mechanical, including photocopying, recording or by any information storage or retrieval system, without permission in writing from the publisher.

First published in 2016 by

 SAGE Publications India Pvt Ltd
B1/I-1 Mohan Cooperative Industrial Area
Mathura Road, New Delhi 110 044, India
www.sagepub.in

SAGE Publications Inc
2455 Teller Road
Thousand Oaks, California 91320, USA

SAGE Publications Ltd
1 Oliver's Yard, 55 City Road
London EC1Y 1SP, United Kingdom

SAGE Publications Asia-Pacific Pte Ltd
3 Church Street
#10-04 Samsung Hub
Singapore 049483

Published by Vivek Mehra for SAGE Publications India Pvt Ltd, typeset in Minion Pro 10/12.5 pt by Zaza Eunice, Hosur, Tamil Nadu, India and printed at Chaman Enterprises, New Delhi.

Library of Congress Cataloging-in-Publication Data

Names: Kohli, Kanchi, editor. | Menon, Manju, editor.
Title: Business interests and the environmental crisis/edited by Kanchi Kohli and Manju Menon.
Description: New Delhi, India; Thousand Oaks, California : SAGE, 2016. | Includes index.
Identifiers: LCCN 2015049014| ISBN 9789351508601 (hardback : alk. paper) | ISBN 9789351508595 (epub : alk. paper) | ISBN 9789351508618 (ebook)
Subjects: LCSH: Sustainable development. | Environmental policy–Economic aspects.
Classification: LCC HD75.6 .B8785 2016 | DDC 338.9/27–dc23 LC record available at http://lccn.loc.gov/2015049014

ISBN: 978-93-515-0860-1 (HB)

The SAGE Team: N. Unni Nair, Alekha Chandra Jena, Shobana Paul and Rajinder Kaur

Contents

List of Abbreviations

ABS	access and benefit-sharing
ARIPO	Africa Regional Intellectual Property Organization
BEF	biodiversity and ecosystem function
BIO	Biotechnology Industry Organization
BMCs	Biodiversity Management Committees
BS	benefit-sharing
BTA	Bengal Tenancy Act
CAG	Comptroller and Auditor General
CBA	cost–benefit analysis
CBD	Convention on Biological Diversity
CCI	Cabinet Committee for Investment
CEA	Central Electricity Authority's
CDM	Clean Development Mechanism
CII	Confederation of Indian Industry
CHM	common heritage of mankind
COP	Conference of the Parties
CSIR	Council of Scientific and Industrial Research
DMIC	Delhi-Mumbai Industrial Corridor
EC	environment clearance
EIA	Environment Impact Assessment
FAC	Forest Advisory Committee
FCA	Forest Conservation Act
FD	Forest Department
FPIC	free prior and informed consent
FRA	Forest Rights Act
GATT	General Agreement on Tariffs and Trade
GBMR	genetic or biological material or resources
GEF	Global Environment Facility

GFC	Global Financial Crisis
GIM	Green India Mission
GIS	Geographical Information Systems
HPC	High Power Committee
ICBG	International Cooperative Biodiversity Groups
ICCAs	indigenous peoples and local communities
ILCs	indigenous and local communities
INC	Intergovernmental Negotiating Committee
IP	intellectual property
IPBES	Intergovernmental Platform on Biodiversity and Ecosystem Services
IPCC	Intergovernmental Panel on Climate Change
IPLCs	indigenous peoples and local communities
IPOs	Indigenous Peoples' Organizations
IPRs	Intellectual Property Rights
ISF	International Seed Federation
IWMI	International Water Management Institute
JBA	Japan Bioindustry Association
JNPT	Jawaharlal Nehru Port Trust
JFMCs	Joint Forest Management Committees
LCL	Lavasa Corporation Limited
LMOs	living modified organisms
LULUCF	Land Use, Land Use Change and Forestry
MDG	Millennium Development Goals
MAF	Million Acre Feet
MDO	mine developer-cum-operator
MEA	multilateral environmental agreement
METI	Ministry of Economy, Trade and Industry
MoEF	Ministry of Environment and Forest
MWRRA	Maharashtra Water Resources Regulatory Authority
NARS	National Agricultural Research System
NBA	National Biodiversity Authority
NCD	Natural Capital Declaration
NGT	National Green Tribunal
NIB	National Investment Board
NPV	Net Present Value
NWDA	National Water Development Agency
OAU	Organisation for African Unity

OSTP	Office of Science and Technology Policy
PES	payments for environmental services
R&D	research and development
RBPH	River Bed Power House
REDD	Reduction of Emissions from Deforestation and Degradation
SRD	Sabarmati Riverfront Development
SSD	Sardar Sarovar Dam
SRFDCL	Sabarmati Riverfront Development Corporation Ltd
TEEB	The Economics of Biodiversity and Ecosystem Services
TNC	The Nature Conservancy
TRIPS	Trade Related Aspects of Intellectual Property Rights
TVA	Tennessee Valley Authority
UBDC	Upper Bari Doab Canal
UNCED	UN Conference on Environment and Development
UNDRIP	UN Declaration on the Rights of Indigenous Peoples
UNEP	United Nations Environment Programme
UNFCCC	United Nations Framework Convention on Climate Change
USAID	United States Agency for International Development
USPTO	US Patent and Trademark Office
USTR	US Trade Representative
WIPO	World Intellectual Property Organization
WTO	World Trade Organization

Preface

This project of putting together a collection of essays on the regulation of nature as a resource has been close to our hearts for over 10 years. During this time, we have engaged with environmental policymaking efforts related to land, water, biodiversity, minerals, forests, and wildlife, sometimes as independent researchers or writers, as members of official committees and as campaigners and activists. However, what finally helped pin down this project were the events that followed the promulgation of the Forest Rights Act, 2006, as the first law in India to "distribute" or return rights over nature to those who had been historically denied legitimate access to their lands. As the process of clarifying this new law with rules and government circulars progressed and the legislation's entanglements with realpolitik came to the fore, we committed to this project.

This collection of essays is inspired by the work done by many scholars on understanding nature and nature–human interactions. It builds on their work by directing the spotlight to the locations and venues where policy discussions on nature are going on and the meanings of nature, its uses, and their costs are being determined. These essays help to understand that, even if nature is understood in diverse ways, the environmental policy meant to work at national and international levels subscribes to secular measurements and a mechanical understanding of nature. The book contains one introductory and eight thematic essays. It asks the question, if nature is no longer available as a limitless resource, how has the policy discourse on the environmental crisis come to view it, value it, and live with it? It introduces four distinct, yet integrated, processes, which define the current policy discourse and the business interest in the environmental crisis. This includes viewing nature as a commodity, introducing principles of valuation, defining clear property rights, and putting in place a regulatory framework that accommodates these principles.

The eight essays are organized into two separate sections. The first four talk about how the policy discourse on the environment creates a distinct form of knowledge about nature by introducing new terms, values, formats for exchange, and formulae. These are being used increasingly to account for the loss of nature and for offsetting this loss. The second set of essays deal with the politics of participation in this discourse. While critiquing such an approach of environmental problem-solving, practitioners look at mechanisms to democratize it for fair and equitable outcomes.

One of the key features of the edited volume is that the essays are written by practitioners in the field of environment, agriculture, and biodiversity. They are all people who are in the midst of policymaking and who can have a significant influence on how these are shaped. They bring to these essays their understanding of the problem of conservation in their fields through specific case studies or historical narratives, and analyze deeply the issues that confront them in their efforts toward conservation and securing biodiversity-based livelihoods. Some essays are ethnographic, in which the authors draw lessons from their ongoing participation in these policy processes and assess the outcomes of these processes so far. Though each of the essays attends to the environmental policy discourse within different sectors, they find comparable concepts and principles that form them. The essays are written in popular essay form and not as academic papers.

One anticipated point of criticism is that the book does not present any alternatives to environmental problems. While some authors critique the framework itself, others try to squeeze out what they believe could be just and equitable outcomes as an alternative to critique and nonpartici-pation. Another expected point of criticism is that nature has always been a commodity and so this work is merely a description of "what is." The writers of the essays would then point out that such an acknowledgment, that today environmental policy is regulating the use of commodities and not nature, is in itself a major epistemic breakthrough for future work on environmental policy.

This publication would not have been possible without the guidance of Shri Ramaswamy Iyer and Praful Bidwai. The project was incubated by the Heinrich Boell Foundation, India. We thank Dr Axel Harneit-Sievers and Sanjay Vashisht for the enthusiastic support and intellectual inputs throughout the project. We have learned immensely about the issues presented in this collection of essays from colleagues in various environmental and human rights organizations and movements that we have worked closely with. Our warmest regards to friends at Kalpavriksh, Namati, Campaign for Survival and Dignity, EIA Resource and Response Centre, Greenpeace, Natural Justice, Grain, Deccan Development Society, and Centre for International Forestry Research. Long discussions and questions posed by them have helped us frame the contours of this project. A special thanks to Heather Goodall, Kiran Asher, Rakesh Kalshian, Rachael Knight, and Vivek Maru for all the time they have spent with us over our emails, notes, and drafts. Most importantly, we express our gratitude to the authors of the essays. They worked with us through every step of the project, with patience. This project has given us an opportunity to get to know their work more closely, and for that we are very honored.

Many thanks to everyone at SAGE and the external reviewer whose comments and support have helped realize this publication. We hope it finds its place among the current debates on the financialization of nature.

Kanchi Kohli
Manju Menon

Introduction: Green and Pink

Kanchi Kohli and Manju Menon

The Business Interest in the Environmental Crisis

The 2014 Forest Asia Summit was held in Jakarta, Indonesia, in one of its tallest buildings, fully air-conditioned and with gigantic chandeliers from high ceilings that were lit up all day. Large ballrooms, decorated with a collection of the most colorful orchids, ferns, and synthetic billboards, were filled by over 2,000 development professionals, agricultural scientists, environment policymakers, natural resource accountants, climate change researchers, students, and philanthropists. They represented governments, political parties, NGOs and academic institutions, consultancy groups, and corporate giants.[1]

Speakers in the first plenary spoke of the decimation of the South East Asian forests due to large-scale land use change, especially by plantations and "misguided" community practices. They attributed the responsibility commonly to all humankind. The second plenary was on green growth in South East Asia, which would help "reduce the gap between the rich and the poor, as well as reduce ecological damage." The solutions that followed celebrated corporate investments for conservation and increasing consumption and prosperity in transition economies to resolve the ecological and food crisis. In the last two decades, these terms have become intimately linked.

The Forest Asia Summit is representative of many such events that have, over the years, acknowledged that we are in the midst or at the edge of a global environmental crisis. International campaigns and governmental accords have affirmed this (Secretariat of Convention on Biological Diversity, 2010; United Nations, 1992; The World Bank Group, 2012). There are few refuting it, which means that the crisis has acquired the power of a scientific fact rather than merely an informed opinion or a lived experience. Large businesses dealing with timber, minerals, pharma, and seeds are on the dock for overusing nature in the production of consumer goods. In 2007, WWF and Coca-Cola announced their partnership to help conserve the world's freshwater resources to offset the water extraction by its manufacturing plants. In 2012, this was expanded as a "Water+" commitment to also protect 11 freshwater basins around the world (Journey Staff, 2012). In the face of visible degradation of habitats that have been at the center-stage of protests, these businesses and governments have had to respond.

The environmental crisis also affects private profits directly. Economic liberalization in many parts of the world allowed private players to enter into sectors that were held exclusively by the state. Several laws on mining, electricity production, and others have been amended to accommodate private corporations in these sectors. Now, their investments dominate these production sectors, either by full ownership of production units or by joint venture policies (Das, 2014; Government of Gujarat, 1997; IUCN, 2012). As a result, they are pushed to respond to the escalating situation that if degradation continues there may be no resources for them to use in their processes. The Confederation of Indian Industry (CII) maintains on its website that business can no longer be pursued as per Milton Friedman's advice "that there is only one responsibility of business: to use its resources and engage in activities designed to increase its profits."[2] They acknowledge that without a green face, both their credibility and profits are at stake (Rio Tinto, 2013; Tata Steel, 2012). They need to chase the "triple bottom line" which includes social and environmental performance along with profits. Solutions are desperately needed and corporations are looking for them.

Several large corporations have been persuaded by their own business prospects and by international organizations that conservation makes economic sense in the long run. International conventions and global congregations on environment, biodiversity, and climate change are setting up formal dialogues between polarized entities such as affected parties and private corporations. Mediating this relationship is a whole host of actors that include scientists, policymakers, economists, legal experts, NGOs, environmental activists, indigenous community leaders, and heads of state. Looking at these conventions and the large crowds that they bring together, there is little doubt that big businesses are now positioned as leaders in resolving the environmental crisis.

The configurations of partnerships or collaborations that emerge from these negotiations rely on commitments between parties—be they nations, regions, or communities. These are similar to fiscal contracts and tender agreements for trading and investments in bioresources, although these efforts to arrive at agreements are presented as philanthropic initiatives of corporations for a better world or greener planet. These partnerships and contracts for environmental projects blur the distinctions between public and private, choice and obligation, processes and commodities, producers and consumers, benefits and costs, and legality and corruption.

This collection of essays lays out the manner in which the policy discourse on the environmental crisis has borrowed economic and trade principles to address the problem, and to what effect. This discourse ties together accountants and ecologists, bankers and biologists, governments and communities, and private sector and international NGOs into a network of expert environmental problem-solvers and ecological philanthropists. As shown by the essays, this network is in action in varied spaces; in villages and cities, in courtrooms, in government chambers, and in corporate boardrooms as well as international conference halls. The discussions and negotiations that take place in these venues are to account for the "scarcity" of nature. If nature is no longer available in plenty, how should one view it, value it, and live with it? These questions are at the root of the conversations at international environmental gatherings. The four key elements that constitute the bulk of these conversations and form the nucleus of this business interest in the environmental crisis are the commodity, the pricing, the ownership, and the regulation. These elements go into creating the global and national policy instruments that respond to local or regional ecological conflicts and provide solutions to global environmental anxieties.

Commodities: Natural Entities or Nature's Goods

Carolyn Merchant, in her work *Death of Nature* (Merchant, 1990), speaks of the moment in history when nature was turned into an inanimate object with a finite set of qualities or traits and was decontextualized from its "habitus." These objects lacked power or agency and gained meaning only by the specific uses that they were put to. While phenomenology understands nature as an organism that lives in a dynamic connection with everything around it, modern scientific disciplines treat nature as a set of substances with limited but specific uses (Latour, 2005). Commodification is the process by which nature is extracted or harnessed, based on one or some of its functions and services made visible or "revealed" while its myriad, unmeasurable qualities remain hidden.

Through human history, the availability of naturally occurring minerals, spices, timber, fiber, or tea has attracted buyers and markets. Such natural commodities have played an important role in the colonization process in many parts of the world (Beinhart and Hughes, 2009). The reliance on these commodities in nation-building exercises in post-independence economies such as India has also been understood and recorded (Lahiri-Dutt, 2014). Commodities have been the engines of growth in both capitalist and communist economies. Commodities of nature, or natural resources as most planning and policy documents call them, are central to the economic strength of nation-states today. In India, entire ministries have been set up to manage natural resources such as water and coal and to distribute them among the population. Special programs under the country's five-year plans have been undertaken to utilize targeted amounts of the resources (Planning Commission, 2012a). Since then, entire regions have turned into cotton centers, energy hubs, and timber markets based on the high and easy availability and extractability of these commodities.

Vinuta Gopal, in her essay, describes coal as a "post-colony" public good. Post-independence, large stretches of Central Indian forests were demarcated as coal-bearing areas under a new legislation. Even today, entire clusters of human habitation and areas important for wildlife are auctioned off and traded as "coal blocks." This has become imperative to fuel the country's growth aspirations.

Similarly, the more recent discourse on energy security within a climate-context has allowed the Indian government to convert the entire

Himalayan landscape into a renewable energy production zone. A large number of power projects are proposed for all the river systems so that energy can be harnessed in a cascading arrangement. Hydropower, the technology that involved long gestation, multi-purpose, large-scale dams and tunnels, with impacts such as displacement and environmental risks, is no longer the same. It creates a new commodity today—valuable green power found only in the Himalayan region and therefore essential for India's energy security (Menon, 2011).

The environment crisis discourse also creates commodities by its focus on atomized life qualities or life processes such as genetic material and carbon molecules. Genes are the new raw material in biotechnology-related research and development. Bhutani shows that the US government began research in the various applications of genetically engineered biotechnology in the 1980s. Tobacco, the first genetically engineered plant, was successfully reported back in 1983. Since then, obtaining biological material and unpacking its genetic framework has been critical to the survival and profits of several MNCs in the pharmaceuticals or agriculture businesses. Their experimentation and creation of new products, gene fragments, are patented and sold or used to raise revenue through technology-user fees or claiming royalties when used by others.

Burte argues that, in modern societies, human beings have also managed to create commodities out of abstract notions. The commodity here is not just land or water, but the idea of the idyllic ecocentric space or traditional knowledge about local biodiversity and its uses. Bavikatte and Robinson write about the translation of nature for its commercial sale and patenting. One of the first efforts of commodification of traditional knowledge resulted in a post facto contract between the San community in South Africa, represented by the South African San Council, and a leading scientific research and development organization, Council of Scientific and Industrial Research (CSIR)-South Africa, to share a percentage of the royalties earned by CSIR by the sale of the patent.

Builders have been able to create a premium value for housing colonies in hill stations near water reservoirs and golf courses. Buyers purchase the idea of a home which allows them good air, long forest walks, and bird calls, all within gated campuses. Wild nature is packaged and delivered within private property. The pursuit of creating such hyper homes—with elevators reaching high and bore wells plumbing depths, expansive imported grass lawns and chlorinated infinity pools, hidden cameras and electronic traffic barriers—is not devoid of its impacts on the human societies who reside in these areas. Burte describes Lavasa, advertised as the first planned post-1947 hill station created in the western state of Maharashtra, where real estate was created by separating nature from the living communities. It is now available for the consumption of a new class of successful but stressed souls, needy of its calming effects. This "slow-motion city" (Ganesan, 2013) celebrates "nature" even though much human, mechanical, and monetary investment is routinely made in manicuring, landscaping, and fencing it from its native human and animal inhabitants.

Valuation: Nature Pricing, Distribution, and Compensation

The cost–benefit analysis (CBA) is a decision-making tool used to ensure that only those infrastructure projects or welfare schemes are undertaken by government that have a net benefit for its communities or the nation (OECD, 2006). It involves identifying the social and financial costs of the proposed venture and the likely benefits that will accrue from it. The Indian regulatory framework on forests has, since 1980, required a CBA to be carried out prior to forest land being diverted for non-forest uses like plantations, road construction, or industrial purposes (MoEF, 2004).

Conventionally, this implied that the costs of "ecological and environmental losses and socio-economic distress caused to the people who are displaced are weighed against economic and social gains," of forest diversion (MoEF, 2004). Much was left to be desired in the application of this tool when decisions around forest diversions took place. Do the items listed under costs take into account all the costs set off by the project, or does it only account for the financial costs to the project? Who selects the items as costs and can they appreciate the entire range of costs? How are the costs and benefits prioritized or graded? Are the benefits inflated due to the counting of indirect ones like human well-being, while only first level costs such as financial compensation are considered? These have been some of the questions that have existed for as long as CBA has been in practice.

The justification to build the first post-independence irrigation dams, including the Bhakra Nangal, that were part of building the infrastructure of independent India, was to convert the rivers into an economic resource that had greater value than what it had under the prevalent local uses. The project was premised on the principle, as Dharmadhikary states, that water flowing free is water going "waste." Redistribution or diverting water for irrigation, even if it caused a disruption in the upstream–downstream continuum, implied enhancing the value of water by putting it to greater and more useful uses. Who were the lowly users of valueless water who were made redundant by this? The fishermen in the delta, the flood plain agriculturists, and the scores of other marginal livelihoods that made way for irrigated cash and food crop farming.

The process of natural resource valuation viewed nature primarily as an empty category and filled it by selecting measurable, economically relevant values over its mixed and multiple uses. This is the only way decisions could be made on allocation of resources, such as rivers, across various sectors. The value of water held back by a dam for irrigation and private entitlements to water for trade are arrived at based on the market for agricultural products and drinking water. In such a marketplace of water commodities, the price of water is the dialogue. This method of valuation resulted in excessive use of water all around the world in the form of water mining, groundwater pollution, disappearance of lakes and ponds, and damming of entire river systems. Now that water shortages are being experienced and the global statistics show that water wars are imminent, we speak of recognizing global water for its full range services to human societies (Goldenberg, 2014).

In order to combat the lack of value or the invisibility of important ecological services in the current valuation methods, new mechanisms in economics have co-evolved with the growing collective expertise in the field of ecology. Jeremy Walker delves into this in his essay in this volume. He writes that in response to the crisis of nature, concepts such as ecosystem services have emerged from literatures of big conservation organizations and international policy at one level, and from journals of conservation biology and ecological economics at another. One of the first efforts at this was the heuristic exercise undertaken by ecological economists as a method of showing how the earth's ecological services taken together are far greater than any economic system, even if priced conservatively. Their calculation marked the total value of earth's ecological services at 33 trillion dollars per year (Constanza et al., 1997). This approach to solve the problem of undervaluation of natural resources used in the development process has spawned off numerous frameworks for natural resource accounting.

The most prominent initiatives among these is the Natural Capital Declaration (NCD) led by the financial sector comprising financial institutions, international banks, lending agencies, and governments (Natural Capital Declaration et al., 2012). The philosophy driving this approach is to appropriately price "Mother Nature" and highlight the real economic cost of her services. Pawan Sukhdev pioneered the phrase "natural capital" and operationalized what he calls the "green economy." In his words, "nature's back office isn't working yet, so invoices don't get issued" (Sukhdev, 2011a). The Natural Capital framework envisages that the high pricing of nature will eventually weed out the wasteful users of nature from the economic system because they will be made to undertake such activities only at substantial financial costs (Sukhdev, 2011b). The NCD requires that national governments incentivize the practice of disclosure of full costs of their investments so that the green economy can function efficiently. Information asymmetry, in their view, is what causes markets to fail in their potential to select the best users of capital—financial and natural. This would involve not just details about environmental costs of a project but details on a range of risks such as "legal liability, credit risk, volatility, unexpected falls in cash flows, and reputational, regulatory and portfolio risks, each presenting different financial pressures requiring additional mitigating measures."[3]

Such disclosure is difficult to come by. Private corporations and investors of extractive industry, dam building, and corporate farming rarely, if ever, state this information as it is bound to provoke conflict with existing users of nature.[4] Firstly, most regions where these activities are undertaken support human societies and their elaborate arrangements with nature for small-scale enterprise and cultural practices. Secondly, nation-states themselves are engaged in a grand performance or exhibition of development and inclusive growth. They choose what they call "high reward–high risk" projects to bring hitherto forgotten areas into the development map so as to "mainstream" them. So, projects in border areas, ethnic territories, and "backward" or remote zones are permitted despite their high use of natural resources (The World Bank, 2003). These projects may have never made it if they came through the perfect market system that NCD envisages.

The new accounting of natural capital used in development processes could emphasize the importance of nature's services that makes living on this planet possible. It may ensure that the costs to nature caused by development are accounted more comprehensively. However, the benefits column of the accounts sheet is prejudiced toward economic growth despite growing protests the world over and a rising demand for limits to growth (Sekulova, 2013; Shrivastava and Kothari, 2012). Industrial-led economic growth is ascribed the status of a universal value, a natural goal of human societies. This belief inherent in cost-benefit calculations pushes for redistribution of natural resources away from local users into the hands of corporations.[5]

This accounting system is secular, in that it does not understand geographical, ethnic, or cultural uses of nature. All users of nature are stakeholders, a term made fashionable by the World Bank style consultations[6] for decision-making on natural resource projects and policy. This system forces all interested parties into a level playing field as a result of which low economic value, localized needs, and community purposes of nature are quashed by those that can pay higher prices for using the same resource. By this system of accounting, nature can exist in its highest ecological form or as dear natural capital only in account books.

If environmentally damaging projects cannot be stopped, something has to be done to offset this damage. Earlier forms of accounting included a mechanism of compensation for offsetting the environmental damage caused by development projects. Governments of hill states have demanded compensations for maintaining their forests and foregoing developmental opportunities (Planning Commission, 2013). In India, this helps to maintain the national forest cover at 33 percent as required by policy (MoEF, 1988). Such offset mechanisms have been in existence and have been implemented by governments in several countries.

In India, forest legislations have incorporated compensatory mechanisms for the last three decades. In the Forest (Conservation) Act, 1980, the system of compensatory afforestation requires the user to compensate for the loss of forestland in physical terms. All proposals seeking approval (with a few listed exceptions) are made with a comprehensive scheme for compensatory afforestation. As per law, compensatory afforestation is to be done over non-forest land equal in area to the forest land diverted for non-forest uses at the cost of user agency. Whenever non-forest land is not available, which is to be certified by the Chief Secretary, compensatory afforestation is to be done over double the extent of degraded forest area at the cost of user agency (MoEF, 2004). But this form of compensation only offsets the loss of forest land and not of the forests itself. A correction to this simple system of compensation was made by the understanding that forests perform vital environmental services over the full period of their life (IEG, 2006). There is a net loss of these services for several years, till the forests created through compensatory schemes grow out fully. The concept of net present value (NPV) was brought into the compensatory mechanism and fixed values were added to the bill of the investor/developer based on the density and type of forest used by the project.[7] Payments received for such forest diversion/redistribution are then invested in creating forests elsewhere. This way, forests are turned into mobile, fungible, mechanical units producing an itemized list of services (Kohli et al., 2011; Menon and Menon, 2013).

Many of these forms of compensation and offsetting of environmental damage are explained within the concept of "payment for environmental or ecological services." At the global level, it was in the 1990s that the term "payments for environmental services" (PES) started to be used in conservation discussions to develop schemes that provide subsidies or similar financial incentives to achieve environmental goals. In her essay, Lovera observes that mechanisms similar to PES have been recorded as far back as the 1930s when the US government established an Agricultural Conservation Program. This was re-formed into the Conservation Reserve Program by the US Agriculture Act in 1954 and remains one of the largest schemes in the world, providing almost US$ 2 billion per year in payments to farmers to move away from cultivation to permanent vegetation in order to reduce risks of erosion.

Over the years, PES has been turned over into a market-based mechanism so that the costs of mitigation and conservation can be built directly into production costs. But, as Lovera and Ghosh establish, the markets are yet to catch on and put money into PES. One of the largest afforestation programs undertaken is the one funded by the Chinese government to increase the tree cover on sloping farmlands. It pays farmers a monetary compensation that is directly credited into their bank accounts for developing plantations on farms (Bennett, 2008). PES schemes such as the UN–REDD and REDD+ are mechanisms devised within the discourse of climate change mitigation (FAO et al., 2011). Since deforestation has been recognized as a significant factor causing climate change, those causing deforestation are provided with a legitimate opportunity to offset or compensate for their act in equal measure. With PES as a basic underlying principle, REDD schemes first calculate the forest capacity for carbon storage and absorption. It then allows mining companies and palm oil plantations to pay for afforestation (REDD) and/or fund conservation programs by which national governments or local communities can be compensated for maintaining forests as carbon stocks (REDD+). Thereby, more carbon can be stored in these areas while industrialization and commercial plantations can legitimately replace forests and forest use in different places.

It allows the private sector users to pay for recreating or retaining environmental services in other possible sites without necessarily restraining the impacts in their existing locations. It also ensures the saleability of nature-based commodities even though they cannot be consumed in the present. Forests, rivers and coal mines are protected as carbon stocks or critical energy reserves until the markets demand them for economic growth. This system has ensured that we stay with the experience of environmental anxiety and manage it as a business opportunity. Such accounting turns nature into commodities that can be traded between developed and developing places, consumers and producers, present and future time. It relies on complex financial planning, accounting, and negotiations by corporations and investors. It cannot be done without the help of experts who understand both ecological processes and econometric models.

Development geographies abound with the absurdity of compensation packages for the damage to health and home of the residents of many places. In Chhattisgarh, a Central Indian state, its majority tribal population lives over large tracts of medium and low grade coal deposits. Some of Asia's largest mines operate in these areas by granting compensation to local people for land acquisition and damaged homes due to mining underground and around and a one-time payment for loss of livestock or livelihood. There is even a *dust bhatta*, or compensation for ill health due to breathing coal dust, offered by the private mining companies.[8]

The most recent of the conservation laws, India's Biological Diversity Act, 2002, promulgated in compliance with the Convention on Biological Diversity (CBD) and its Nagoya Protocol, promises "benefit-sharing" (BS). One of the most popular BS mechanisms implemented so far in countries like India is by monetary payments made either to institutions set up under the law or to communities who share their knowledge and access to local biodiversity with research bodies or pharma companies. It is a vague compensation mechanism that is based on a contested definition of what constitutes a bioresource. Such a compensation mechanism can assess neither the full economic value of the resource (biodiversity or knowledge) nor the full range of profits and opportunity costs to the community or investor that accrue from the commercial utilization of the resource through production and patents. It also assumes a single set of benefit claimers at the community level even though the same resource may be used in the same ways by many groups of people across landscapes and national boundaries.

India's National Biodiversity Authority (NBA) has spent 10 years developing guidelines in an effort to address the above questions (Kohli and Bhutani, 2013a). The April 2014 draft guidelines of the NBA warns that "carrying out benefit sharing at every stage of the value chain will discourage its use" (NBA, 2014). So the new procedures envisage a single point through which benefits-sharing contracts of the monetary and non-monetary kinds [such as technology transfer and sharing of Intellectual Property Rights (IPRs), and capacity building] can be administered. Once these contracts are administered, either with a government institution under the BD Act or a single community user, no competing claims by other communities will be entertained. The implementation of compensatory mechanisms under the ABS regime of the BD Act is poised to unravel the social meanings of the terms biodiversity and benefits.

Property Rights: A Universal Form of Resource Ownership

The third element of these new fiscal arrangements relates to the creation of new sets of resource rights and clearly defined exclusive owners/users of nature. The need for legitimate and legally clarified relationships with nature has come to be essential for protecting new investments to solve the environmental crisis. Both proprietary or ownership rights and monetary values for discrete "products" of nature, say a species or a service of a forest, offer the possibilities of secular accounting and contractual trading of nature in a culturally diverse world that understands and perceives it in very different ways.

Rights over nature have always been difficult to establish because it is an entity created in a shared space. Its specific uses have been demarcated through soft boundaries and informal institutions or the relationships of co-operation and contest between different user groups, whether they are "original" inhabitants or migrants. Small farms are often used by seasonal graziers post-harvest; forests are more often than not commonly accessed by a multiple groups of villagers and rivers have users along the length of its flow. This is made further complex by the emergence of technology-driven commercial application of nature. The use of new extractive technologies creates commodities such as bottled water and genetically engineered food grains that are decontextualized and filled with a whole new set of values such as purity and resilience. Such hybrid products created from degrees of experimentation and research create a dense multiplicity of ownership claims. But to administer contracts that give legitimacy to new users of nature, some claimants have to be made owners.

The creation of rights has also become an unquestionable ally in several social and environmental struggles as well as assertions by indigenous communities. For one set of actors, it is a way of getting a foot in the door or "getting a seat at the table"[9]; it is the only way to be able to create a stake in an extractive business paradigm and not be left out as an affected party or a victim of development. Seeking patents before the corporations do, recording land rights for better compensations, legal marking of forest claims demanding the right to give conditional consent are all steps to be taken in response to the threats of exploitation and resource grab. They are now part of counter-control strategies and assertions such as in the case of forest rights claimed by the Dongria Kondh, a particularly vulnerable tribal community in the Niyamgiri Hills, Odisha. The campaign for community forest rights by the communities fighting against a coal block in Singrauli, Madhya Pradesh, demanded that the legal clauses of rights recognition and consent be followed prior to allowing mining operations (Kohli and Menon, 2014; Sahu, 2010; Sethi, 2013).

The complexities involved in the creation of property from nature are explored through two ongoing debates around the recording of land rights and seeking recognition for forest rights. In April 2014, a large number of international organizations sent an open letter seeking that the "Right to Land and Property" be included as one of the new United Nations Millennium Development Goals (MDG). In this open letter, there is a clear emphasis on securing property rights to all individuals, both women and men. Securing rights to land, forest, and pastures, argues the letter, would reduce poverty and ensure sustainable development (OSF and Namati, 2014).

Letters such as the above emphasize what agencies such as Liberty Institute in India, the World Bank, and others espousing libertarian philosophies have been advocating. They view the grant of individual rights and the creation of property out of land, water, forests, and biodiversity so that transactions or negotiations can be undertaken without the involvement of the state. Parceling off land to individual owners would allow for a direct linkage to land markets, doing away with the transaction costs of state intervention for facilitated acquisition and compensations (Deininger, 2012; Deininger et al., 2007; Mitra and Mitra, 2014).

The above does not take into account the issues of large-scale land grab, land acquisition, and distress sales that are taking place the world over. Having access to a piece of land to cultivate or derive forest produce from does not ensure a continued secure tenure on the same. Further, it does not also ensure that policies will remain conducive for an individual and/ or family to continue to practice agriculture. Small and marginal farmers are finding it increasingly difficult to carry out agriculture due to India's agricultural policy being driven more toward large-contract farming as well as land consolidation (Planning Commission, 2012b).

What is interesting, however, is that policy processes around land rights worldwide has seen a marriage of radical groups challenging land grab and historical forest injustices with libertarian groups to promote a technical form of stakeholder politics. While the former seek a right to participate in a context where land continues to be premium commodity, the latter believe that attributing ownership is the conclusive way to rise above poverty or destitution. Although both these groups use land rights and community tenure interchangeably, there is a fundamental difference between the logics of common land stewardship and the market-based land property regimes. The former is an effort to link community-based access and conservation through local governance. In the latter, land is parceled into little units that can only be used as bankable assets. Both corporations and governments alike, who seek to consolidate their land ownership, often push for clearly defined tenurial rights rather than have to deal with messy overlapping custodianships.

Many scholars have highlighted the limits of tenurial security in achieving conservation (Robinson et al., 2011) and that a tenure creates willing stakeholders in large-scale land use change (Ritter, 2009). Those who lament the loss of the common land stewardship in this discourse of land rights include wildlife ecologists/conservationists, for whom fragmented landscapes mean the certain death of some species especially large mammals, the allies of marginalized farm and forest based enterprises, and the practitioners of traditional occupations like fisheries. They fear that property making and the taking over of productive landscapes by industry will turn these places into dead sites without culture, ecology, and enterprise.

The Scheduled Tribes and Other Traditional Forest Dwellers (Recognition of Forest Rights) Act, 2006 (FRA), came as a success story for the communities and groups that had been locked in struggles with the State over the historical process of reservation and enclosing of forests since colonial times. The FRA has been a significant yet controversial addition to forest governance laws in India. The legislation recognizes and vests both individual and community forest rights and the occupation of forestland in forest-dwelling communities (both tribal and non-tribal). There are different sets of criteria for the eligibility of tribal and non-tribal forest-dwelling communities over forests that they may have used (Kohli and Menon, 2014).

For a growing neoliberal state that brings more and more marginal areas under its controversial development map, this new success is not merely the transfer of rights to forests from the Forest Department (FD) to forest dwelling families. It is a much more profound act that allows the transformation of forests from the government property held in trusteeship or the commons to the creation of forest plots as private property. This is especially so when forests are claimed as individual rights, which has been the priority area of focus for villagers and government departments in the process of implementing the law (Bandi, 2013; MoTA, 2014). In effect, it is truly what Goldman describes as the "tragedy of the commoners" (Goldman, 1993). Migrant users of forests, those without written records or evidence of forest use and those against whom social prejudices exist, have been unable to make claims or are rendered ineligible by this legal process.

Following the passing of the legislation, there is a general agreement on its objectives between developmental experts in the World Bank, national governments, and NGOs with revolutionary forest rights groups. Many of the FRA activists were part of leftist formations that eschewed private property to varying degrees. It would be naive to imagine that nature-based markets are or can be freed of the State, or that owning property can ensure rights to decision-making on it. If at all, the State has a much greater role to play in inventorying, standardizing, valuing, and certifying commodities. In fact, titles issued under FRA come with the conditions that land use is not to be changed. There is no purpose in commodifying land into property if it cannot be transacted. The poor forest dweller will remain poor and bound with that piece of land if the title cannot be freed up for transaction. It leaves the title holder in a disadvantaged position with the land becoming commodified and their right over it having no capital premium. Our national laws for land acquisition will continue to ensure what can be sold and cannot and the fact of private property has never stopped this from happening. With land, forests, or water being compartmentalized into individually owned plots or use rights, the thicket of multiple "commons" claims that the large industrial users of forests had to deal will have been cleared.

Much of the literature on the political economy of development has written about the effects of technocratic, managerial development projects that turn citizens into victims. Now, with two decades of experience on globalization and rights discourses, the project of development is being investigated in new ways. It is shifting attention from studying the politics of resistance to the nuanced art of negotiation. The rights discourse and participatory approaches of governance have allowed citizens who are likely to be impacted by development, a "seat at the negotiating table." Will they be successful in altering power relations? What kinds of imprints will the participants of this process have on the project of development and on the environment deserves close scrutiny and analysis.

Environment Regulation: Bringing Marginal Nature into Active Production

Regulation is understood as a rule or law which is designed to create limits, define rights, and govern the behavior of the holders of these privileges. With new possibilities of extracting nature out of its dense web of social relations and turning it into commodities, resource, or capital, it is indeed the task of regulation to ensure that rules of extraction are put into place. Regulation is the statement of intent to allow the use of nature in a unidimensional form, as a resource, and yet remain valuable and necessary to human societies. The network of commodities, buyers, and sellers and the conditions of exchange and trade are meant to operate in most economies within the framework of regulatory systems.

In India, as in most parts of the world, environment regulation lays out stepwise procedures for access to resources or investments in natural capital. This involves processes such as mapping, inventorying, documenting, consultative processes, and expert appraisals. They overlay the constitutional or legal protections already assigned to places and people in the name of creating a level playing field or inclusive growth. So areas that received protections for decades under the Constitution's Sixth Schedule or the special reservations that protected forest habitats along with the primitive tribal groups (PTGs) that live there are reduced to a fact without context in an Environment Impact Assessment (EIA) Report. This EIA report is deliberately devoid of any social complexity as it caters to the mind of a technocrat who is looking for numbers that can help make decisions on returns on investment. Be it the trees that will be cut, the acreage of land to be acquired, or the people who are to be displaced. James C. Scott argues that the actual social patterns of human interaction with nature are bureaucratically indigestible in their raw forms. They need to be simplified and made legible to enable the state to interact with them (Scott, 1998). The state, private corporations, and communities all have a role to play in creating legibility and making nature available for use. Land entitlements are to be surveyed and demarcated, and biological resources are meant to be mandatorily recorded in "official" registers. This makes trading simpler and more efficient. For example, common lands in large parts of India have been termed wastelands (Singh, 2013). With this they are made easily available to investors because they have already been labeled as useless or unworthy. Investments on commonly used resources of any form are seen as improving their value. They are acquired or bought at very low prices or compensations.

Regulation is to ensure efficient and targeted extraction of resources. Mapping technologies have become very significant in regulatory processes. These help to decide areas of extraction and conservation (energy hubs, power houses, no-go areas, PAs), permissible limits (pollution standards and minimum forest cover, carrying capacity), and technologies of extraction (underground mining, Run of the River projects) and mitigation. These aspects of regulation require high levels of expert knowledge on the environment such as disciplinary specialists in hydrology, geology, and life sciences. This takes decision-making away from its professed goals of participation and decentralization. However, there is yet to be a careful assessment of whether such efficient and regulated extraction has helped to reduce the use of nature or increased its consumption, as warned by the Jevon's paradox. While regulation of resource use may be essential in today's times, it needs a moral compass provided by normative values of how we would like to live with nature.[10]

An interesting element of the policy discourse on environmental crisis is the creation of a range of environmental regulations. All environmental international conventions and national laws today come with the stated objectives for conservation as well as policies for extraction coupled by the language of "trade-offs" and "balance." New regimes of managing the crisis are meant to save them by putting in place elaborate procedures for the assessment of resource, efficient extraction with least environmental and social impacts, and supported by mitigation measures where impacts are unavoidable. For instance, the objective of India's Forest (Conservation) Act, 1980, is that of conserving forests. However, what it actually details out is a regulatory process through which forests can be systematically diverted for non-forest use. Procedures such as CBA, compensatory afforestation, and payment of NPV allow for legal uses of forests for development. The BD Act, 2002, whose first stated objective is conservation, lays out a clear process of recording, accessing, and compensating for the use of bioresources and people's knowledge. While the national implementing agencies are still working out the best principles for benefit-sharing following a legalized access, communities have taken coal companies to court seeking a share in their profit. They not only demand that the coal company pay them from the profit of accessing this fossil fuel, but have put pressure on the NBA that such systems of financial payments be institutionalized through guidelines (Kohli and Bhutani, 2013b, 2014).

Climate change policies around REDD and REDD+ schemes have formalized offset mechanisms in exchange for continued carbon emissions. Both these concepts emerge from 1992 United Nations Framework Convention on Climate Change (UNFCCC), which has recognized the role of forest conservation in climate mitigation. With this, forests are to be globally managed for their carbon value. So countries and corporations can offset deforestation by either funding afforestation programs (REDD) or conservation enclosures (REDD+) anywhere across the world. The idea sold to governments and communities with good forests is that if forests are viewed as stocks and priced well then they can be conserved as well as earned from.

There have been recent debates in India on the decision to appoint an independent environment regulator to implement environmental laws. This has been the responsibility of the Ministry of Environment, Forests and Climate Change and this move is to separate law-making and implementation functions. Much as this may appear a move toward efficient regulation, it has been pointed out that outsourcing environmental decisions to experts will result in negative environmental outcomes and undemocratic processes when regulation still legitimizes environmental damage and the need for trade-offs (Menon and Kohli, 2014).

The Dilemma for Environment Justice

The official approach to environmental issues within the principle of limitless growth has been to treat local uses of nature as wasteful or inefficient distribution of resources. The approach tries to reallocate, by "proper" costing and fair procedures of exchange between a set of distinct owners and buyers, these resources to more economically valuable uses such as development projects, conservation schemes and industry.

This reallocation, made legitimate by environment policy and laws, turns land, water, forests, human, and animal and plant life into commodities that can be bought and sold. Objects that the environment regulatory system mobilizes for the commodity market are not only a matter of a different nomenclature, but are entirely new entities. Land is a site, water is hydro resource or bottled drinks, forests are carbon stocks, human bodies are construction or forest migrant labor, animal and plant life are genetic material, enzymes, and hormones. They are all fungible, mobile, and tradable commodities. When reallocated for "efficient" production, they become unavailable or scarce when needed for local consumption, expressions of enterprise, creativity, culture, and leisure. Such reallocation not only allows for valuation of objects of cultural importance, identity, history, and memory, but calls any resistance to valuation as irrational, anti-development, or against public purpose.

The climate debates have ratcheted up nature conflicts to a global level. Now we are warned of the perils of not taking care of the planet as a result of which the useful "functions" that special ecosystems perform will be lost to us. Now these functions, and not just the objects that perform these functions, are on the market. This step may have brought corporations and conservationists as allies, but the problem remains that the global economy subsumes nature as its subset. Mechanisms like the

PES promise to make "growth at all costs" a reality by bringing all values of nature into the account books. Notwithstanding the acceptance of cultural, aesthetic and moral meanings of nature, they have been assigned exchange values. Today, markets have been tied to nature even more tightly such that the risks to one inevitably make the other vulnerable.

The interest that big business has in rejigging its image, from being part of the problem to becoming the creators of the solution, pulls everyone engaged in environmental work to respond. All of us, the writers in this publication, have been drawn into it as willing or reluctant participants, even as we critique this approach. We are engaged in the tasks of finding solutions, framing alternatives, developing replicable models, coordinating better plans, measuring compliance, and so on. We have formed allies of one sort or another in our work but we are forced to think about the extent to which these are helpful to advance environment justice in today's times. While some of us define our role as working actively with businesses open to a reformist agenda, others work at designing more equitable trading conditions that favor the local community. Some of us try to improve the official processes of valuation, while others collaborate to enhance the local values of nature by engaging in enterprise building. Colleagues in the fields of engineering, design, and energy systems offer alternative ways of dealing with supply, while many encourage ways of reducing demand.

This collection of essays is a contribution to understanding how nature is viewed by market mechanisms to resolve the environmental crisis. The essays are reflective pieces by environmental activists and researchers who have closely watched or participated in the efforts of businesses to find solutions to the environmental crisis. While much as the high profile negotiations between big business and conservation groups continue to present win-win possibilities, these pieces clearly highlight the political and ecological limits of such business-led solutions.

Notes

1. Details of the Forest Asia Summit, including the videos, are available on http://www.cifor.org/forestsasia/ (accessed on November 14, 2015).
2. Website of Confederation of Indian Industries and section on environment, http://www.cii.in/Sectors.aspx?enc=prvePUj2bdMtgTmvPwvisYH+5EnGjyGXO9hLECvTuNtI5sIDkU3GehZCDzrCfdL4 (accessed on June 17, 2014).

3. "About Natural Capital and the Finance Sector" available on http://www.naturalcapitaldeclaration.org/about-natural-capital-and-the-finance-sector/ (accessed on June 17, 2014).

4. Environment impact assessments that are mandatory by law routinely furnish false and misleading information about impacts and risks. This is despite the legal clauses that nondisclosure or wrong information will attract rejection of the report and project.

5. This systematic process of dispossession of the poor has resulted due to a "shared vision of economic development and industrial growth as progress" by the judiciary and legislators in India. This has resulted in a reactionary demand for land rights as well as pushed for the amendments to the draconian Land Acquisition Act of 1894. See Wahi (2012).

6. Several World Bank funded projects introduced the idea of stakeholder consultations where representatives of local communities, government, NGOs and investors/project developers, and project consultants were brought together for a consensus on the project or plan. It was in reaction to such consultations that indigenous and local communities pushed for their "free prior informed consent" as a part of the decision- making processes (Colchester and Ferrari, 2007; Laplante and Spears, 2008).

7. On March 28, 2008, the Supreme Court of India fixed the rates at which NPV for forest land falling in different Eco-classes and density sub-classes. The rates vary from ₹10.43 lakh per hectare to ₹4.38 lakh per hectare. For the use of forest land falling in the National Parks and Wildlife Sanctuaries, the NPV is payable at 10 times and 5 times respectively of the normal rates of NPV. On May 9, 2008, the Supreme Court also granted some exemptions for the payment of NPV which includes use of up to one hectare of land for schools, hospitals, village tanks and other such act; relocation from protected areas, collection of boulders and silt from river beds and a few other instances (Judgment dated March 12, 2014 in I.A. I.A. NOS. 2143 WITH 2283, 3088, 3461, 3479, 3693 IN 2143, 827, 1122, 1337, 1473 AND 1620 AND 1693 IN 1473 AND 3618 in Writ Petition (Civil) 202 of 1995).

8. Interview with Sudha Bharadwaj, a public interest lawyer and civil rights activist based in Bilaspur, Chhattisgarh. March 11, 2014.

9. We are grateful to Heidi Norman for her presentation, titled "Getting a Seat at the Table": The NSW Aboriginal Land Council and the Rush to Extract, at the Academy of the Social Sciences in Australia Workshop, The Coal Rush, and Beyond: Comparative Perspectives, on December 12 and 13, 2013.

10. The limits to growth principle is one such example that has acquired much public attention and support.

References

Bandi, M. (2013). "Implementation of the Forest Rights Act: Undoing Historical Injustices." *Economic and Political Weekly, XLVIII*(31), 66–69.

Beinhart, W. and L. Hughes. (2009). *Environment and Empire (Oxford History of the British Empire Companion Series)*. Oxford, UK: Oxford University Press.

Bennett, T.M. (2008). "China's Sloping Land Conversion Program: Institutional Innovation or Business as Usual?" *Ecological Economics, 65*(4): 699–711. May 1, 2008. ISSN 0921-8009, http://dx.doi.org/10.1016/j.ecolecon.2007.09.017.

Colchester, M. and Ferrari, M.F. (2007). *Making FPIC Work: Challenges and Prospects for Indigenous Peoples*. Gloucestershire, United Kingdom: Forest Peoples Programme, Moreton-in-Marsh.

Costanza, R., d'Arge, R., de Groot, R., Farber, S., Grasso, M., Hannon, B., Limburg, K., Naeem, S., O'Neill, R., Paruelo, J., Raskin, R., Sutton, P. and van den Belt, M. (1997). The value of the world's ecosystem services and natural capital." *Nature, 387*(6630), 253–260.

Das, K. (2014). "Modi Exploring Breakup of Coal India, Opening up Sector–sources." *Reuters*, May 21, 2014.

Deininger, K. (2012). Land Rights and the World Bank Group: Setting the Record Straight. Available at: http://blogs.worldbank.org/ (Accessed on June 20, 2014).

Deininger, K., Jin, S., and Nagarajan, H.K. (2007). *Land Reforms, Poverty Reduction, and Economic Growth: Evidence from India*. USA/New Delhi: The World Bank Group.

FAO, Food and Agricultural Organization of the United Nations, UNDP, United Nations Development Programme and UNEP, United Nations Environmental Programme. (2011). *The UN-REDD Programme Strategy 2011–2015*. Available at: http://www.un-redd.org/AboutUN-REDDProgramme/tabid/102613/Default.aspx (Accessed on June 20, 2014).

Ganesan, R. (2013). Lavasa: Slow motion city. *Business Standard*. June 8, 2013.

Goldenberg, S. (2014). Why global water shortages pose threat of terror and war. *The Guardian/The Observer*, February 9, 2014.

Goldman, M. (1993). Tragedy of the commons or the commoners' tragedy: The state and ecological crisis in India. *Capitalism Nature Socialism, 12*(4), 49–68.

Government of Gujarat. (1997). *Build-Own-Operate-Transfer (BOOT) Principles under Port Policy, 1995*. Gandhinagar, Gujarat: Gujarat Maritime Board, July 29, 1997.

Institute for Economic Growth. (2006). *Report of the Expert Committee on Net Present Value*. New Delhi: IEG.

IUCN Business and Biodiversity Program. (2012). *IUCN Business Engagement Strategy*. International Union for Conservation of Nature (IUCN), April 2012.

Journey Staff. (2012). *Renewing Our Partnership. Expanding Our Impact*. Available at: http://www.coca-colacompany.com/stories/converging-on-water-an-innovative-con-servation-partnership (Accessed on June 17, 2014).

Kohli, K. and Menon, M. (2014). The making of forest (re)publics: Popular engagement with official decision-making on forest conversions. In Sharachchandra Lele and Ajit Menon (Eds.), *Democratizing Forest Governance in India*, pp. 261–298. New Delhi: Oxford University Press.

Kohli, K. and Bhutani, S. (2013a). *The "Balancing" Act: Experiences with Access and Benefit Sharing under India's Biodiversity Regime*. India: Kalpavriksh and Swissaid.

———. (2013b). The legal meaning of biodiversity. *Economic and Political Weekly, XLVIII*(33), 15–17, August 17, 2013.

———. (2014). Biodiversity Management Committees: Lost in numbers. *Economic and Political Weekly, XLIX*(16), 18–20, April 19, 2014.

Kohli, K., Menon, M., Samdariya, V., and Guptabhaya, S. (2011). *Pocketful of Forests: Legal Debates on Valuating and Compensating Forest Loss in India*. New Delhi: Kalpavriksh and WWF-India.

Krishnakumar, A. (2003). A deal blocked. *Frontline, 20*(2), 18–31, January 2003.

Lahiri–Dutt, K. (2014). *The Coal Nation: Histories, Ecologies and Politics of Coal in India*. United Kingdom: Ashgate.

Laplante, L.J. and Spears, S.A. (2008). Out of the conflict zone: The case for community consent processes in the extractive sector. *Yale Human Rights and Development Law Journal, 11*(69). Available at http://digitalcommons.law.yale.edu/cgi/viewcontent.cgi?article=1070&context=yhrdlj.

Latour, B. 2005. What is given in experience? A review of Isabelle Stengers 'Penser avec Whitehead'. *Boundary 2, 32*(1), 222–237.

Menon, M. (2011). Up for grabs: New sites for private hydropower production in Northeast India, dialogues, proposals, stories for global citizenship accessed from http://base.d-p-h.info/en/fiches/dph/fiche-dph-8952.html on January 13, 2016.

Menon, M. and Kohli, M. (2013). A pocketful of forests. *Current Conservation, 6*(1), 20–23, June 2013.

Merchant, C. (1990). *The Death of Nature: Women, Ecology, and the Scientific Revolution,* Reprint. New York: HarperCollins.

MoEF, Ministry of Environment and Forests. (1988). *National Forest Policy.* New Delhi: Ministry of Environment and Forests, Government of India.

_____. (2004). *Handbook of Forest (Conservation) Act, 1980 (with amendments made in 1988), Forest (Conservation) Rules, 2003 (with amendments made in 2004), Guidelines and Clarifications (up to June, 2004).* New Delhi: Ministry of Environment and Forests, Government of India.

MoTA, Ministry of Tribal Affairs. (2014). *Status Report on Implementation of the Scheduled Tribes and Other Traditional Forest Dwellers (Recognition of Forest Rights) Act, 2006 [for the period ending 30 April 2014].* New Delhi: Government of India.

Mitra, B. and Mitra, M. (2014). *Recognising Right to Property: An Agenda for Reforming Land Related Laws and Policies.* Available at: http://righttoproperty.org/blog/?p=351 (Accessed on April 30, 2014).

NBA, National Biodiversity Authority. (2014). *Guidelines on Access to Biological Resources and Sharing of Benefits Arising from their Utilization.* NBA, April 2014.

Natural Capital Declaration, Secretariat–UNEP Finance Initiative, Global Canopy. (2012). *The Natural Capital Declaration.* Available at: http://www.naturalcapitaldeclaration.org/ (Accessed on April 28, 2014).

OECD, The Organisation for Economic Co-operation and Development. (2006). *Cost-Benefit Analysis and the Environment: Recent Developments.* United Kingdom: OECD.

OSF (Open Society Foundations) and Namati. (2014). *Justice Should Be Included in the Post 2015 Development Goals.* Washington, United States: OSF and Namati.

Planning Commission. (2012a). *Twelfth Five Year Plan (2012–2017): Faster, More Inclusive and Sustainable Growth (Volume I).* New Delhi: Government of India.

_____. (2012b). *Twelfth Five Year Plan (2012–2017): Economic Sectors (Volume II).* New Delhi: Government of India.

_____. (2013). *Report of the Committee to Study Development in Hill States arising from Management of Forest Lands with Special Focus on Creation of Infrastructure, Livelihood and Human Development.* New Delhi: Government of India, November 2013.

Rio Tinto. (2013). *Rio Tinto Sustainable Development 2013.* Available at: riotinto.com/sustainabledevelopment2013 (Accessed on June 17, 2014).

Robinson, B.E., Holland, M.B., and Naughton-Treves, L. (2011). Does secure land tenure save forests? A review of the relationship between land tenure and tropical deforestation. CCAFS Working Paper no. 7. CGIAR Research Program on Climate Change, Agriculture and Food Security (CCAFS). Copenhagen, Denmark. Available online at: www.ccafs.cgiar.org

Ritter, D. (2009). *The Native Title Marketplace*. Australia: University of Western Australia Press.

Sahu, G. (2008). Mining in the Niyamgiri Hills and Tribal Rights. *Economic and Political Weekly, XLIII*(15) April 12, 2008.

Scott, J.C. (1998). *Seeing Like a State: How Certain Schemes to Improve the Human Condition Have Failed*. New Haven, CT: Yale University Press.

Sethi, N. (2013). Tribal interests, norms ignored for Mahan coal block. *The Hindu*, September 21, 2013.

Singh, S. (2013). *Common Lands made Wastelands: Making of the Wastelands into Common Lands*. Anand, Gujarat: Foundation for Ecological Security.

Secretariat of the Convention on Biological Diversity. (2010). *Global Biodiversity Outlook 3*. Montreal, Canada: Secretariat of the Convention on Biological Diversity.

Sekulova, F., Kallis, G., Rodríguez–Labajos, B., and Schneider, F. (2013). Degrowth: From theory to practice. *Journal of Cleaner Production, 38*(2013), 1–6.

Shrivastava, A. and Kothari, A.. (2012). *Churning the Earth: The Making of Modern India*. United Kingdom: Penguin.

Sukhdev, P. (2011a). "Put a value on nature." Transcript of the TED talk in December 2011. Available at: http://www.ted.com/talks/pavan_sukhdev_what_s_the_price_of_nature/transcript (Accessed on April 28, 2014).

_____. (2011b). Putting a price on nature: The economics of ecosystems and biodiversity. *Solutions, 1*(6), 34–43, January 2011.

Tata Steel. (2012). *Measuring the Impact of Sustainable Policies (Principle 6: Environment)*, Annual Report 2011–2012 of Tata Steel, India.

The World Bank. (2003). *Water Resources Sector Strategy: Strategic Direction for World Bank Engagement*. USA: The World Bank.

The World Bank Group. (2012). *Toward a Green, Clean, and Resilient World for All: A World Bank Group Environment Strategy 2012–2022*. Washington, DC: The World Bank Group..

United Nations. (1992). *United Nations Framework Convention on Climate Change*. Available at: http://unfccc.int/resource/docs/convkp/conveng.pdf (Accessed on June 17, 2014).

Wahi, N. (2012). State, private property and the Supreme Court. *Frontline*, 9(19).

Zimmerman, M.E. (1990). *Heidegger's Confrontation with Modernity, Technology, Politics, Art*. Bloomington and Indianapolis: Indiana University Press.

Section I
Examining "Nature" in Business

1

Bringing Liquidity to Life: Markets for Ecosystem Services and the New Political Economy of Extinction

Jeremy Walker

This chapter attempts to situate the rise of market-based conservation policy, and its associated theoretical and policy frameworks such as The Economics of Biodiversity and Ecosystem Services (TEEB), within a wider history of what might be termed *financialization*. Outlining a new chapter in the long history of ontological adjustment of ecological science to dominant accounts of political economy, this chapter explores the emergence of a novel political economy of extinction. This can be analyzed in the transformations of theory: the reframing of the sixth extinction crisis within the neoliberal idiom of "natural capital" and "ecosystem services" reflects a history of the reprocessing of political and scientific ecological discourse in order to better accommodate it to reigning economic doctrines. TEEB and other articulations of market-based conservation do little to question the dominant economic theory that has licensed the financialization of social, political, and economic life and led to our current global economic crisis. As a species of power, it can also be analyzed in the social connections of the corporate boardroom, where the professional authority, executive expertise, epistemic frameworks, and political projects of senior conservation ecologists increasingly converge with those of the world's most powerful bankers.

Introduction

If economists continue to debate whether there is enough "global growth" in evidence to declare the Great Recession that followed the financial crisis of 2008 officially over, it may be a moot point for the multitudes living its effects in the "real economy." The vast quantities of central bank money creation that have kept financial markets liquid have had their counterpart in rising public debt, austerity, insecurity, unemployment, and declining real wages. A more ominous crisis of global growth, however, continues in the background. The biosphere is in "negative growth territory," continually being reduced in size, diversity, and complexity. In the material world of the "real economy," deforestation, land clearing, and the mining of oceanic fisheries continue apace. Greenhouse emissions continue their exponential rise, and climate change threatens to unravel abiding biotic relationships in existing refugia.

Coral reefs, "the rainforests of the sea," are so threatened by warming events and ocean acidification that some marine scientists are calling for the rapid upscaling of a raft of prophylactic ocean-engineering technologies. These range from covering vast areas of reef with giant pool covers, to capturing and re-releasing reef species after genetically engineering them to tolerate heat and acidity stress beyond the range to which they have evolved to withstand (Rau et al., 2012). Calculating rates of extinction is a dark art; biologists suggest that the consignment of species to extinction is now occurring at somewhere between 100 and 10,000 times the "normal" deep time rate, with the range of estimates for actual species extinctions being between 50 and 36,000 per year (Lawton and May, 1995; Pimm and Raven, 2000; Stork, 2010). In the deep geological time of evolutionary history, the biosphere finds itself on the precipice of the sixth mass extinction crisis since life emerged (Barnosky et al., 2011).

The biopolitical project of the "crisis discipline" of conservation biology (Soule, 1985, p. 727) once proceeded on the ethical ground of opposition to the heedless destruction of forms of life. The ethics of intrinsic value, in which life-forms exist of themselves and for themselves independent of human meaning systems, was married to the quest for a meticulously value-free scientific account of the parts and wholes of biotic communities and ecological systems: a rigorously nonanthropocentric ethos and episteme devoted to the preservation of the extra-economic fundament of life from the depredations of "the economy." It is widely recognized that attempts to reduce the gathering pace of extinction under the aegis of the 1992 Convention on Biological Diversity (CBD) and the ethos of the protected areas paradigm have failed. While only the most naïve idealists would interpret this as a pure failure of philosophy, a sense of pragmatic inevitability has pervaded the transformation of conservation politics by the inexorable rise of the concept of "ecosystem services" to the influential heights of international policymaking over the last decade. A now familiar revolution has occurred within conservation biology and its institutional practices, a move to fully subordinate it to the sine qua non of anthropocentric policy languages: marginalist economics[1] as reconfigured by the political philosophy of neoliberalism, which elevates it to a cosmological prime Adam Smith's armchair anthropology of a constant human "propensity to barter, truck, and exchange one thing for another."

As the realization slowly dawns that ecological erosion is in lockstep with climate change, of which it is both cause and effect, and that it will fundamentally threaten the lifeworld of human populations, so too does the knowledge that it is too late for conservation alone to preserve a minimally functioning biosphere. The 10 percent of the Earth's surface inside protected areas must be complemented by a grand project of systematic restoration to reconnect eroding and isolated remnants of the relatively "wild" biosphere. Since the return to ecological pasts implied by "conservation" and "restoration" is, given the irreversibility of extinction and global warming, strictly impossible, the shift in focus becomes the ethically agnostic problem of re-engineering the resilience of the directly economic functions of undestroyed ecosystems, which have lately been discovered by conventional economic thought and reframed within it under the term "ecosystems services."

The shift in the philosophy of extinction accomplished by these developments is notable: the biosphere is no longer to be protected from the depredations of economic growth, to be allowed to "let live" in a separate, delimited space and a sphere of values, as in the protected areas paradigm, or in the theoretically unlimited sovereign protection of the US Endangered Species Act. As Australian Environment Minister Peter Garrett put it in a speech to conservation professionals,

> With 1,750 species on the threatened list it is time Australian governments began to deal with regional ecosystems rather than adopting a band-aid approach to dealing with species under stress[...]. While[...]we'll have to act in an urgent way from time to time to prevent their extinction, it won't always be effective to keep tackling them one by one. We shouldn't focus solely on the sick and dying, but should work to build the resilience of ecosystems and landscapes, to ensure, if you like, that the hospital waiting rooms are a little less full and the health care a lot more preventative. (Gray, 2009)

Perhaps nothing signifies what is at stake more clearly than the name of the CBD's new transnational scientific institute dedicated to collating, analysing, and advancing state-of-the-art scientific knowledge to inform the political community: the Intergovernmental Platform on Biodiversity and Ecosystem Services (IPBES). The model organization for this is of course the Intergovernmental Panel on Climate Change (IPCC), but there is a notable difference. In its quest to communicate state-of the-art climate science, the IPCC did not think to preemptively subordinate its scientific mission to neoliberal styles of thought by dubbing itself the "International Panel on Climate Services."

What is to be done with what remains of the "wild type" biosphere, and how to retain certain of its useful side effects? Among the list of "services," we find the "supporting services" that underwrite the very possibility of life, such as nutrient cycling, seed dispersal, pollination and primary production, and "regulating services" such as flood mitigation, climate moderation, and disease control. The biosphere is no longer to be protected *from* the market economy as a vital reserve of fundamental, priceless value; the biosphere is now to be properly evaluated through full internalization *within* the calculative apparatus of the financial markets, with all its biodiversity and ecosystem functions to be priced, privatized, securitized, and traded as "vital infrastructure assets."

The emergence of "ecosystem services" is attested to by a mushroom-cloud-shaped literature across the gray literatures of big conservation and international policy fora, and the journals of conservation biology and ecological economics where it has wide if often uneasy professional acceptance. On the ground, private and state actors foster a host of experimental biodiversity banks, markets for ecosystems services and biodiversity "offsets," and development projects involving payments for ecosystem services. At the level of the United Nations, this has culminated in attempts to theorize and codify "The Economics of Ecosystems and Biodiversity" (TEEB) as a governmental policy language (Bishop, 2012; Sukhdev et al., 2010; ten Brink, 2011). Certainly, the problems this literature seeks to address are serious. How to re-establish habitat connectivity between the isolated islands of "biosphere reserves" across landscapes privately owned and dedicated to economic production, without a massive program of land nationalization? How to finance the maintenance of existing biosphere reserves and national parks and indeed increase their reach in the postcolonial South, given their vulnerability to the permanent fiscal crisis of the state brought on by structural adjustment, volatile capital flows, and the exhortation to export primary commodities to service debt? Who among us would not hope to witness, after a bit of microcredit and "social innovation," a flourishing of small, medium and large conservation providers, the rise of a productive sector specializing in mass ecological restoration, and long-term prudential ecological management of carbon sinks? Wouldn't it be wonderful to live in a world where it was so profitable to nurture the well-being of the biotic community that "providers" of "ecological services" could outbid coal miners for land containing coal?

In order to savor this improbable utopia, this chapter seeks to situate the rise of the "economics of biodiversity and ecosystem services" within a wider history of "financialization." Concisely, the term financialization refers to the "process whereby financial services, broadly construed, take over the dominant economic, cultural, and political role in a national economy" (Phillips, 2006, p. 268). A consequence is the penetration of global financial markets into the intimate texture of everyday life, exemplified in the securitization of household debts, and the numerous ways in which ordinary wage-earners are enjoined to manage their increasing exposure to global financial risk by becoming a kind of finance capitalist of oneself as a portfolio of precarious assets and liabilities (Martin, 2002; Martin et al., 2008). This process is coterminous with "globalization" insofar as the denationalization and liberalization of finance has been a continuous project of US foreign policy, IMF structural adjustment policies, WTO provisions, and other supranational trade treaties.

In this chapter, my account of "ecosystem services" begins with the observation that this re-translation of the problem of biosphere destruction is seamlessly adapted to the reigning mode of political economy. The essence of neoliberalism as a political philosophy is derived from the social epistemology of the Austrian economist Friedrich Hayek, who stuck fast to the view that society and nature are both so complex that market prices are the only reliable form of collective information gathering, processing, and distributing. Its inscrutable "decisions" on how to organize economic life, even if they seem irrational, cruel, and unjust, in fact always surpass the expert knowledge assembled by democratic institutions or scientific organizations, regardless of popular desires for social justice or other purposes. "Ecosystem services" offers little resistance to the Hayekian view of the market as a kind of omnisciently efficient hive mind organizing the impenetrable complexity of the world according to an inscrutably distributed epistemic vantage point that no mere individual or institution can hope to occupy. Nor does it quibble with the standard neoclassical economists view of the economy as an object modelled to mathematical perfection as a frictionless market eternally returning to timeless equilibrium—yet whose natural destiny is to "grow" constantly and infinitely increase the output of consumer products, and thereby that portion of the earth where we come across fossil-fuelled industrial technomass and its manifold side effects.

That there is a long history of conceptual exchange between the disciplines of ecology and economics is not known nearly well enough, suffice to say that ecology has always been politically subordinate, and a debtor in the relationship. In accepting "ecosystem services" as common language, the ecological scientist thus risks becoming too well attuned to the neoliberal ontology of nature, knowledge, and political morality, unwittingly enrolled in the production of a neoliberal science, and a neoliberal nature.

In Hayek's mature philosophy, which fortified itself by drawing upon the sciences of biological complexity to which ecologists like C.S. Holling (1973) were key contributors, the market is *like* the biosphere, insofar as it is an evolving, nonlinear and complex adaptive system. It is an emergent order too complex and resilient for any centralized form of knowledge to comprehend, much less to predict or control, one that thrives spontaneously upon its own catastrophic turbulence (Walker and Cooper, 2011). For Hayek, the market is the highest level attainable of collectively organized human knowledge, inaccessible to actual humans apart from concise price signals. And yet, because we can only know nature or society through the information distilled and distributed by our own subjective "environment" of prices, we can never really know if the biosphere is in crisis, or whether it is worth doing something about it, until it is actively traded for profit in private exchange.

The new political economy of extinction, represented by proposals for markets in ecosystem services, thus reframes the problem in the familiar neoliberal fashion as a "market failure," traceable *not* to the inherent inappropriateness of private-profit seeking as the solution to particular collective social problems such as the sixth mass extinction, but rather a political failure of government to foster the market's autonomous proliferation of novel market formats, property rights, and financial products (i.e., "financial innovation") in the spirit of the Mont Pelerin Society member and Chicago School economics-law scholar Ronald Coase (1960).

The idea that our only hope to conserve and restore the biosphere is to have social interactions with nature, mediated and "self-regulated" by financial market prices, is "grounded" in the Chicago School finance theories of rational expectations and the "efficient markets hypothesis" (Fama, 1970; Lucas, 1972; Sargent, 1973). Numerous analysts have linked the EMH to the phenomena of "financialization" and thus causally to the ongoing world economic crisis. Thus, it is, on the face of it, wholly surprising that a body of financial theory that has failed so spectacularly in the sphere of finance policy should now be called upon to effect the missing transvaluation of ecological values that we so desperately need to prevent "the economy" from taking the biosphere down altogether.

A Brief Genealogy of Ecosystem Services

The standard neoclassical model of permanent growth in equilibrium denies any direct role for natural resources in the economic process: market economies "naturally" converge upon a steady rate of growth. Responding to the "limits to growth" debate of the 1970s, mainstream economists tended to dismiss the problems of pollution and the exhaustion of natural resources (presumed to be strategic minerals in almost every case), as exciting opportunities for entrepreneurs to cash in with the next technological *substitution*. Such was the faith in a generic abstract "technology," that some predicted that the consequence of an inexorable depletion of minerals and fossil energy would be a miraculous future "age of infinite substitutability" (Goeller and Weinberg, 1978).

The mainstream economist's response was to re-frame the problem as an inquiry into the market conditions conducive to "optimal growth paths" and "optimal rates of depletion" (Solow, 1974; Stiglitz, 1974a, 1974b). Reflecting the rising influence of Chicago finance theory, a common thread in these papers was the Hayekian conjecture that real economic problems were not biophysical but informational: the crisis was in fact the absence of futures markets for natural resources. As Dasgupta and Heal put it:

> [M]any of the difficulties that are involved in the making of policy recommendations about the rate of depletion of exhaustible resources stem from the fact that crucial aspects of this problem are inherently uncertain, and it is not clear that an adequate class of contingent markets exists. (1974, p. 4)

Redirecting the question of the limits of "natural resources" away from an abiotic pre-occupation with strategic minerals, the term "ecosystem services" was coined by publicly engaged ecologists and conservation biologists in the 1980s as a pedagogical device to try to get across to conventional economists the point that neither human life nor "the economy" could exist without the biosphere in something resembling its present form. As Lovelock (1979) has observed, without the geo-transforming effects of the biosphere, the Earth would have an oxygen-less atmosphere of 98 percent carbon dioxide, and an annual average temperature of around 290°C.

Against orthodox techno-optimism, Ehrlich and Mooney (1983) insisted that certain "keystone" species, were vital, irreplaceable, and nonsubstitutable. Critical as partners in so many symbiotic, mutual relationships across the web of life—food, habitat, pollination, seed dispersal, soil structuring, ecological engineering—their loss could cascade in a kind of extinction multiplier effect, which could degrade and irreversibly alter ecosystems, curtailing their productivity and abundance, ultimately unravelling crucial planetary *ecosystem functions* such as temperature regulation, soil formation, and the cycling of water, nitrogen, phosphorus, and carbon. Extinction events ("losses of biodiversity") are not atomized, discrete events, but are themselves time-delayed causes of further local, regional, and global extinctions, as recognized in the concept of "extinction debts" (Tilman et al., 1994). In one of the earliest papers to conceptualize "ecosystem services," published before the neologism "biodiversity" had been coined, the causal link between extinction and "human well-being" was baldly asserted:

> [A]ll [ecosystem services] will be threatened if the rate of extinctions continues to increase (*italics in original*, Ehrlich and Ehrlich, 1981 cited in Maier, 2012, p. 187).

In practice, this move disclosed a knowledge problem: the precise causal relations between any particular species and its environment, between biodiversity (species richness, genetic diversity, community diversity) and the ecosystem functions that emerge from and condition biotic existence, are radically under-determined. Part of the problem is attributable to the classical division of scientific labor between the organismic perspective (of community, evolutionary and population ecology), and the abstracted biochemical and biophysical approach of systems ecology. This gulf can be attributed in part to the sheer complexity of ecological causality, given the temporal and spatial openness of real ecosystems. Conservation biologists thus argued that, in light of our ignorance of the precise causal relations between biodiversity loss and ecosystem failure, a rigorous precautionary policy was warranted toward *every particular extinction*.

The lack of clarity as to how species loss might generate changes in global ecosystems, or how biodiversity was related to global biomass "productivity" modeled by the International Biosphere–Geosphere Program, has given rise since the early 1990s to a whole new sub-discipline in ecology called biodiversity and ecosystem function (BEF) research. These studies emphasize the *functions* of species in biogeochemical or ecosystem processes and attempt to directly assess their role in ensuring the reliable function of ecosystems (Naeem et al., 2009).

Since the 1980s, ecologists have made serious efforts to work with mainstream economists. This has happened in convocations such as the Beijer Institute of Ecological Economics and in multi-authored papers that have used "ecosystem services" as a means to cobble together some common intellectual ground (Arrow et al., 1995). One widely discussed paper co-authored by leading BEF ecologists and environmental economists (Costanza et al., 1997) estimated the annual monetary value of the biosphere's contribution to human well-being on the order of $US33 trillion, although most of it was "outside the market."

Ehrlich's student, Gretchen Daily, has been one of the most important popularizers of ecosystem services (Daily et al., 2002). But it was the publication of the UN Millennium Ecosystem Assessment (2005), which adopted the idiom of ecosystem services for its policy framework, that did the most to catalyze the mushroom-cloud shaped literature on "ecosystem services" across journals like *Conservation Biology* and the increasingly mainstream *Ecological Economics*, the "gray" literatures of governments and natural resource management, big environmental NGOs (ENGOs) such as The Nature Conservancy, Conservation International and World Wildlife Fund, global development institutions (UNEP, WB, etc.), and the transnational networks where scientific and policymaking coalitions are forged. Tacitly acknowledging the abandonment of scientific materialism at stake in the neoliberal conflation of "the economy" with financial markets, the UNEP Finance Initiative (UNEP–FI, 2012) undertook a quest to "demystify materiality," the better to "hardwire biodiversity and ecosystems into finance." Numerous experiments involving markets and other systems of payment for "ecosystem services" are underway. Along with various "species banks" there are also a range "offset" schemes underway such as the US market for wetlands, which in theory trades habitat loss against restoration projects under a "cap and trade" no net loss arrangement (Pawliczek and Sullivan, 2011; Robertson, 2004). Then there is the global Business and Biodiversity Offsets Program initiated by a consortium of mining and logging interests in what is claimed as voluntary "self-regulation."

Given its origins in a plea for the irreplaceability of natural species and communities, and the absolute irreversibility of extinction, it is more than a little ironic that "ecosystem services" has become a technology of security designed to increase the biosphere's "liquidity" from the point of view of financial markets. By "securitizing" ecological units and processes into financial assets that can be negotiated, exchanged, or substituted on capital markets for cash or other forms of financial capital (the "biodiversity offset," for example, which trades an act of present destruction for a promise of ongoing conservation or future restoration), "extinction debts," which are by definition strictly unpayable, can become profitable sites of financial innovation and portfolio investment. But of course it must be remembered that liquidity also presumes the possibility of instantaneous *disinvestment*. In a world where biodiversity protection is to be mediated by global markets for ecosystem services, the process of identifying expendable species via triage becomes not so much a case of the kind of Taylorist scientific analysis of species utility, as it does in the BEF literature (Kareiva and Levin, 2003), but of rational business decisions to write off unprofitable investments, or in the larger market context, according to the speculative effect of euphoria or panic that constitutes volatile financial market sentiment.

One consequence is a shift in the site of the determination and execution (or not) of environmental policy from government corridors to the boardrooms of transnational corporations, and a privatization of an increasingly scarce ecological health.

Financialization: A Cautionary Tale

It seems worthwhile to note that many of the key actors involved in the push to reframe ecological protection, conservation, and restoration as financially profitable business activities also have senior roles in the global investment banks at the center of the financial crisis. While the ecosystem-services literature often claims to be merely providing a means to evaluate biodiversity in land-use decisions, the logical extension of the strange idea that "nature has to pay for itself" (Daily and Ellison, 2002) is the project to transform the worlds ecosystems into natural capital assets capable of yielding flows of "services" that can be privatized, securitized, and profitably traded in global financial markets (Chichilnisky and Heal, 2000). The risk of extinction and ecological meltdown is at stake in the effort to construct a global market in ecosystems services, in the transformation of the figure of the conservationist from a woolly naturalist to a consummate banking insider. This transfiguration is complete in the person of Pavan Sukhdev, the leader of the UNEP Green Economy initiative and its project to codify TEEB. An international career banker and financial "innovator," Sukhdev's credentials include having:

> [W]orked with Deutsche Bank for 14 years. [...] While at Deutsche Bank in India, Pavan founded and later chaired [the] Global Markets Centre, Mumbai "[...] It is being used by Deutsche Bank's originations, derivatives structuring, trading and distribution teams in equities, credit, fixed income and foreign exchange around the globe. (TEEB, 2012)

An eloquent activist for the cause of mainstreaming biodiversity and ecosystem erosion, Sukhdev was a key figure in the successive rounds of liberalization of Indian financial markets and was instrumental in India's currency and interest rate and derivatives markets from 1993 till 1998. More recently, he has chaired the World Economic Forum's Global Agenda Council on Ecosystems & Biodiversity and currently serves on the boards of Conservation International and the Stockholm Resilience Centre. The purpose of TEEB is to internalize the economic values of nature into decision-making at all levels using market pricing (Spash and Aslasken, 2012; TEEB, 2010, pp. 3, 14). The Synthesis Report indicates that TEEB intends

> creating a common language for policymakers, business and society that enables the real value of natural capital, and the flows of services it provides, to become visible and be mainstreamed in decision making. (TEEB, 2010, p. 24)

We learn about the form of this common language in *Ecological and Economic Foundations* (Pushpam, 2010), the key theoretical book in the TEEB series:

> In economics, "value" is always associated with trade-offs–that is something only has (economic) value if we are willing to give up something in order to get or enjoy it. The common metric in economics is monetary valuation.

As Spash and Aslucken (2012) understand it, TEEB is congruent with a philosophy in which corporations can do no wrong.

> TEEB employs the political rhetoric of "getting the price right" to allow markets to function efficiently. This involves explaining that, waste sinks have no cost for the private sector, and non-market benefits provide no reward to the market investor. In this neo-liberal framing private companies that destroy and pollute are innocent victims of a failing price system and cannot be blamed because they lack the right incentives for ecologically sustainable management. So we are told that, "Companies do not clear-cut forests out of wanton destructiveness or stupidity. On the whole, they do so because market signals [...] make it a logical and profitable thing to do." (TEEB, 2010, p. 9)

Proponent for the privatization of natural capital and the construction of new markets to finance ecosystem service provision have not, it seems to this author, addressed the problems generated by financialization. To illustrate, we might look at the food crisis that broke in the period 2007–2008, when the global prices of basic food commodities—rice, maize and wheat—soared amid an unprecedented amplification of volatility in the world's grain markets. The price of rice, for example, almost tripled between March 2006 and the peak of the spike in May 2008.

Millions of poor, worldwide, accustomed to spending much of their income on food staples, were immediately thrust into destitution and hunger. According to one estimate, of the roughly two billion people across the world who spend more than 50 percent of their income on food, 250 million people joined the ranks of the hungry in 2008, bringing the total of the world's "food insecure" to a peak of one billion people (Kaufman, 2011). Food riots broke out from Haiti to Cairo and social unrest simmered. Northern media attention turned to the stunning collapse of Wall Street banks in September 2008 and the *Götterdämmerung* of the Bush administration bailing out the banks at the center of the roiling of global financial markets. Even after grain prices eased in world markets, prices did not fall in numerous local and national contexts in the South, restricting the poor from accessing food with varying degrees of intensity.

Noting that grain production continued to keep up with grain consumption, and that prices of local millets and other grains not traded in world futures markets did not rise, the Indian economist Jayati Ghosh isolated the seismic price shifts and the ongoing rise in food prices to the generation of a highly profitable price bubble. Seeking exposures uncorrelated with the US finance and real estate sector as the subprime crisis unfolded, hedge funds and investment banks including Deutsche Bank and Goldman Sachs, piled into staple food futures markets, which in the United States had been deregulated in 1999 by the Commodities Futures Trading Commission (Ghosh, 2010). Billion dollar bets on price rises become a self-fulfilling prophecy. Olivier De Schutter (2011), UN special rapporteur on food security, has linked the financialization of food markets to the global land grab that is driving up the price of land rights in many Southern contexts, especially Africa, pushing local farmers off the land in favour of transnational exports to countries with surplus US dollar holdings and inadequate long-term food security, such as China and Saudi Arabia (Figure 1.1).

Figure 1.1

Index numbers of world trade prices of food grains

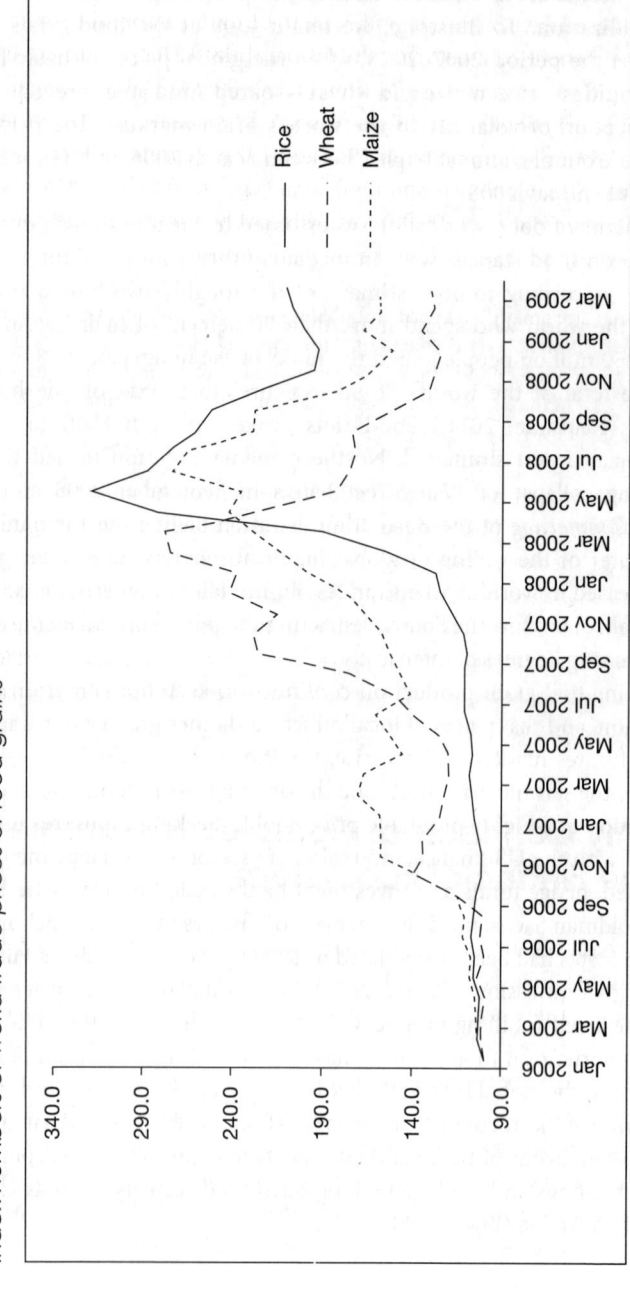

Source: Ghosh (2010, p. 76).

It is not incidental, I think, that the most influential advocates of market-based environmental policy are to be found amongst the financial elites that benefitted most from the dismantling of Depression-era banking law and public interest legislation, such as the 1933 Glass–Steagall Act, and the international restrictions placed on financial speculation in the Bretton Woods system between 1944 and 1971. Repealed under pressure from Wall Street lobbyists and neoliberal economists, these reforms had for generations, at least in the West, effectively minimized the situation J. M. Keynes had described in the *General Theory*:

> Speculators may do no harm as bubbles on a steady stream of enterprise. But the position is serious when enterprise becomes the bubble on a whirlpool of speculation. When the capital development of a country becomes a by-product of the activities of a casino, the job is likely to be ill-done. (Keynes, [1936] 2009, p. 142)

Since our concern is the capital (re)development of the biosphere as such, the stakes are very high indeed. Thus it seems at best naïve to argue that the risk of species extinction should be transferred to the financial markets and managed on a for-profit basis through biodiversity derivatives (Mandel et al., 2009). It is not too difficult to imagine particular conservation investments being written down, or vulnerable species "shorted" to extinction in accordance with the ultra-short term investment horizon of speculative finance.

Highly Connected: Complex Hierarchies in the Financial Ecosystem

Whilst bankers such as Pavan Sukhdev are conceiving of a comprehensive suite of financial markets for the risk management of ecological turbulence, there is also a coterie of senior ecologists engaged in applying cutting-edge ecological theory to the analysis of systemic financial risk. Although the two projects, which form an inverted mirror of each another, are yet to be explicitly articulated, their protagonists move in the same circles, an elite milieu in which the volatilities of a stressed biosphere and of deregulated global finance are routinely conflated.

The mainstream economics profession has tended to adopt a position of defensiveness and radical innocence with regard to its intellectual complicity in authorizing runaway financialization (Mirowski, 2013). The post-crisis debate has nevertheless catalyzed a reappraisal of the neo-classical presumptions of perfect information, infinite foresight, instantaneous and frictionless returns to equilibrium after exogenous shocks, complete markets and risk-free financial contracts, linear predictability and the utter uniformity of the representative agent, assumptions programmed into the computable Dynamic Stochastic General Equilibrium model, which became a mainstay of government and central bank policy-making prior to the crisis. The Global Financial Crisis (GFC) has brought to the fore a movement which seeks not to provide a radically alternative policy analysis, but to rather extend and completely re-found the ontology of finance and macroeconomics away from the pale imitation of Newtonian physics, and to bring financial economics into conformity with developments in the cutting edge sciences of biological complexity.

In 2009, Andrew Haldane, the Bank of England's Executive Director of Financial Stability, argued for the integration of complex systems theory (particularly as developed in the field of ecosystems science) into the toolkit of financial regulation. Haldane's project was mentored by the veteran systems ecologist Robert May, himself an official scientific advisor to the Bank. Unfolding the logic of connectivity that is germane to complexity theory, Haldane highlighted the systemic parallels between the contagion effects of infectious disease, ecological crisis and bank failures occurring in critical nodes of the global financial markets:

> Both events [the failure of Lehman Brothers and the unfolding of the SARS epidemic] were manifestations of the behavior under stress of a complex, adaptive network. Complex because these networks were a cat's-cradle of interconnections, financial and non-financial. Adaptive because behavior in these networks was driven by interactions between optimizing, but confused, agents. Seizures in the electricity grid, degradation of ecosystems, the spread of epidemics and the disintegration of the financial system each is essentially a different branch of the same network family tree. (Haldane, 2009)

Haldane went on to suggest that regulators should abandon the general equilibrium models of orthodox economics and instead "rethink the financial network as a complex adaptive system" characterized by nonlinear dynamics and susceptible to sudden changes of phase state or so-called "tipping point" during periods of stress. Shortly before he delivered his speech, a group of senior ecologists including Robert May, Simon Levin, and George Sugihara published a paper in *Nature* which outlined the usefulness of complex systems ecology as a model for bankers during the gathering sub-prime crisis (May et al., 2008). Both financiers and ecologists emphasize that they are only drawing analogies between what they speak of as formally similar but ontologically discrete worlds of money and life in general. Yet the history-making interactions between the eroding biosphere and the financial markets is precisely what is at issue for the advocates of biodiversity derivatives and markets for ecosystem services.

The career of the marine ecologist George Sugihara personifies the epistemic and professional convergence of the conservation biologist with the figure of the financial innovator. An expert in the population modelling of plankton and fisheries as chaotic, complex systems, Sugihara was "seduced" in the mid-1990s by Deutsche Bank and spent several years in their derivatives arm working on a secret "black-box project" to develop novel instruments and trading strategies (Dalton, 2005). On his return to the Scripps Institute of Oceanography, he began work on a project to set up a market to conserve fisheries by allowing fishers to profit from trading in fish futures, options, and catch rights—an alternative to catching and selling fish. Fish markets are subject to large volatilities of price and catch volume, offering ideal conditions for derivative trading which thrives on critical events. His outlines of derivative contracts for such an exchange are, quite fittingly for the privatized knowledge technologies of financial innovation, the subject of patent applications.

The ecologist Peter Kareiva is head scientist of The Nature Conservancy (TNC), and an author of the methodology of ecosystem services valuation developed by the Natural Capital Project. The acronym "TNC" aptly symbolizes the transnational reach and corporate organization of the Big Three conservation NGOs (the other two being Conservational International and World Wildlife Fund) which since the mid-1980s, a period widely noted for the drying up of conservation funds, have come to control perhaps a half of the finance available for conservation globally (Chapin, 2010). Notably, it was during the 1980s' Third World Debt crisis, which precipitated a rapid increase in the rate of deforestation in the tropics, as IMF "structural adjustment" programs replaced import substitution with "export led development" and fiscal contraction, that conservation NGOs such as World Wildlife Fund, Conservation International and the Nature Conservancy gained international high finance experience in the form of the "debt for nature swap," buying out portions of "distressed" sovereign debt on secondary markets in exchange for commitments to fund protected areas (Reilly, 2006).

Self-described prior to the sub-prime crisis as "Nature's Real Estate Company," TNC eschews the environmentalist role of public policy critique in favor of the bequest and purchase of private land for conservation corridors and easements. While the effectiveness of this global effort is beyond our present concerns, TNC has been accused of not being above some environmentally questionable land speculation in a series of articles in the *New York Times*, of allowing oil drilling on donated land, and of involvement in the Bush era rewrite of the Endangered Species Act, which introduced cost–benefit criteria into the process of listing endangered species and devolved enforcement from the EPA to an assortment of local agencies. Scientists such as Kareiva and Gretchen Daily are well outnumbered on the TNC Board, which includes senior executives from the "keystone" predators of the global finance ecosystem: the hedge fund Blackstone, Barclays Bank, Goldman Sachs. The Conservancy's current CEO, Mark Tercel, was previously the executive responsible for the Goldman Sachs Centre for Environmental Markets. And while it declines to publish the names of its hundreds of corporate donors, the advisory "Business Council" listed on the Conservancy's website includes ExxonMobil, Dow Chemical, Duke Energy, Weyerhauser, Monsanto, corporations who are significant opponents of environmental law, and noted funders of neoliberal think tanks and counter-science media campaigns. As Naomi Klein (2013) has noted, Conservational International and TNC invest considerable portions of their substantial funds directly in the fossil fuel sector, which does seem something of an ethical contradiction.

For our purposes, perhaps the most illustrious political insider and figure of neoliberal conservation is the billionaire Hank Paulson, who prior to his fateful appointment by President G.W. Bush as US Secretary of Treasury, served simultaneously as CEO of Goldman Sachs and Chair of the TNC Board. It is in the latter capacity that he wrote:

> It is clear that a system of market-based conservation finance is vital to the future of environmental conservation. (Levitt, 2005)

Three years later, in a move antithetical to the public neoliberal narratives of the small state and efficient markets, Paulson sought from Congress exceptional powers of sovereign debt creation and wealth transfer from taxpayers to private banks.

The Secretary is authorized to purchase, and to make and fund commitments to purchase, on such terms and conditions as determined by the
Secretary, mortgage-related assets from any financial institution having its
headquarters in the United States. (From the original 5 page draft of the
Troubled Assets Relief Program, 2008, cited in Kolb, 2010, p. 317)

As US Federal Reserve Chair Ben Bernanke said in 2008 after Lehman's
collapse, the risk was that, without immediate, extreme intervention,
"there will be no economy on Monday." One wonders what kind of crisis
would generate an immediate intervention to prevent the possibility of
there being "no biosphere" for the next generation.

Prior to the GFC, explicit attempts to move economic theory beyond
the unrealistic assumptions of neoclassical equilibrium had been almost
exclusively directed at financial price phenomena, as "rocket scientists" with superior mathematical skills were hired to develop trading
strategies for hedge funds. But in the wake of the crisis, the Hayekian
vision of the market as a complex system spontaneously evolving in
far-from-equilibrium conditions has arguably come into its own in the
general re-founding of risk management in the terminology of resilience,
"tipping points," and epistemic limits to prediction that had already been
accomplished in the spheres of adaptive environmental management,
critical infrastructure security, counter-terrorism, and disaster response
(Walker and Cooper, 2011).

The extraordinary resilience of neoliberalism post-crisis, I would
suggest, is partly due to its metaphorical shift from outdated "balance of
nature" and "equilibrium" metaphors drawn from mechanics and energy
physics as the ideal image of scientific explanation, to the life sciences
of biological complexity. Neoliberals cognizant of the Austrian focus on
emergent processes are apt to find themselves awed by hedge funds, with
their breathtaking generation of "financial biodiversity" or fancifully
conflating public banks with "species" doomed to extinction (Ferguson,
2009; Lo, 2005). The lesson is clear: finance capital is not only the natural extension of the deep evolutionary history of the biosphere, but an
immanent expression of its selective evolutionary filter.

Given the prevalence of such soporific memes, there was something
refreshing in the study conducted by several experts in the mathematics
of network topologies (Vitali et al., 2011). Their analysis of newly available cross-ownership data of 43,000 transnational corporations led them

to identify a "super-entity" of 147 supra-national finance corporations at the core of the global economy, with Barclays, Deutsche Bank, and Goldman Sachs close to the top of the list. On their analysis, these banks and funds exert a profoundly concentrated degree of control over the global network of corporations in the "real economy." Indeed, according to their analysis, "network control ... is much more unequally distributed than wealth. In particular, the top ranked actors hold a control ten times bigger than what could be expected based on their wealth" (2011, p. 6).

The release of the report coincided with the peak of the Occupy Wall Street protests against the increasing convergence of financial and political power in the aftermath of the financial crisis. Journalists reporting on the study sought the views not, as one might expect, of economic historians or political theorists but rather of exponents of the mathematics of complexity theory. One of these was financial insider George Sugihara, who while admitting that it was "disconcerting to see how connected things really are," nevertheless brought the gravity of complexity science to bear, arguing that the study was "strong evidence that simple rules governing TNCs give rise spontaneously to highly connected groups," and assuring us that there is no point worrying about the increasing concentration of political power in the hands of a small band of billionaires, as "such structures are common in nature" (Coghlan and McKenzie, 2011). Sugihara was referring to "power laws," a staple of the Santa Fe "complexity" school of financial economics. His common natural structures, however, rather trace back to the social sciences, and to one of the founding neoclassical economists, Vilfredo Pareto, who developed a logarithmic formula to describe the "natural fact" that "in all countries and at all times the extreme distribution of income and wealth follows a power law distribution" (Farmer and Geanokoplos, 2008). For Pareto, inequalities of wealth "naturally" coalesced around a distribution wherein the wealthiest 20 percent of the population control 80 percent of wealth, a distribution which, while alarming on the surface, would be something of a socialist utopia in comparison to the far more polarized wealth of contemporary financialized America (Domhoff, 2013). The "Pareto Principle" is widely cited is a prelude to the discovery of power laws, which are held to have universal application in theorizing extreme deviations from Gaussian probability in events such as earthquakes, financial crises, and tellingly for our narrative, mass extinction events (Sole and Manrubia, 1996).

Who Will Buy My Rain?

In 2008, Canopy Capital, a London-based private equity firm, purchased the rights to market the ecosystem services of the Iwokrama nature reserve, a protected tract of rainforest in the Guyana Shield. While the firm and the government of Guyana declined to publicize the terms of their agreement, or to clarify to the forests' indigenous owners by what sovereign power the state first exclusively possessed and then denationalized these rights, it was noted that these ecosystem services included rainfall production, water storage, and weather moderation provided by a 1,432 square mile patch of rainforest. Canopy Capital suggested it was looking at marketing "ecosystem services" through an "Ecosystem Service Certificate" attached to a 10-year tradable bond, the interest from which will pay for the maintenance of the Iwokrama forest.

On the Australian leg of his TEEB world tour in 2010, Pavan Sukhdev put up a slide that showed a relief map of the South American continent, and demonstrated the necessary dependence by farmers in the temperate crop growing regions of the continent on the rainfall generated by the tropical rainforests of the tropical north. Noting that the "Amazon Rainforest Water Pump" puts 20 billion tons of water in the atmosphere, some of which falls on the Rio Plata Basin, Sukhdev posed the rhetorical question, "What does the granary of Latin America pay for its freshwater?" As your present author, who was in attendance, happened to be puzzling through the problem of how Canopy Capital would generate the income to meet the coupon payment on its rainforest bonds necessary to attract private investment, it seemed that Sukhdev had provided the answer. When I asked him if he knew how Canopy Capital intended to exclude nonpaying farmers from rainfall, he was merely irritated and called for the next question. However, as Canopy Capital's website darkly hints, recalling the disastrous social triage effected by the water-privatizations imposed by the IMF and the World Bank upon Bolivia, "[i]f we continue not to pay for this public eco-utility, its services will simply be cut off" (Canopy Capital, 2013).

The financialization of the biosphere is at this point but a speculative project, one that acknowledges the contribution of global financial architectures to destructive economic practices, and the desperate need for massive, long-term investment in conservation and restoration. Yet, it does this in such a way as to disarm any radical critique of corporate capitalism in its contemporary finance dominated expression. "Ecosystem services" abandons the potentially radical point of view of earlier conservationism, which understood ecological breakdown as the result of the dominant economic model of permanent industrial growth in conditions of presumed market equilibrium. The implication that economic theory and practice would need to accept that the "economy" was a subset of the biosphere, and the recognition that this would require a reformulation of macroeconomic doctrines so that they were subordinate to ecology, no longer in flagrant contradiction with the earth sciences, has been neutralized. Something almost the reverse has happened, a process in which ecologists themselves have played an essential part. The political effects of the collapse of the distinction between markets and life may include the naturalization of global financial crisis, and the speculative financialization of extinction.

In the wake of the 2008 financial crisis, no serious reform of transnational finance has been contemplated: the socialization of the speculative losses of private banks in the form of government debt, bailouts, and austerity measures has rather furthered the concentration of wealth in finance houses at the center of the crisis, banks which are also key players in the discursive construction of markets for ecosystem services. As evidenced by the ongoing global economic crisis, a crisis which has itself undermined market-based responses to climate change, capital markets are not capable of self-regulation, much less of determining the "optimal mix" of species and ecosystems composing the biosphere. Just as the environment of national economic policy is increasingly subject to the power of private finance capital and their alumni in central banks in and through crisis, increasingly the environment of the "environment" is the financial markets.

Note

1. Marginal utility theory refers to the currently hegemonic form of economics which takes the explanation of price formation in terms of the preferences of a representative "individual" as more or less exhausting the methodological scope of a "scientific" economics. Whilst the classical political economy of Smith, Ricardo, Mill, and Marx analyzed the production and distribution of wealth, drawing upon history, law, and the natural sciences to understand the political and material transformations wrought by industrial capitalism, the "marginalist revolution" of the 1870s, Leon Walras, William Stanley Jevons, and Carl Menger, attempted to establish a pure economics through a depoliticized analysis of market dynamics. The term includes both neoclassical and Austrian economic theory, despite their respective differences in approach.

References

Arrow, K., Bolin, B., Costanza, R., Dasgupta, P., Folke, C., Holling, C.S., Jansson, B., et al. (1995). Economic growth, carrying capacity, and the environment. *Science, 268*(28): 520–521. Retrieved November 18, 2015, from http://www.precaution.org/lib/06/econ_growth_and_carrying_capacity.pdf.

Barnosky, A.D., Matzke, N., Tomiya, S., Wogan, G.O.U., Swartz, B., Quental, T.B., Marshall, C., et al. (2011). Has the Earth's sixth mass extinction already arrived? *Nature, 471*(7336), 51–57.

Bishop, J. (Ed.). (2012). *The Economics of Ecosystems and Biodiversity in Business and Enterprise.* New York: Earthscan.

Canopy Capital. (2013). *What is the nature of the deal between Canopy Capital and the Iwokrama International Centre (IIC) that has been widely reported in the media?* Retrieved March 12, 2013, from http://canopycapital.co.uk/page.asp?p=5452.

Chapin, M. (2010). A challenge to conservationists. In D. Rose and J. Elliot (Eds.), *The Earthscan Reader in Poverty and Biodiversity Conservation* (pp. 214–230). London/Washington, DC: Earthscan.

Chichilnisky, G. and Heal, G. (2000). Securitizing the biosphere. In G. Chilchilnisky and G. Heal (Eds.), *Environmental Markets* (pp. 169–179). New York: Columbia University Press.

Coase, R. (1960). The problem of social cost. *Journal of Law and Economics, 3*(October), 1–44.

Coghlan, A. and MacKenzie, D. (2011, October 19). Revealed: The capitalist network that runs the world. *New Scientist.*

Costanza, R., d'Arge, R., de Groot, S., Farber, M., Grasso, B., Hannon, S., Naeem, K., et al. (1997). The value of the world's ecosystem services and natural capital. *Nature, 387*, 253–260.

Daily, G., Ellison, K., and Myers, N. (2002). *The New Economy of Nature.* Washington, D.C.: Island Press.

Dalton, R. (2005). Conservation policy: Fishy futures. *Nature, 437*, 473–474.

Dasgupta, P. and Heal, G. (1974). The optimal depletion of exhaustible resources. *Review of Economic Studies*, Special Issue, *41*(128), 3–26.

De Schutter, O. (2011). The green rush: The global race for farmland and rights of land users. *Harvard International Law Journal, 52*(2), 504–559.

Domhoff, G.W. (2013). *Wealth, income and power.* University of California at Santa Cruz. Retrieved May 4, 2013, from http://www2.ucsc.edu/whorulesamerica/power/wealth.html.

Erlich, P. and Mooney, H. (1983). Extinction, substitution and ecosystem services. *BioScience, 33*(4), 238–254.

Fama, E. (1970). Efficient capital markets: A review of theory and empirical work. *Journal of Finance, 25*(2), 383–417.

Farmer, J.D. and Geanakoplos, J. (2009). The virtues and vices of equilibrium and the future of financial economics. *Complexity, 14*(3), 11–38.

Ferguson, N. (2009). An evolutionary approach to financial history. *Cold Spring Harbor Symposia on Quantitative Biology, 74*, 449–454.

Ghosh, J. (2010). The unnatural coupling: Food and global finance. *Journal of Agrarian Change, 10*(1), 72–86.

Goeller, H. and Weinberg, A. (1978). The age of substitutability. *American Economic Review, 68*(6), 1–11.

Gray, S. (2009, August 17). Put ecosystem first, says Garrett. *Sydney Morning Herald.*

Haldane, A.G. (2009). *Rethinking the financial network.* Speech delivered at the Financial Students Association, Amsterdam. Retrieved December 6, 2010, from http://www.bankofengland.co.uk/publications/speeches/2009/speech386.pdf.

Holling, C.S. (1973). Resilience and stability of ecological systems. *Annual Review of Ecology and Systematics, 4,* 1–23.

Kareiva, P. and Levin, S. (Eds.). (2003). *The Importance of Species: Perspectives on Expendability and Triage.* Princeton: Princeton University Press.

Kauffman, F. (2011, April 27). How Goldman Sachs created the food crisis. *Foreign Policy.* Retrieved November 16, 2015, from http://www.foreignpolicy.com/articles/2011/04/27/how_goldman_sachs_created_the_food_crisis.

Keynes, J.M. ([1936] 2009). *General Theory of Employment, Interest and Money.* Chennai: Atlantic.

Klein, N. (2013, May 20). Time for big green to go fossil free. *The Nation.*

Kolb, R.W. (2010). *The Financial Crisis of Our Time.* London: Oxford University Press.

Lawton, J. and May, R. (Eds.). (1995). *Extinction Rates.* Oxford: Oxford University Press.

Levitt, J. (Ed.). (2005). *Walden to Wall Street: Frontiers of Conservation Finance.* Washington, DC: Island Press.

Lo, A. (2005). Reconciling efficient markets with behavioural finance: The adaptive markets hypothesis. *Journal of Investment Consulting, 7*(2), 21–44.

Lovelock, J.E. (1979). *Gaia: A New Look at Life on Earth.* London: Oxford University Press.

Lucas, R. (1972). Expectations and the neutrality of money. *Journal of Economic Theory, 4*(2), 103–124.

Maier, D. (2012). *What's So Good about Biodiversity? A Call for Better Reasoning about Nature's Value.* Dordrecht: Springer.

Mandel, J., Donlan, C., and Armstrong, J. (2009). A derivative approach to endangered species conservation. *Frontiers in Ecology and the Environment, 8*(1), 44–49.

Martin, R. (2002). *Financialization of Daily Life.* Philadephia: Temple University Press.

Martin, R., Rafferty, M., and Bryan, D. (2008). Financialization, risk and labour. *Competition & Change, 12*(2), 120–132.

May, R., Levin, S., and Sugihara, G. (2008). Complex systems: Ecology for bankers. *Nature, 451*(7181), 893–895.

Millennium Ecosystem Assessment. (2005). *Synthesis Report.* Washington, DC: Island Press.

Mirowski, P. (2013). *Never Let a Serious Crisis Go to Waste: How Neoliberalism Survived the Financial Meltdown.* London: Verso.

Naeem, S., Bunker, D., Hector, A., and Loreau, M. (Eds.). (2009). *Biodiversity, Ecosystem Functioning, and Human Wellbeing: An Ecological and Economic Perspective.* New York: Oxford University Press.

Pawliczek, J. and Sullivan, S. (2011). Conservation and concealment in SpeciesBanking.com, USA: An analysis of neoliberal performance in the species offsetting industry. *Environmental Conservation, 38*(4), 435–444.

Phillips, K. (2006). *American Theocracy: The Peril and Politics of Radical Religion, Oil and Borrowed Money in the 21st Century.* New York: Penguin.

Pimm, S. and Raven, D. (2000). Biodiversity: Extinction by numbers. *Nature, 403*(6772), 843–845.

Pushpam, K. (Ed.). (2010). *The Economics of Ecosystems and Biodiversity: Ecological and Economic Foundations.* London/Washington, DC: Earthscan.

Rau, G., McCleod, E., and Hoegh-Guldberg, O. (2012). The need for new ocean conservation strategies in a high-carbon dioxide world. *Nature Climate Change, 2*(10), 720–724.

Reilly, W. (2006). Using international finance to further conservation: The first 15 years of debt-for-nature swaps. In C. Jochnick and F. Preston (Eds.), *Sovereign Debt at the Crossroads: Challenges and Proposals for Resolving the Third World Debt Crisis* (pp. 197–214). Oxford: Oxford University Press.

Robertson, M. (2004). The neoliberalization of ecosystem services: Wetland mitigation banking and problems in environmental governance. *Geoforum, 35*(3), 361–373.

Sargent, T. (1973). Rational expectations, the real rate of interest and the natural rate of unemployment. (Brookings Papers on Economic Activity, No. 2). Washington: Brookings Institute.

Sole, R. and Manrubia, S. (1996). Extinction and self-organized criticality in a model of large-scale evolution. *Physical Review E, 54*(1), R42.

Solow, R.M. (1974). Intergenerational equity and exhaustible resources. *Review of Economic Studies*, Special Issue, *41*(128), 29–34.

Soule, M. (1985). What is conservation biology? *BioScience, 35*(11), 727–734.

Spash, C.L. and Aslaksen, I. (2012). Re-establishing an ecological discourse in the debate over the value of ecosystems and biodiversity. (Discussion Papers, 2012/05) Vienna: University of Economics and Business.

Stiglitz, J. (1974a). Growth with exhaustible natural resources: Efficient and optimal growth paths. *Review of Economic Studies*, Special Issue, *41*(128), 123–138.

_____. (1974b). Growth with exhaustible natural resources: The competitive economy. *Review of Economic Studies*, Special Issue, *41*(128), 139–153.

Stork, N. (2010). Re-assessing current extinction rates. *Biodiversity and Conservation, 19*(2), 357–371.

Sukhdev, P., Wittmer, H., Schroter-Schlaack, C., Nesshover, C., Bishop, J., ten Brink, P., Gundimedia, H., et al. (2010). *The economics of ecosystems biodiversity: Mainstreaming the economics of nature: A synthesis of the approach, conclusions and recommendations of TEEB.* See http://www.teebweb.org/our-publications/all-publications/

TEEB (2012). The economics of ecosystems and biodiversity: TEEB study leader. Retrieved November 16, 2015, from Teebweb.org/training/about/teeb-study-leader.

ten Brink, P. (2011). *The Economics of Ecosystems and Biodiversity in National and International Policy Making.* Washington, DC: Earthscan.

Tilman, D., May, R.M., Lehman, C.L., and Nowak, M.A. (1994). Habitat destruction and the extinction debt. *Nature, 371,* 65–66.

UNEP-FI (United Nations Environment Program, Finance Initiative). (2010). CEO briefing: Demystifying materiality: Hardwiring biodiversity and ecosystem services into finance. October 2010. Retrieved June 8, 2012, from http://www.unepfi.org/fileadmin/documents/CEO_DemystifyingMateriality.pdf.

Vitali, S., Glattfelder, J.B., and Battiston, S. (2011). "The network of global corporate control." *PLoS ONE, 6*(10), e25995. doi:10.1371/journal.pone.0025995.

Walker, J. and Cooper, M. (2011). Genealogies of resilience: From systems ecology to the political economy of crisis adaptation. *Security Dialogue, 42*(2), 143–160.

2

Claiming Benefits, Making Commodities

Shalini Bhutani

The Problem: "Benefit-sharing"

Biological resources are unequally spread across unequal countries.[1,2] Inequality amongst countries refers here not only to the historicity of asymmetric economic and political power amongst them that determines their interactions even today, but also to the dissimilarities and unevenness in their biological endowments [such as that between India and the United States of America (USA)]. The naturally occurring bioresources do not recognize territorial limits and political boundaries. But people and more so governments do. Local biodiversity-keepers within their communities may be able to *share* (i.e., make joint use of a resource), however imperfectly, in locally defined spaces and through self-made rules.

At the global level, the rule-making for sharing genetic resources between countries has been an ongoing negotiation under the multilateral environmental agreement (MEA) the Convention on Biological Diversity (CBD). An international regime (the IR) has been developed as a supplementary agreement to the CBD. It is called the *Nagoya Protocol on Access to Genetic Resources and the Fair and Equitable Sharing of Benefits Arising from Their Utilization to the Convention on Biological Diversity* (in short, hereinafter, "the Protocol"). It is meant to settle the issue of access and benefit-sharing (ABS) in the context of exchange between countries.[3] In the CBD, "access" acquires a specific meaning of obtaining genetic or biological material or resources (GBMR), or people's pre-existing biodiversity-based knowledge, for purposes of formal research and development (R&D) as well as commercialization.

The CBD and its Protocol are meant to ensure that fair and equitable benefit-sharing accrues whenever access takes place (Berne Declaration and others, 2013). It requires the accessor of GBMR or people's knowledge to share the benefits derived from the use of those resources, with the communities in the country of origin of the resources, in fair and equitable measure. The purpose of ABS regimes is to effect biodiversity justice by preventing access without permission, compensation, or acknowledgement of the provider country. For the CBD, signed at the United Nations (UN) Earth Summit in Rio 1992, did two major things. First, it declared that states had sovereign rights over their own GBMR. With CBD, it was being said that, then onward, though the concern is shared but the resources no longer are. Second, the CBD prescribed member countries to undertake regulation of ABS vis-à-vis GBMR. This required governments to move toward regulatory governance in hitherto unregulated areas.

This chapter attempts to lay out how, at the global level the IR regime under CBD and at the national level the regulations under it have become a space to negotiate contracts between different sets of actors with often opposing world views—the users/accessors and the providers of bioresources or related knowledge. It traces the debates in and around the CBD which led not only to the propertizing of bioresources and people's knowledge, but also to the setting up of the marketplace where these are to be traded. The author draws from the decade-long experience of the Indian ABS law—the Biological Diversity Act.[4] Domestic legislations in many countries in compliance with the CBD are brought about in the name of conservation but are really about trade in local resources (Kohli and Bhutani, 2013). The chapter thus seeks to point out how the IR and the implementation of its concept of "benefit-sharing" might very well be part of the problem. With the ABS regime offering "protection" to both biodiversity and its keepers through commodification of resources hitherto regarded as heritage (Bhutani, 2012), this chapter questions whether real "benefits"—understood as something that promotes well-being—to conservation and local communities can be truly claimed, as is the case by those pushing the regime.

Common Heritage

Prior to the CBD, it was convenient for some to keep perpetuating the idea that the biological wealth of the planet is *shared* and held in common. The presumption of such a *res communis* state of affairs meant that biological resources belonged to all, yet was corrupted by practice to mean freely accessible to all. This principle of international law, instead, implies that these resources were not open to unrestricted appropriation. For common heritage also implies common responsibility. However, insistence on this aspect by provider countries is not always possible, given their unequal power relations with user countries.

In the 1960s, the principle of common heritage of mankind (CHM) had found its way into the UN lexicon in the context of discussions on the seas.[5] The CHM status of biodiversity was assumed but not expressly articulated; it allowed technology-rich countries to access another country's biological material as a *shared* resource without having to acknowledge the source or recompense for its use in any way.

CHM was thus an ethical principle that was not backed by law as far as the biodiversity sector was concerned. Thus, there were little or no legal obligations to share back with the provider country. There were no regulations in force or institutions in place, at the international or even the national level, for any wealth generated from the use of genetic resources to be so shared.[6] The gap in global law and policy on sharing was itself flagged as a problem. The CBD changed the legal status of GBMR from CHM to put an end to the free-for-all access.

Technology Concerns

In the years leading up to the UN Stockholm Declaration of 1972, the degradation of the natural environment had come to be considered a major concern calling for global action.[7] This required global agreement for the protection of species, landscapes, and ecosystems. Specific international conventions on conservation, such as of wetlands (Ramsar, 1971) and migratory species (CMS, 1979) and that of trade in wildlife (CITES, 1975) were put in place.[8] The role of technology in conservation was also duly recognized in these conventions.

Another possible risk to environment on the horizon at the time was from emerging science and technology itself. This was only in part acknowledged by the *Asilomar Conference on Recombinant DNA*

Molecule Research in 1975, supported by the National Academy of Sciences of USA.[9] The conference comprising scientists—mostly molecular biologists—a few lawyers and some media persons from across the world was held in Asilomar, California. The participants also included senior researchers from research divisions or corporate-funded laboratories of General Electric, Merck, Roche, and Searle (Peterson, 2010). Its main focus was the possible biohazards from rDNA research and it made recommendations for laboratory precautions in research and acceptance of risk categories, but not all the broader social and ecological implications of modern biotechnology were addressed. In fact, for the proponent scientists the success of the Asilomar Conference was in being able to prevent any regulation by the US Federal Government on rDNA experiments.

Industry by now had a fair idea of the many practical applications of the technology and how with manipulating genetic materials new kinds of life forms and "new" products could be created. The technology also gave industry a very different lens from that of indigenous peoples and local communities (IPLCs) through which to view biological resources, breaking them down into their genetic components dismembered from people's knowledge systems and decontextualized from their local settings. The genetic reductionism, to be later synergized by economic reductionism, would eventually lead to the commercialization of the smallest now broken up components of bioresources.

Loss of biodiversity in general had emerged as an area of concern in the 1980s. In November 1988, the United Nations Environment Programme (UNEP)'s Governing Council convened the first *Ad Hoc Working Group of Experts on Biological Diversity* toward developing a global legal framework on the issue.[10] In May 1989, this was followed by meetings of an *Ad Hoc Working Group of Technical and Legal Experts*. This latter group was tasked to prepare an international legal instrument for the conservation and sustainable use of biological diversity, taking into account "the need to share costs and benefits between developed and developing countries."[11]

In the 1980s, the government of the USA had begun supporting research on biotechnology. In 1983, researchers from Miami reported success in developing the first genetically engineered plant—GE tobacco. Thereon, the US Federal Government began developing regulatory frameworks for "new" products derived from modern biotechnology. In 1984, the White House Office of Science and Technology Policy (OSTP) proposed a *Coordinated Framework for the Regulation of Biotechnology.* This was issued in 1986 by the President's Domestic Policy Council Working Group on Biotechnology through the OSTP. The framework established the US government's intent to be the first-mover in the commercialization of potential products from modern biotechnology. In 1986, the OSTP gave regulatory approval for GE plants.

Meanwhile, in 1980, the US Supreme Court had given a favorable ruling for the MNC, General Electric Co., allowing it to patent a human-made GE bacterium developed by its microbiologist "inventor" Ananda Chakrabarty.[12] The US Patent and Trademark Office (USPTO) that had originally rejected the patent application on ground that living biological material is not patentable subject matter, had to grant the patent in 1981. The Court ruling that made living (modified) organisms patentable was also a push toward the commodification—meaning hitherto non-saleable things, in this case life forms, being considered commercial products that could be bought and sold.

This was to have major ramifications outside the United States too, for the idea was pushed into multilateral agreements regulating international trade. It would go on to influence the implementation of MEAs such as CBD as well. The Uruguay Round of trade talks through 1986–1994 conducted within the framework of the General Agreement on Tariffs and Trade (GATT) for the first time included intellectual property (IP) in global trade rules. This took the form of the Agreement on Trade Related Aspects of Intellectual Property Rights (TRIPS) in the GATT successor—the World Trade Organization (WTO).[13]

Bioprospecting

Around the same time, another issue of equal urgency was being raised by biodiversity-rich countries, particularly through their IPLCs—that of bioprospecting (ETC Group, 1995). Bioprospecting, the scouring of the biological world for possible new crops, cattle types, cures, cosmetics, and so on, for commerce, had taken on a new proportion. For modern biotechnology had by then moved from being merely a scientific endeavor to being an entrepreneurial science. Industry had begun to view the very building blocks of biological life forms—the genes—with new commercial value. But this idea was not in line with the cosmovision of many IPLCs and governments in the "South,"[14] which were the sources for such genetic material. Even though they may have been previously trading other resources with the outside world, to them both commercialization of certain living bioresources, patenting of plants and animals per se, or even privatizing biodiversity related-knowledge domains, was considered incomprehensible.

Accessors, however, did not always respect the diversity of views or wait for global rules on bio-trade to come into place. Countries such as the USA have continued to access GBMR regardless. In 1992, a worldwide bioprospecting initiative called International Cooperative Biodiversity Groups (ICBG) was started jointly by the US National Institute of Health, National Science Foundation, and United States Agency for International Development (USAID).[15] This too was hit with controversy.[16] After its lead US ethnobiologist was accused of unethical practices in the documentation of the biodiversity of Chiapas, Mexico and the knowledge of the Mayan people, that particular ICBG was shut down in 2001.[17] But the bioprospecting consortium is still operating in seven countries in Latin America, Africa, Indonesia, Philippines, and the Pacific Islands. Those associated with it claim that what *differentiates this search today from the way it has been done in past decades is the recognition that the process and its potential rewards should provide benefits to the source country and local communities that are the stewards of those resources.*[18] The ICBG has its own set of principles on ABS as well as on intellectual property.[19]

The emergence of modern day MNCs in this area too hastened commercialization. For, driven by business imperatives and shareholder interests, they accessed purely to maximize profits. Global trade rules pushed along by MNCs are also a major factor in the globalization of standards and practices of bio-trade between countries. Since they seek uniform operating conditions across the globe, they seek similar contractual arrangements irrespective of location. Universal trade rules have been one way of eroding more "traditional" forms of governance over local bioresources. Foreign MNCs also became the leitmotif in popular struggles against "biopiracy," though this may be changing today to include public sector researchers and even smaller domestic companies that access intra-country. US seed companies such as RiceTec, Inc. (that patented Basmati rice lines and grain) and pioneer biotech MNCs such as Monsanto (that introduced their GE constructs into cotton to India) became household names in India in the 1990s.[20]

Biological material and its local know-how was being used by the "life science" industry—whether private or public—to develop new products previously not bought and sold at a global scale. Local NGOs and farmers' groups campaigned against what they saw as "intellectual piracy, resource piracy, and economic piracy" (Shiva and Bhutani, 2001). On the other hand, there was equal pressure on governments to respond to the demands of the biotechnology industry. The industry that continued to resist regulation on biosafety wanted regulatory regimes from governments on two fronts—access laws on genetic resources and laws on intellectual property protection for their technology and their products made from the use of genetic resources. By the mid-1990, UNEP formed a new *Sub-Working Group on Biotechnology* with the purpose of making a Convention, that is, the CBD. The Convention was to prepare terms of reference on such matters as biotechnology transfer and access to genetic resources.[21] Thus, from the outset, the CBD had the onerous task of having to balance divergent interests.

Accessor Responsibilities

Conservation on a global scale is possible only with shared responsibilities world over. What the CBD did not change is that conservation of biological diversity remains *a common concern of humankind*. Nonetheless, as per the CBD, countries do have differentiated responsibilities, depending on whether they are provider or user countries. Over and above conservation, the responsibilities of user countries include providing reciprocal access to technologies in exchange for genetic resources (Article 16), technical and scientific cooperation (Article 18), distribution of benefits derived from biotechnology (Article 19), legislative, administrative or policy measures for benefit-sharing with the provider countries [Article 15(7)], and financial resources (Article 20).

Many of the accessor countries, under legal obligation to share benefits, do not have access laws in place till date. The USA has chosen not to become a member of CBD. The precise mention of biotechnology in the Convention text kept the USA from becoming a member. For the US delegation was against any regulation of living modified organisms (LMOs). While several offending clauses were referred to in the US Declaration opposing the CBD, the US representative reiterated the Bush administration position that "[a]s a matter of substance, we find particularly unsatisfactory the text's treatment of intellectual property rights ... technology transfer and biotechnology."[22] To date, the US government is not party to either the CBD or its rules on ABS and biosafety developing under its protocols, while it was one of its original proponents (Johnson, 2012).

The European Commission has only in 2013 proposed a regulation establishing rules governing ABS to enable the European Union to ratify the Nagoya Protocol and formally become a party.[23] Japan's Basic Act on Biodiversity, came as late as 2008; in any case, it deals primarily with local actions. Japan's access rules are still a set of voluntary guidelines—"the Guidelines on Access to Genetic Resources for Users in Japan" developed in 2005 by its Ministry of Economy, Trade and Industry (METI) in consultation with the Japan Bioindustry Association (JBA). The JBA has been "helping" its private sector and scientific community to develop relations in India while the latter develops its ABS regime (Sumida, 2008).

The pressure to make an ABS system work in practice is relatively more on countries supplying the bioresources and they may choose additional onerous responsibilities on themselves with expectation of benefits. Access-heavy implementation has also meant that much less care goes into ensuring that benefits received are channeled back for local good, including conservation. In many states in India, "local biodiversity funds" envisaged under the law have not yet been operationalized. This makes it difficult for any monetary benefits, if and when received, to reach the provider communities in their area. The fact of access does not automatically mean downstream benefits.

The Protocol requires a provider country of GBMR to set up the necessary national authority and national legislation to effect ABS. In the South Asian region, only India and Bhutan have such access laws in force.[24] These are predominantly about facilitating access to bioresources (by other than locals), rather than prioritizing local conservation and community control. The implementation of ABS laws very quickly becomes about state management of biological resources, that too as a precursor to put them on the market. The state-centric paradigm had by then also shifted to a market-centric economic paradigm. So, state attention was on facilitating the rights of accessors, rather than insistence on their responsibilities.

There are currently no processes in place in India to monitor the use of the material after access has been granted. There are no means to cross-check if the terms and conditions in the ABS agreement are being adhered to or that the user is in line with the prescriptions for "sustainable use" as envisaged by the CBD and the BD Act. The matter if and when it arises has to be dealt with as a breach of contract, also invoking the penalty provisions of the BD Act. While noncompliance of the ABS requirements is a punishable offence that can attract the penal provisions of the BD Act, there is little political will to push the big players. Only one or two state-level biodiversity boards (SBBs) in India have dared to put the penal provisions to test by insisting on benefit-sharing by companies.[25] Internationally too there is no legal recourse under CBD. User countries like the USA have also consistently resisted the two key measures that both India and the Nagoya Protocol insist upon—establishing national checkpoints and a certificate of compliance. In any case punishing for noncompliance does not have the effect of restoring a bioresource to its previously non-commodified state.

Beneficial Language?

The language of CBD (Article 1) expressly makes conservation one of the three objectives of the Convention, along with sustainable use and fair and equitable sharing of the benefits arising out of the utilization of genetic resources. The language favorable to accessors is that these objectives are to be fulfilled taking into account all rights not only over those resources but also to technologies. But access itself is *not* one of the stated objectives. Yet most national governments are pre-occupied with first setting up the access regimes under their national legislation. They are meant to streamline the due procedures for approval and the formats of the contractual agreements, as well as setting up of new institutional structures by which these access processes can be legally carried out.

India's BD Act is no exception. It envisages one kind of structure, the biodiversity management committee (BMC), to be set up in every local body. When the act was notified in 2002, the language of Section 41 therein on BMCs appeared broad enough to give space to local communities to exercise sovereignty vis-à-vis the biological heritage in their areas. In 2004, when the implementing rules were notified by India's Environment Ministry, the role of BMCs in the text of the rules had been reduced to providing data in the government exercise of documentation of biological resources and related knowledge.[26] There are no express rights or responsibilities of local communities toward biodiversity conservation detailed in the Central BD Rules. Instead, the BMC's main responsibilities are essentially that of book-keeping, to prepare people's biodiversity registers in consultation with local people, to maintain data about the local *vaids* and practitioners using the biological resources and to maintain a register giving details of the access to biological resources and traditional knowledge granted, details of the collection fee imposed and details of the benefits derived along with the mode of their sharing.

IPLCs, whether participant in the official CBD processes or campaigning outside, have been seeking legal recognition for their ways of life as they are. It is the limitation of the CBD and its times that their demands are only responded to by the grant of a right to "benefit" from the trade of bioresources. The language of "rights" introduced in the CBD suggests how it accommodates the dominant discourse. Today's rights come with a particular culture of individualism (Kneen, 2009); this can be antithetical to the collective experiences that CBD was meant to safeguard. The CBD recognizes rights of states, but atomizing these rights to identify a set of "benefit claimers" can lead to the break-up of biodiversity-dependent societies itself. For with shared bioresources, it cannot be said that one particular individual or local group alone can be associated with them.

Yet, implementation of law is as much about interpretation. Though the language of CBD may appear balanced, yet in actual practice, ABS regimes are tilted in favor of the bioprospectors. And even where countries have collectively organized against the imbalance, as did the Organisation for African Unity (OAU) with its Draft Model Law[27] more conducive to African realities, these efforts have been scuttled through not only diplomatic channels but also propping up of alternative industry-drafted texts on intellectual property rights (IPRs). For example, the Africa Regional Intellectual Property Organization (ARIPO) in 2013 has proposed an Africa-wide draft plant breeder's law.[28] Universalism is used by many Western states to negate the validity of local systems of law and governance and erode their own lexicon. Meanwhile, the language in which an ABS contract can be universalized is a matter under consideration of the IR.

Gene Economy

No economic system can function without the law. The gene economy too is propped up by the legal system. Access laws constitute the set of rules that guarantee the supply of raw materials to the manufacturers of products using genetic material. The accessor countries expect that global IR rules that are domestically implemented streamline the manner in which their businesses and researchers can legally acquire genetic resources, particularly for biotechnology. The gene-centered economics drives the implementation. The dominant technology made *genetic* resources visible as potential tradable commodities.

Genes, the smallest units of heredity of a living organism, are now big business. Viewed merely from their use in an economy, sans locating them in the ecological context of the biosphere or the social contexts of IPLCs, genetic materials can very narrowly be regarded as mere resources. As the secretariat of the CBD explains, the key attribute of genetic resources, which differentiate them from biological resources, is their replicability. DNA carries genetic information. Unpacking DNA, despite the inadequacy of scientific knowledge of it even to date, is crucial to understanding the characteristics of all living forms and can that lead to new discoveries from which to make new products. And if a business enterprise can own and control the very blueprint of life, it has immense business opportunities, particularly in the agriculture and health sector. CBD clearly lays down that access to genetic resources cannot be denied by a country.[29]

Given their potential, collecting genetic resources as well as inventorying their known uses has found much government support. In fact there is a specific CBD obligation toward "identification and monitoring" of components of biological diversity (Article 7). Annex I of the CBD has an indicative list of categories to maintain and organize, which apart from ecosystems, habitats, and species, includes "described genomes and genes of social, scientific or economic importance." Documentation and data-basing has also been the emphasis in the implementation of the BD Act in India as in other countries. To store the physical collections, state institutions within the national agricultural research system (NARS) and the Botanical Survey of India, Zoological Survey of India have been designated as national repositories under the act.[30] Many of these institutions date back to the British times when they were set up by colonial powers to survey the resources of the Indian empire (Pati and Harrison, 2001). In present day India, any person who discovers a new taxon in the country—be it a plant, animal, or any other organism—is mandatorily required to report it to and deposit a voucher specimen in these repositories.[31] Nation-wide exercises on the compilation of pre-designed people's biodiversity registers are also underway in India. In the national stock-taking of genetic wealth, nothing can remain unaccounted for.

That the genetic code of all life forms ought to be freely available to all is taken as a given by many across the globe. Yet the gene economy relies on patent laws to allow an accessor who first isolates it and/or finds a use for it to claim exclusive rights over it. A longstanding policy of those who come to bear on international law, such as the US government, has been that scientific discoveries of naturally existing genes can be patented for private profits.

But the debate over patenting living genes is still not settled. The contentious issue of gene patents in the biopharmaceutical industry has come to the fore again with the Myriad Genetics case in the USA.[32] Through IP, the company claims to own the rights to *any* test for the presence of the two critical genes associated with breast and ovarian cancer, thus being able to charge several thousand dollars for the diagnostic test. The matter was heard by the Supreme Court of the USA, which expressed serious doubts about the legality of a company's exclusive patent on the cancer genes.[33] In its judgment in June 2013, it held that naturally occurring human genes cannot be patented. However, the Court allowed for patent protection over a modified form of DNA called complementary DNA (cDNA). The Court did not specify what extent of modification will warrant patentability. Though the judgment has created confusion in the industry, it is certainly not the curtain call on patenting life forms. In fact, despite the Court ruling, Myriad Genetics, Inc. has filed legal suits against its competitors alleging that their new breast cancer screening tests infringe its patents.[34]

The patenting of genes and microorganisms is of critical importance to biotechnology MNCs. The global seed businesses organized into the International Seed Federation (ISF) *urges the negotiators of the international treaties on biodiversity to respect the international agreements on intellectual property and to be mutually supportive of those agreements.*[35] In being able to virtually own fragments or the constituent parts of a whole living organism, the LMO manufacturer can claim royalties or technology user fees from anyone using it in any form anywhere. The US MNC Monsanto Company Inc. has become the global motif of the perversion of the patent system, in holding several thousand patents many of which are on genes and seeds.[36]

The global Biotechnology Industry Organization (BIO), of which companies such as Monsanto are members, keeps a vigilant eye world over what might negatively bear on its business interests. For instance, it has repeatedly expressed concern over specific foreign government's weak IP enforcement efforts, following the Office of the US Trade Representative's (USTR) release of its Special 301 Report. "The USTR's Special 301 Report illuminates the failings of India, China, Brazil and

Canada, among others, to provide adequate IP protection for biotechnology companies creating novel and innovative products," said Joseph Damond, BIO's Senior Vice President, International Affairs.[37] The industry also preempts any national or local-level law-making that may work to its disadvantage, by developing its own rules, as is the case with BIO's *Guidelines for Members Engaged in Bioprospecting.*[38]

The CBD processes have embraced businesses as important stakeholders in the convention implementation. CBD members see this as crucial in achieving the Aichi Biodiversity Targets.[39] A meeting on conservation mechanisms that could be adopted for the post-2010 biodiversity targets was held in Jakarta, Indonesia at the end of 2009. It led to the Jakarta Charter on Business and Biodiversity, 2009, which amongst other things prescribes:

> The value of biodiversity and ecosystem services needs to be better reflected in economic models and policies, bearing in mind that sustainable management of biodiversity and ecosystem services are a source for future business operations as well as a condition for new business opportunities and markets.

The CBD's Tenth meeting of the Conference of the Parties (COP 10) responded to this with a decision on business engagement that among other things, called for "the establishment of national and regional business and biodiversity initiatives, and to strive toward a global partnership on business and biodiversity."[40] Thereafter, the CBD Secretariat facilitated the setting up of a global platform on business and biodiversity.[41]

Trade-Friendliness

Global trade—the exchange of goods and services across international borders is claimed by those who believe in "free" trade, as being beneficial for people's needs. The WTO Secretariat itself explains that the multilateral trading system has to get progressively freer, lowering trade barriers over time through negotiations (Jawara and Kwa, 2003). Trade-led economic growth is what most governments today are keen to pursue.

The CBD frame does not challenge the very idea of forever trade in biological heritage, while the CBD Secretariat and its member countries are mindful of the impacts of trade liberalization on biodiversity, for instance specifically on agricultural biodiversity.[42] Nonetheless, CBD perpetuates the idea that trade will generate benefits for both conservation and local communities. This perspective is carried through in the implementation of biodiversity legislation within countries. These laws at most try and make the trade better, by requiring ethical behavior and due procedure to be followed. Thus, law-makers and administrators alike have got busied in organizing the marketplace for bioproducts and those selling them.

Quite clearly, as other CBD member countries (with the exception of Bolivia), India's CBD-compliant national law, the BD Act, is not averse to global trade in India's GBMR or in related people's knowledge. It only requires that, if and when trade takes place, due approval be taken from the National Biodiversity Authority (NBA) and the prescribed fees be paid. In fact, the NBA sees ABS as a "large scale financing mechanism" to generate monies.[43] And given that India has been a country at the very center of the problem of "biopiracy," it is surprising that even the provisions in the act which give NBA the power to challenge piracy of Indian resources/knowledge in another country have never been invoked.[44]

The SBBs have also been tasked with processing requests and granting approvals for any commercial utilization by Indians. In this exercise, the BMC becomes a mere economic agent rather than a political space. It is the point of transfer of the bioresources/knowledge upon an access request. The entire institutional structure is built on the premise that genetic material is to be used for research and/or commercial purposes; this is normative in the sense that it institutionalizes the transfer of community-managed bioresources to the market economy.

CBD was conceived as a conservation treaty in a pre-WTO era. But it came to maturity only after trade liberalization through its implementation was cemented. Meanwhile, trade liberalization under domestic economic "reform" policies had already begun in India since 1991. Formal negotiations of the Intergovernmental Negotiating Committee (INC) for CBD also began in 1991. Just as CBD was entering into force in many countries, the WTO and its trade agreements came into force in 1995. Under its trade rules, plant and animal genetic resources and knowledge of the living world were brought under the trade regime. These were hitherto not regarded as resources to be traded. In the absence of state regulation, these resources had been left for either public use or local community decision-making.

There is a role that other trade-oriented international fora, such as the World Intellectual Property Organization (WIPO), also play in keeping CBD on the trade track. WIPO maintains a database of all model ABS contracts and actual agreements.[45] It also seeks to assist users and providers of genetic resources with the negotiations of access and benefit-sharing agreements, wherein examples of model agreements and actual contracts are listed.

Therefore, it is of little surprise that CBD's implementation itself has become increasingly preoccupied with biotrade. National legislations of CBD countries have had to follow suit; it is through them that CBD is implemented. For instance, under India's BD Act the term "commercial utilization" in the context of bio-resources is defined in the act. Amongst other things it includes *genes used for improving crops and livestock through genetic intervention*.[46] Allowing for genetic resources to be traded is considered a necessary pre-condition for bargaining for benefits.

Biodiversity management too is subject to trade interests. The influence of trade and macro-economic policies in the general scheme of things in state actions cannot be over-emphasized. By express wording in the BD Act, the NBA is bound by the directions given by the Central Government on questions of policy.[47] For that reason, there has also been much discussion amongst government officials in India to keep certain bio-resources within the legal category of "normally traded commodities" (NTCs).[48] This exempts trade in the listed 190 bio-resources from what are seen by industry as burdensome ABS requirements, if and when they are traded as commodities.

Another important aspect of trade is protecting intellectual assets and the ability to own them to the exclusion of others. Harmonization of patent standards worldwide has been a constant endeavor of the industry. The WTO TRIPS also specifically laid down that patents can be sought in all fields of technology.[49] Countries like India and Brazil that initially resisted this could have continued to put up a united front at the talks leading up to TRIPS. But they were assailed with "aggressive unilateralism" by the USA (Shukla, 2000). Even after WTO was created, the US administration initiated a complaint against India at the WTO's dispute settlement body, compelling it to amend its IP laws to be in compliance with TRIPS.[50] IP systems were originally conceived of to "protect" and incentivize innovation. But the "South" has come to realize that IP is about protecting property rights and facilitating trade. And in fact, Southern governments and the public research systems in their jurisdiction themselves aspire for such IP capital.

The TRIPS and CBD relationship is pre-disposed to be trade-friendly. The Convention's language on intellectual property does not challenge the global IP regime as contained in TRIPS. Countries that choose to be members of CBD (recognize) *that patents and other intellectual property rights may have an influence on the implementation of this Convention,* but they are also legally bound to *cooperate in this regard subject to national legislation and international law in order to ensure that such rights are supportive of and do not run counter to its objectives.*[51] Taking a more pragmatic approach in the Trade Negotiations Committee at the WTO, countries such as India suggest changes in the TRIPS text, not as much to reign in the IP regime, but to make TRIPS and CBD "mutually supportive."[52] This is partly explained by the fact that the CBD provisions make access to and transfer of technology to biodiversity-rich countries subject to them recognizing the technology-holders IPRs (Article 16).

The "Biodiversity Amendment" of TRIPS proposed by countries such as India, also accommodates trade.[53] The proposal does not challenge IPRs on living forms or knowledge, but only insists that, if and when patents are sought on either of them then, three conditions need to be fulfilled, namely prior informed consent be taken, the country of origin of the resource/know-how be acknowledged, and benefit-sharing arrangements be in place. India's domestic laws—BD Act read with the (amended) Patent Act 1970—make these a legal requirement. Nevertheless, the BD Act does not prohibit any IPRs, including patents on an invention based either on bio-resources or knowledge from India. It only requires that the approval of the NBA be taken.[54] Grant of IPR/patents is part of the process that leads to the commoditization of these resources.

Under the BD Act, the NBA itself processes applications for IP on any invention based on any research or information on a bioresource from India. Amongst all the access applications received by the NBA, those on IPRs far outnumber the others (575 out of a total of 844 as of August 31, 2013).[55] Since the introduction of the BD Act up to August 2013, 117 ABS agreements have been signed by the NBA, out of which over 63 pertain to approval for IPRs on Indian GBMR. Under the *Guidelines on Access to Biological Resources and Associated Knowledge and Benefit Sharing Regulations 2014,* the idea of joint ownership of IP, is also suggested as an option for monetary benefits.[56]

But a more serious demand for the long pending review of the sub-paragraph [Article 27.3(b)] of TRIPS, which deals with whether plants and animal inventions should be covered by patents, is yet to be completed.[57] The said provision of TRIPS was to be reviewed in 1999. Even the Ninth Ministerial Conference (MC9) of the WTO and its resulting

Bali Declaration failed to make mention of any of the concerns of the South vis-à-vis TRIPS.[58] It merely states that member countries of WTO will not initiate non-violation complaints till 2015.[59]

New trade-friendly terminology has also emerged in the CBD lexicon in the context of finances. This was after the call for "innovative financing mechanisms" was given in the convention.[60] One of the four priorities for national and international action in this area is:

> ([M])obilize private funding through innovative financial mechanisms by fostering biodiversity entrepreneurship and enabling biodiversity entrepreneurs to experiment, invest and expand creative economic activities that contribute to addressing biodiversity challenges.[61]

This gives quite a free-run to those experimenting with financialization and commodification of bioresources, whether through nature derivatives, biodiversity offsets, green bonds, ecosystem services, and so on. Monetization is a key strategy and with it is the use of language that brings ecology into the domains of economics and accountancy (Sullivan, 2012). It is justified as necessary to generate wealth to be channeled back for the health of the natural world.

But a real problem, which has both practical and political dimensions, is arriving at a value for the bioresource that is accessed. A system pre-occupied with monetization and conceptualizing "benefits" in monetary terms, also seeks economic evaluation of the resources. Several efforts are on globally and within India, such as by the NBA with (t)he Economics of Ecosystems and Biodiversity (TEEB).[62] It gives added impetus to the incorporation of monetized ecological values into national and corporate decision-making and accounting practices, and is welcomed as such in the CBD's current strategic plan.[63] In the ongoing UNEP–GEF–MoEF ABS Project, the identification of bio-resources or with potential for ABS from selected ecosystems, such as forests, wetlands and agriculture, and their valuation (estimation of the real value) is an important task in the project.[64]

Sui Generis Options

The CBD, without express mention of the term "sui generis", actually allows countries to design their own system of protection for collective bioresources and intellectual heritage. The phrase finds mention in India's BD Act in the context of protection of people's knowledge:

The Central Government shall endeavor to respect and protect the knowledge of local people relating to biological diversity, as recommended by the National Biodiversity Authority, through such measures, which may include registration of such knowledge at the local, State or national levels, and other such measures for protection, *including sui generis system.*[65]

While in general use, sui generis means "of its own kind." The phrase is borrowed from TRIPS wherein express mention of sui generis was meant to give countries options if they were against the idea of patenting of life forms. It logically follows that if a country opts out of granting IP-protection to plants, animals and other living organisms, then it has the freedom to design a unique non-IP system of protection which is better suited to its particular socio-economic conditions. A real sui generis system would then not commodify life as the IR does today. At the least it would be based on a respect of the time-honored relationships that local biodiversity-keepers have with their bioresources. Some argue that commercialization of bioresources and related knowledge leads to their wider application, as encouraged by the CBD. But the Convention text at least does not mandate that commerce alone can keep alive biocultures.

State Sovereignty

Sovereignty is understood in many ways. It can mean the power to make rules, it can mean having authority over a defined geographic area, and it can mean the state of being independent so as to determine one's affairs and be self-governing. The indigenous or local community is by definition a nation in itself comprising a group of people who share a common culture and perspectives of their biological world.

CBD's contribution in international law is seen as having recognized the *sovereign rights of states over their own bio-resources.* CBD presumes a self-governing political entity, the country under whose territorial jurisdiction the resources are under. This reiterated the idea that the country's resources *belonged* to someone. And that it was their prerogative to use and allow others to use the said resources that belonged to them. The "benefit-sharing" regime, at least in India, has not settled the question of whom the local resources actually belong to. And in fact it can be argued that even today, despite the CBD,[66] the relationships of local communities with their biological heritage are not entirely secure.

In current realities, the exercise of this sovereignty is largely by a central government agency. And with it the traditional state-based politics as against a people's politics is only re-emphasized. This can have two opposite effects, either that of the treatment of bioresources as a "commons" (with near free-for-all access without due respect to local relationships with resources) or its commercialization (with national biodiversity regimes justifying it to generate national wealth). Both can be equally problematic to IPLCs. The notion that CBD permits governments to exercise such authority is antithetical to the notion of community sovereignty that local populations and indigenous groups strive for.

Armed with the sovereignty principle, governments have been able to assert ownership-like authority in permitting resource use by "outsiders," while they are to hold the same in trust for their peoples. It has also allowed much more state regulation in areas previously ignored and relatively less interfered into by the administration. The "public trust" doctrine has not been expressly articulated in biodiversity legislation. In India, it was left behind in the Parliamentary Committee discussions on the final draft of the India BD Bill.[67] For a state today, post-CBD vis-à-vis GBMR/knowledge, nothing can any longer be *res nullius* or ownerless.

A concomitant of sovereignty is that, in the context of CBD, it gives the provider country the basis to ask for a "benefit" in return from the user country. It remains a process of negotiation nonetheless, that too of commercial nature, and not sans its political implications. In that sense, the state preoccupies itself with gathering monies as a proxy for the real work of building communities. Through CBD-compliant ABS procedures, the law attempts to settle matters that have been contentious, but in a no less contentious manner. The ABS regime is both willingness to sell genetic materials and willingness to pay for them (Kloppenburg and Rodriguez, 1992).

Legally permitting communities to collect economic rent from their resources or integrating them into the global marketplace is seen as empowering them. From colonial to even post-colonial times, the state has stopped short of guaranteeing community sovereignty over local bioresources. It has in different natural resource sectors granted entitlements by law in varying degrees, whether through forest rights or the right to compensation for land acquisition.[68] But none of these have been sans first commodifying the underlying resource(s). In the biodiversity law too, the opportunity to legally place these resources under pre-existing collective stewardship has been lost. Community members who have reconciled to commercialization may themselves aid bioprospectors in hope of a piece of the pie. The modern community with the nation-state, often fails to legislate recognition of traditional resource rights (Tilahun and Edwards, 1996).

There are inherent contradictions in the convention itself which remain unresolved. On the one hand its raison d'etre is conservation of biodiversity. It also requires countries to respect, preserve and maintain the knowledge, innovation and practices of IPLCs, but it does not put an end to the individual sale of the components of biodiversity that take away the conditions for the above. Another contradiction, which in part explains the direction that the CBD has taken, is that it talks of state sovereignty at a time when state autonomy is most challenged by globalism and its economic forces.

Staking Claims and the "Claimers"

A claim is generally understood as an ask or a demand that stems from either what is due or comes by virtue of a right. A claim is also criticized by many as being dependent on someone else for it to be fulfilled, if at all (Kneen, 2009). Moreover, a claim by itself does not give substance to a right. Its realization is another matter altogether. The case with guaranteed return of "benefits" upon sharing access is quite the same. Merely being identified as a bona fide claimant does not imply that the benefits are assured.

In the biodiversity sector, there are several types of claims that are pitted against one another. The first is the claim over biological material or its related knowledge per se. This is contested ground, for access laws, while focusing on the inter-country exchange by and large, have not resolved long-standing intra-country disputes over resources. ABS laws of various kinds acknowledge that the primary biodiversity-keepers have a legitimate claim to a share in benefits. CBD gives recognition to the relationship of local communities with local bioresources, particularly those which their knowledge, innovation, and practices help to conserve. But the negotiations of biodiversity-keepers with their own governments in most biodiversity-rich countries are a matter of ongoing struggles. Cases where the national system permits domestic accessors to directly negotiate with the provider communities can be equally lop-sided in their power relations.

Meanwhile, the claim of industry is that it renders "added value" or develops something "new," for which both their "inventions" and the investment made in them need to be granted protection. At a fundamental level it instead commodifies what was earlier not, giving it economic value but at the cost of its social functions and cultural significance. People's knowledge is not seen in the same light. It is instead regarded as something passively passed on from one generation to the next without any incremental effort from the present generation of practitioners. Even from the point of view of conservation, its value of ecological suitability and climatic adaptability thus gets lost. This is most obvious in the case of local seeds and indigenous breeds of cattle and livestock. The message this gives out is that biodiversity is valuable (to the economy) only if it is creating commodities.

The sharing of benefits is made dependent on the generation of "benefits" from commercial utilization of the commodities produced, including profits generated from any IP obtained. The CBD entitles IPLCs to a share in benefits. As the experience with ABS in the past decade in India has shown, the benefit-sharing agreements have yet to yield real benefits for local communities.

The BD regime lays down how users can supposedly recompense India and the local communities for the access, through monetary and non-monetary terms. While "benefit claimers" are defined in the law, the term "benefit" is not specifically defined in laws relating to biodiversity. As in the Indian BD Act, different scenarios are presented. The concept is open to contextual interpretation. What are benefits may vary greatly, depending on where one is placed. For claimants with a legal interest, it boils down to the terms of the ABS contract mutually agreed to, to be able to claim "benefits."

Negotiating the contract can itself be a challenge. For "benefit claimers" can find themselves in two equally problematic positions. One, in which a central or regional state agency, such as the NBA/SBBs in India, negotiates the quantum and nature of the "benefits" they are to get from the accessors. Pre-existing power relations will invariably come into play, particularly when prior informed consent procedures are either not prescribed or adhered to; the intended beneficiaries can be left with very little say in the finalization of the access agreement, and dependent on "higher" state authorities for the actual delivery of those benefits to them.[69]

Upon approving access, the NBA is to determine the terms and conditions of benefit-sharing as it may deem fit to impose in each case. It is also required to negotiate a benefit-sharing agreement for the "benefit claimers" (or the custodians/stewards of the assets/knowledge who are sharing it). The BD Act [Section 21(2)] lists over six types of benefit-sharing that are legally possible when either access takes place or approval for IPRs is granted. The NBA's Benefit Sharing Regulations of 2014 provide an indicate list of both monetary and non-monetary benefit-sharing options, which are essentially drawn from the Nagoya Protocol.[70]

Potential benefit claimers may also be left to fend for themselves when confronted with a potential accessor. The BD Act empowers BMCs to charge fees *from any person for accessing and collecting any biological resource for commercial purposes from areas falling under its territorial jurisdiction.*[71] Though the law may give the power there is both little "capacity" and clout on the ground to be able to truly bargain. In fact, several governments, particularly in Africa and Asia, are seeking support from donor agencies as well as expecting accessor countries to put in money for the "capacity building" of not only its ABS administrators but local populations.[72]

In national jurisdictions which might not have an ABS law in place, there too the law of contract can easily fill the gap as has been advised by national focal points of the CBD. So either way, be it in the lack of legislation or even if there is an ABS law in place, contractual arrangements are fast becoming the norm.

In common law it is required that both parties offer some consideration for a contract between them to be binding. What is offered as consideration must have legal value. For the ABS regime (which is premised on contractual agreements) to work today, attribution of commercial value to bioresources and assignment of property rights are inevitable. Confronted with the choice of whether to commodify or not, as the South African San-Hoodia case illustrates, communities and women in them may well choose financial rewards for sharing of knowledge (Wynberg et al., 2009). Women and other marginalized sections of a community who have been pushed to the fringes of a cash economy may see this as the only way out for "progress." It is left to them to make that (non)choice, with or without fully understanding the pros and cons of commodification, the state agency being the choice architect.

The Nagoya Protocol actually gets down to the brass tacks of how best to negotiate the contractual agreements.[73] It advocates compliance with mutually agreed terms (MAT) (Article 18) and Model Contractual Clauses (Article 19). The NBA however is aware of the problems, including high transactions costs of negotiating and enforcing contracts. The NBA's Draft Guidelines on Access (2013) had clearly stated their objective was that *the process of granting approval by the NBA is time-bound and hassle-free* for the applicant.[74] India eager not to antagonize potential accessors, while not wanting onerous conditions put on its scientists/businesses when it turns user/accessor, is contemplating model contract templates.[75]

Mere participation in the process of negotiation of the share of the benefit, does not take away from the fact that local bioresources will eventually be brokered. In the much quoted "first" ABS case from India pre-CBD the Kani tribe was not even one of the negotiators or parties.[76] Given that most biodiversity-keepers (who at least in India by and large remain dormant stakeholders) are not otherwise involved in the making of the national law that prescribes these ABS procedures, their PIC can often get reduced to a mere paper formality rather than translating into meaningful participation.

The "benefit claimers" are defined by the BD Act as conservers of biological resources and their by-products, and creators and holders of knowledge and information relating to the use of such biological resources, innovations and practices associated with such use and application [Section 2(a)]. However, benefit claimers are not so easily identifiable. Often users/accessors source the material from middlemen or the gray market. In fact, in the parallel economy, resources might be already commoditized before they are done so by law. While all the agreements specifically mention that fees, royalty, and benefit-sharing will be charged on a case-by-case basis and will be regulated by the ABS Guidelines, they all are basically about collecting monies.[77] Non-monetary benefits have not been genuinely explored.

Concluding Thoughts: Making Commodities

The ABS regime under CBD is expected to be a step toward biodiversity justice. Justice in the context of the Convention language is defined as "fair and equitable sharing of benefits." This is meant to reverse and recompense for the injustices of (mis)appropriation of local resources by non-locals, sans due process, permission and profit(s) resulting to the countries of origin of the said resources or knowledge and, more so, the communities from whom it is sourced. Previously unregulated bioprospecting, which became unacceptable, is sought to be made more acceptable through the schema of benefit-sharing.

Yet it is perhaps the ABS concept itself that is leading to the continuing public auction of biological resources to external bidders outside local communities. The problem in the manner in which it is framed, that of illegal trade, is sought to be corrected by legalizing those trade transactions. The solution challenges neither trade nor the so-called "benefits" or technologies that are offered in return. At a more fundamental level, it does not question the privatization of people's knowledge or the commodification of their resources. Benefit-sharing within the ABS regime is about being able *ex ante* negotiate one's share in the hope of a small part of the spoils of commodification *ex post*.

To commodify implies turning something than cannot or ought not to be owned into something that can be bought and sold. Commodification refers to those processes through which social relations are reduced to an exchange relation, or as Karl Marx (1978) refers to it in the *Communist Manifesto*, as "callous cash payment." The current emphasis of ABS laws, policies, and implementation is on putting in place an architecture that allows for commodification of biological heritage to happen. The different stages of the commodity chain are evidenced in the initial gathering, prospecting, and documenting of the resources, then in transforming them into goods that can be offered in the market, thereafter attributing to them property rights, and determining their economic value and selling them at a price. At the end of this entire cycle ABS regimes assume a "trickle-down" effect to the provider of the biological material/knowhow by a cash payment or payback in kind. Even sans a classical Marxist lens, while viewing the construction of this marketplace, the significance of global economic forces is clearly to be seen.

IPLCs world over had hoped that biodiversity rules would arrest "bio-piracy" in all its dimensions. Yet, today many remain sceptical with the idea that it is possible to make bioprospecting ethical. Precariously poised, while some are beginning to co-operate, others are still resisting co-option. The state-sponsored exercise to claim benefits may not only dismember resources but also fragment communities. These are times when market forces are challenging the cohesiveness of communities themselves. Institutionalizing the commerce of the very components of their collective biological heritage can only complicate matters. This can go to the heart of their identities and well-being. Claiming instead that it will get them "benefits" is, to say the least, misleading. In fact, experiences from the ground have shown that trade does not stop to wait till real "benefits" accrue to the provider communities or until their ideas of development are realized.

Herein come the centrality of commercial principles and the law of contracts in biodiversity management. But here too the contractual agreements are inherently imbalanced. They give more legal certainty to the accessors, not in equal measure to the provider countries or their communities. At the national level, oft times weak governmental agencies are reluctant or incapable of going after power-wielding accessors in cases of violation of terms and conditions. Whereas, provider governments do not wish to appear investor-unfriendly so they refrain from imposing terms and conditions that might be seen as too stringent by industry. Meanwhile, at the global level, there is no forum to take defaulting users or those who violate ABS procedures. Wrongfully granted IPRs also still have to be fought on a case-by-case basis at foreign patent offices.

The use of legal instruments and contracts brings into sharp focus the part that law plays in the entire process of commodification. As much as it highlights law-makers and the role of the state, the ABS rules can give a semblance of the state being in control, which is not exactly so. As the discussions in the previous sections would have shown, there are forces other than the regulatory state at play that not only construct, but also control the market. State agencies become a mere conduit for these market forces. Sovereign rights of states over their resources are redefined as the right to trade them. But it would be wrong to assume that states are passive agents in global structures that give such a definition. Trade is welcomed by governments as a means to generate funds. Thus there is considerable buy-in into the concept by Southern governments who see it as an opportunity to profit from their natural capital. But there are implications for the social capital and ecological futures.

Thus more than the ABS contracts and their clauses per se, their deeper implications need to be fully fathomed. The loss must not only be understood as a mere breach of contract or non-fulfilment of an ABS agreement. When biodiversity heritage is removed from its locale and de-contextualized from the biocultural landscape in which it has originally developed, it becomes merely raw material for global trade. This is a departure from what up till now were the time-honored relations with local resources. Contracts can very quickly over-write local customary practices and beliefs. With it is the continual lack of control over decision-making regarding local resources/knowledge. This takes people further away from the idea of sovereignty.

Even the most perfect of ABS laws may not be the perfect solution, for they might remain incapable of restoring to the rightful biodiversity-stewards something that has been traded away or surrendered to a contractual arrangement. It is also a betrayal (breach of faith) by the state in being unable to safeguard resources/knowledge of people as it exists. Another breach that gets far little attention is the intergenerational aspect. The effect of commodification is bound to have impacts far into the future. Future generations could be born in a time that know no other way to relate to their living world and biological inheritance, other than to own, buy or sell it. If the CBD and its implementation are to remain both relevant and sustainable, then a long-term view of the impacts of the ABS regime will have to be taken. For "benefit-sharing" fundamentally relies on the commodification of biodiversity to conserve it. That is a problem, not the solution.

Notes

1. Resource is meant to denote the source from which benefits are repeatedly produced and which a country or an institution uses as a factor of production from which to derive income from. The author does not necessarily subscribe to the viewpoint that biological heritage should be treated as a "resource."
2. The terms country and States have been used here interchangeably as in the text of the Convention on Biological Diversity. A State here refers to a self-governing political entity that has national jurisdiction or control over biological resources. The term State differentiates between an independent country and a regional economic integration organization, such as the European Union. "Nations"—culturally homogeneous groups of people with a shared language, traditional institutions, and historical experience that may exist within countries—are covered by the CBD under the phrase "indigenous and local communities."
3. The Protocol was agreed to at the CBD's Tenth Conference of the Parties (COP10) at Nagoya, Japan. It came into force on October 12, 2014 after 50 ratifications; as of date 64 countries including India have ratified the Protocol. http://www.cbd.int/abs/.
4. The full text of the Biological Diversity Act, 2002 can be downloaded from the Government of India's India's Ministry of Environment and Forests' Forests' website. http://envfor.nic.in/division/biodiversity (as accessed in November 2013).

5. The 1970 UN General Assembly Resolution 2749 (XXV) on Declaration of Principles Governing the Seabed and the Ocean Floor, and the Subsoil Thereof, beyond the Limits of National Jurisdiction solemnly declared that these areas are CHM.

6. See even the dilemma of the (provider) Hawaiian state within a user country USA not a party to the CBD: http://lrbhawaii.info/lrbrpts/05/biocon.pdf (accessed on January 5, 2016).

7. Declaration of the United Nations Conference on the Human Environment–United Nations Environment Programme http://www.unep.org/Documents.Multilingual/ Default.asp?documentid=97&articleid=1503 (accessed on November 18, 2015).

8. Convention on Wetlands; Convention on the Conservation of Migratory Species of Wild Animals; Convention on International Trade in Endangered Species of Wild Fauna and Flora.

9. Paul Berg Meetings that changed the world: Asilomar 1975: DNA modification secured Nature 2008 http://www.nature.com/nature/journal/v455/n7211/full/455290a.html (accessed on November 18, 2015).

10. The group was set up by decision 14/26 of the Governing Council of the UNEP, to "to investigate the desirability and possible form of an umbrella convention to rationalize current activities in this field." The group comprised experts from 25 countries, including USA. http://www.cbd.int/doc/?meeting=BDEWG-01 (accessed on November 18, 2015).

11. See History of the Convention http://www.cbd.int/history/ (accessed on November 18, 2015).

12. Diamond versus Chakrabarty http://en.wikipedia.org/wiki/Diamond_v._Chakrabarty (accessed on November 18. 2015).

13. WTO website http://www.wto.org/english/tratop_e/trips_e/trips_e.htm (accessed on November 18, 2015).

14. The Mātaatua Declaration on Cultural and Intellectual Property Rights of Indigenous Peoples, 1993 that emerged from what is regarded as the "First International Conference on the Cultural and Intellectual Property Rights of Indigenous Peoples" held at Whakatane, New Zealand, called for a moratorium on the commercialization of indigenous medicinal plants and human genetic materials until IPLCs had developed 'appropriate "appropriate protection mechanisms". http://www.ngatiawa.iwi.nz/cms/ view/mataatua-declaration.aspx (accessed on November 18, 2015).

15. ICBG website http://www.icbg.org/index.php

16. GRAIN June 1997 Biopiracy's Latest Disguises Seedling http://www.grain.org/article/ entries/270-biopiracy-s-latest-disguises (accessed on November 18, 2015).

17. See the Maya ICBG bioprospecting controversy on Wikipedia http://en.wikipedia.org/ wiki/Maya_ICBG_bioprospecting_controversy (accessed on November 18, 2015).

18. Read Joshua Rosenthal's A Benefit-sharing case study for the Conference of Parties to Convention on Biological Diversity. www.cbd.int/doc/case-studies/abs/cs-abs-icbg.pdf (accessed on November 18, 2015).

19. Principles for Accessing Genetic Resources, the Treatment of Intellectual Property and the Sharing of Benefits Associated with the ICBG-Sponsored Research http://www. icbg.org/program/principles.php

20. In 1997 the MNC RiceTec, Inc. was granted US Patent No. 5,663,484 on "Basmati rice lines and grains" by the USPTO.

21. United Nations Non-Governmental Liaison Service E&D File, Vol. 1 No. 4, Feb 95 www. un-ngls.org/orf/documents/pdf/ED/biodiv.pdf (accessed on November 18, 2015).

22. United States: Declaration Made at the United Nations Environment Programme for the Adoption of the Agreed Text of the Convention on Biological Diversity, reprinted in 31 I.L.M. 848 (1992).

23. Text of the Draft Regulation can be downloaded from here: http://eur-lex.europa.eu/legal-content/EN/TXT/?uri=CELEX%3A32014R0511 (accessed on January 5, 2015).

24. Bhutan's Biodiversity Act, 2003 & ABS Policy, 2012. Drafts of proposed ABS/Biodiversity laws in Bangladesh, Nepal, Pakistan and Sri Lanka are merely texts not in force.

25. The orders of the Madhya Pradesh Biodiversity Board insisting on payments by coal and other local industries are sub judice in cases pending before India's National Green Tribunal at Bhopal. Likewise, the Board has initiated action against Hershey India Private Limited for not doing the legally mandated benefit-sharing.

26. Biological Diversity Rule 22 on Constitution of Biodiversity Management Committees.

27. In 1998 the Organisation for African Unity adopted a Model Law for the Protection of the Rights of Local Communities, Farmers, Breeders and Regulation of Access to Biological Resources. This offers a framework for OAU Member States while developing a national level legislation suited to their local realities. Following this in 1999 the African Group asked WTO that TRIPS be revised to prohibit the patenting of life forms and that national sui generis laws on the issue be allowed.

28. Draft ARIPO Legal Framework for the Protection of New Varieties of Plants. The text can be downloaded from the ARIPO website here: http://www.aripo.org/resources/laws-protocols (accessed on January 5, 2015).

29. Article 15(2) of the CBD states that (e)ach Contracting Party shall endeavor to create renditions to facilitate access to genetic resources for environmentally sound uses by other contracting parties and not to impose restrictions that run counter to the objectives of this convention.

30. Section 39 of the BD Act.

31. Section 39 (3) of the BD Act.

32. Myriad Genetics, Inc. is a molecular diagnostic company founded in 1991 and based in Utah, USA. It was a defendant in a case: Association for Molecular Pathology versus Myriad Genetics, Inc. et al. at the Supreme Court of the United States. For the first time in US legal history, two of the company's patents on the BRCA1 and BRCA2 genes were ruled invalid on March 29, 2010 by a District Court in Southern District of New York, USA.

33. In a unanimous ruling by Justice Clarence Thomas in the Myriad case decided by the Supreme Court on June 13, 2013 it was held so.

34. Myriad Genetics Presses Ahead on Patents After "Misunderstood" Supreme Court Ruling: Law Blog *Wall Street Journal* July 12, 2013 http://blogs.wsj.com/law/2013/07/12/myriad-genetics-presses-ahead-after-high-court-ruling-on-patents/ (accessed on November 18, 2015).

35. ISF View on Intellectual Property, adopted in Brazil, June 28, 2012 http://www.worldseed.org/cms/medias/file/PositionPapers/OnIntellectualProperty/View_on_Intellectual_Property_2012.pdf (accessed on November 18, 2015).

36. Monsanto's Patents: A List of seed monopolies–Greenpeace (accessed on November 18, 2015).

37. BIO shares USTR's International Patent Concerns http://www.bio.org/media/press-release/bio-shares-us-trade-representatives-international-patent-concerns

38. BIO's Bioprospecting Guidelines http://www.bio.org/articles/bio-bioprospecting-guidelines

39. Aichi Biodiversity Targets http://www.cbd.int/sp/targets/(accessed on November 18, 2015).
40. Decision X/21 on Business Engagement adopted by the CBD COP10 in Nagoya, Aichi Prefecture, Japan http://www.cbd.int/decision/cop/default.shtml?id=12287 (accessed on November 18, 2015).
41. CBD's Global Partnership on Business and Biodiversity http://www.cbd.int/en/business/global-partnership (accessed on November 18, 2015). The first meeting of the Global Platform on Business and Biodiversity was scheduled in Tokyo, Japan on December 15–16, 2011.
42. Secretariat of the CBD (2005) *The Impact of Trade Liberalisation on Agricultural Biodiversity*, Domestic support measures and their effects on agricultural biodiversity Montreal, SCBD, p. 47 (CBD Technical Series No.16).
43. NBA Docket.
44. Section 18(4) of the BD Act.
45. Biodiversity-related Access and Benefit-sharing Agreements http://www.wipo.int/tk/en/databases/contracts/list.html (accessed on November 18, 2015).
46. Section 2(f) of the BD Act defines "commercial utilization" as end uses of biological resources for commercial utilization such as drugs, industrial enzymes, food flavors, fragrance, cosmetics, emulsifiers, oleoresins, colors, extracts, and genes used for improving crops and livestock through genetic intervention, but does not include conventional breeding or traditional practices in use in any agriculture, horticulture, poultry, dairy farming, animal husbandry or bee keeping.
47. Section 48 of the BD Act.
48. Section 40 of the BD Act gives power to the Central Government to exempt certain biological resources from the purview of the Act. As per a notification of the Environment Ministry dated October 26, 2009, there are 190 NTCs that have been categorized as: medicinal plants, spices, and horticultural crops (which include fruits, vegetables, root, tuber and bulbous crops, flower crops, plantation crops, medicinal crops, and aromatic crops), which on the basis of requests from state governments and the wisdom of the Union Government qualify for such exemption.
49. Article 27.1 of TRIPS http://www.wto.org/english/docs_e/legal_e/27-trips_04c_e.htm (accessed on November 18, 2015).
50. Dispute DS50 Complaint filed by USA Against India on the issue of Patent Protection for Pharmaceutical and Agricultural Chemical Products http://www.wto.org/english/tratop_e/dispu_e/cases_e/ds50_e.htm
51. Article 16(5) of the CBD.
52. Read the full proposal: Draft Decision to Enhance Mutual Supportiveness between the TRIPS Agreement and the Convention on Biological Diversity TN/C/W/59 dated April 19, 2011.
53. See TRIPS – Close Call in Geneva Seedling October 2008 GRAIN http://www.grain.org/article/entries/711-trips-close-call-in-geneva
54. Section 6 of BD Act.
55. http://nbaindia.org/text/24/TOTALAPPLICATIONRECEIVED.html (accessed on November 18, 2015)
56. These were issued by India's Environment Ministry on November 21, 2014. The full text can be downloaded from http://nbaindia.org/uploaded/pdf/Gazette_Notification_of_ABS (accessed on November 18, 2015).
57. For more details please read this section on the WTO website: http://www.wto.org/english/tratop_e/trips_e/art27_3b_background_e.htm (accessed on November 18, 2015).

58. By the time this book went into print the WTO's MC10 had been held in Nairobi, Kenya in December 2015. There too the "Nairobi Package" adopted by member countries on December 19, 2015 likewise agreed not to initiate non-violation complaints till any further decision. No substantive decisions, on the review of TRIPS, etc. were taken with respect with issues around IPRs.

59. TRIPS Non-violation and Situation Complaints: Ministerial Decision. WT/MIN(13)/31 — WT/L/906.

60. Refer to Decision XI/4, Paragraph 19 as well as the Strategic Plan for Biodiversity (2011–2020) of the CBD.

61. Note by the Executive Secretary, CBD Document UNEP/CBD/WG-RI/2/4 dated 16 May 2007. The full text can be read here: https://www.cbd.int/doc/meetings/wgri/wgri-02/official/wgri-02-04-en.pdf (accessed on January 5, 2015).

62. http://www.teebweb.org/ (accessed on November 18, 2015).

63. Strategic Plan for Biodiversity 2011-2020 http://www.cbd.int/sp/ (accessed on November 18, 2015).

64. A National Consultation Meeting on Economic Valuation of Biological Resources for the purposes of access to genetic resources and benefit-sharing was organized under this project 9-10 December 2013 at Chennai in Southern India. Therein experts proposed that "value chain analysis and identification of economic/resource rent" of bio-resources based products is more appropriate in estimating the real value of bio-resources. http://nbaindia.org/gallerycontent/642/gallerycontent/1/NationalConsultatio.html (accessed on November 18, 2015).

65. Section 36(5) of the BD Act, 2002.

66. Article 8(j) of the CBD.

67. As mentioned in the report of the Indian Parliamentary Committee on Science & Technology, Environment & Forests, dated December 4, 2001, the committee considered insertion of the following new sub-clause 3A on "Public Trust Doctrine" in the Biological Diversity Bill, 2000:

> All biodiversity shall be held by the Union of India in trust for the people of India to be conserved, used and sustained in the public interest consistent with principles of sustainable development and equitable sharing, especially for local groups and communities and to enhance community control over biodiversity resources.

On the advice tendered by the Ministry of Law & Justice (Department of Legal Affairs), the committee discussed the matter and decided not to insert the clause.

68. The Scheduled Tribes and Other Traditional Forest Dwellers (Recognition of Forest Rights) Act, 2006 http://tribal.nic.in/WriteReadData/CMS/Documents/20121129033 2077861328File1033.pdf;
The Right to Fair Compensation and Transparency in Land Acquisition, Rehabilitation and Resettlement Act, 2013; http://dolr.nic.in/dolr/downloads/pdfs/Right%20to%20Fair%20Compensation%20and%20Transparency%20in%20Land%20Acquisition,%20Rehabilitation%20and%20Resettlement%20Act,%202013.pdf

69. See *Unfair Share, Uncertain Futures* http://www.themalaysianinsider.com/mobile/breakingviews/article/unfair-share-uncertain-futures-shalini-bhutani-and-kanchi-kohli/ (accessed on November 18, 2015). This is the seaweed access case from Southern India, wherein despite the NBA having got a large sum of money from the accessor company (Pepsi India Ltd.), the same had not reached the communities.

70. Some of the benefit-sharing options in Annexure 1 of the Regulations (2014):

    1. Monetary benefits—upfront payments, milestone payments, funds, supply contracts/linkages, IP benefits, etc.
    2. Institutional benefits—such as venture capital funds, enterprise development
    3. Capacity building—at various levels
    4. Access to and transfer of technologies
    5. Sharing and exchange of scientific information.

71. Section 41(3) of the BD Act.
72. Article 20 of the CBD.
73. Section 39 (3) of the BD Act.
74. Draft Access Guidelined issued by the National Biodiversity Authority under Section 18(1) of the Biological Diversity Act, 2002.
75. As mentioned in the Draft Guidelines on Benefit Sharing issued by the NBA, a good contract template could be one that contain seven basic aspects:

    1. Direct payments in cash or knowledge exchanges (equipment, training, technological know-how).
    2. Payment of a significant percentage of the initial budget of the project (10 percent) and the returns of the commercialization of the products (50 percent).
    3. Cooperation clauses that stipulate the gradual translation of the investigation processes to the supplier country, in order to create new jobs and the achievement of industrial development.
    4. Minimum exclusivity.
    5. Agreement on the samples property and patents property.
    6. The use of chemistry synthesis, semi-synthesis and domestication of the living sources, in order to avoid the continuous extraction of the biotic material.
    7. Legal mechanisms that will provide protection to both parties.

76. Know How Licencing Agreement between The Tropical Botanic Garden and Research Institute, Kerala, India (TBGRI) and The Arya Vaidya Pharmacy (Coimbatore) Ltd, Coimbatore, India (the PARTY), dated November 10, 1995 http://www.wipo.int/tk/en/databases/contracts/texts/tbgri.html
77. The benefit-sharing formulae vary in each case.

References

Berne Declaration, Bread for the World, ECOROPA, Tebtebba, TWN. (2013). Nagoya Protocol on Access to Genetic Resources and the Fair and Equitable Sharing of Benefits Arising from their Utilization: Background and Analysis, p. 168.

Bhutani, S. (2012). *Prized or Priced: Protection of India's Traditional Knowledge related to Biological Resources and Intellectual Property*, WWF-India, Delhi.

Biswamoy, P. and Harrison, M. (Ed.) (2001). *Health, Medicine and Empire: Perspectives on Colonial India*. New Delhi: Orient Longman Ltd.

CITES. (1975). Convention on International Trade in Endangered Species of Wild Fauna and Flora. Available from https://www.cites.org/eng/disc/text.php (accessed on January 5, 2016).

CMS. (1979). Convention on the Conservation of Migratory Species of Wild Animals; Legal citation 1651 UNTS 333; 19 ILM 15. (1980); ATS 1991/32; BTS 87 (1990), Cm. 1332. Available from http://www.cms.int/en/convention-text (accessed on January 5, 2016).

ETC Group. (1995). *Bioprospecting/Biopiracy and Indigenous Peoples*. Canada: RAFI (now ETC). Available at: http://www.etcgroup.org/content/bioprospectingbiopiracy-and-indigenous-peoples (accessed on November 20, 2015).

Jawara, F. and Kwa, A. (2003). *Behind the Scenes at the WTO: The Real World of Trade Negotiations*. London and New York: Zed Books.

Johnson, S. (2012). UNEP: *The First 40 Years: A Narrative*. United Nations Environment Program, Nairobi. Available at: http://www.unep.org/40thAnniversary/ (accessed on November 20, 2015).

Kloppenburg, J. and Rodriguez, S. (1992). Conservationists or Corsairs? *Seedling* (July) GRAIN. Available at: http://www.grain.org/es/article/entries/489-conservationists-or-corsairs (Accessed on November 20, 2015).

Kneen, B. (2009). *The Tyranny of Rights, The Ram's Horn*. Ottawa, Canada: The Ram's Horn.

Kohli, K. and Bhutani, S. (2011). *Chasing "Benefits": Issues on Access to Genetic Resources and Traditional Knowledge with reference to India's Biodiversity Regime*, p. 28. New Delhi: Kalpavriksh and WWF-India.

_____. (2013). *The 'Balancing' Act*. New Delhi: Kalpavriksh & Swissaid.

Peterson, M.J. (2010). "Asilomar Conference on Laboratory Precautions." International Dimensions of Ethics Education in Science and Engineering. Available at: www.umass.edu/sts/ethics.

Ramsar (Iran) (February 2, 1971). Convention on Wetlands of International Importance especially as Waterfowl Habitat. UN Treaty Series No. 14583. As amended by the Paris Protocol, December 3, 1982, and Regina Amendments, May 28, 1987. Available from http://www.ramsar.org/sites/default/files/documents/library/scan_certified_e.pdf (accessed on January 5, 2016).

Schiebinger, L. (2004). *Plants and Empire: Colonial Bioprospecting in the Atlantic World*. Cambridge: Harvard University Press.

Shiva, V. and Bhutani, S. (2001). *An Activist's Handbook on Intellectual Property Rights and Patents Research Foundation for Science, Technology and Ecology*. New Delhi: Research Foundation for Science, Technology and Ecology.

Shukla, S.P. 2000. "From GATT to WTO and Beyond." Working Papers No. 195, The United Nations University/WIDER, August 2000, Helsinki, Finland.

Sullivan, S. (2012). *Financialisation, Biodiversity Conservation and Equity: Some Currents and Concerns*. Malaysia: Third World Network, ISBN: 978-967-5412-69-1.

Sumida, S. (2008). Bioindustry and the convention on biological diversity: Japan experience. *Asian Biotechnology and Development Review*, *10*(3), 37–48.

Tilahun, S. and Edwards, S. (Ed.) (1996). *The Movement for Collective Intellectual Rights Institute for Sustainable Development*. Addis Ababa/London: Institute for Sustainable Development/The Gaia Foundation.

Wynberg, R., Schroeder, D., and Chennells, R. (2009). *Indigenous Peoples, Consent and Benefit Sharing Lessons from the San-Hoodia Case*. Netherlands: Springer.

3

The Abstract Nature of Building[1]

Himanshu Burte

The perspectival argument in this chapter is guided by a common theme: connectedness, or more specifically, relationality. The chapter focuses on the erosion of relationality in contemporary planned urban development, both in the way the developmental imagination understands reality and in the substance of the reality it creates. In particular, it examines what plans, discourse and outcomes on the ground reveal about the way nature, society and their interrelationship in place are viewed by the developmental imagination. To do this, two key strands of the debate on space are brought into conversation. One is the idea of place from the geographical and urban planning literature. I have chosen to approach "place" through an extension of the concept of relationality that Marc Auge (1995) uses in an anthropological sense: while Auge uses the idea of relationality in the sense of social relatedness, I extend it to include a relatedness with nature. The other is a set of key theoretical insights offered by the Marxist philosopher and social theorist, Henri Lefebvre in *The Production of Space* (1991).

I argue that the current neoliberal economic system, in India, as elsewhere, is increasingly focused on producing what Lefebvre thinks of as abstract spaces made paradoxically real (henceforth, real abstract spaces) to enable capital accumulation. These resemble Auge's "empirical non-places" quite closely (1995, p. viii). This spatiality, first invented with a more progressive rhetoric by the modernism of the 20th century, is marked by an apparently willful (and often exploitative) disconnection with the historically evolved socio-ecological system of their site, as well as the planet as a whole. Here it is relevant to note that 20th-century modernism, for all its democratic rhetoric, was itself inspired significantly by the values and methods of scientific management, a philosophy that organizes the managerial logic of 20th and 21st-century capital (Guillen, 2006).

To anchor the argument that follows, I shall briefly introduce three high profile projects that involve the production of real abstract space as part of a broader urban and developmental strategy in different parts of India: the Sabarmati Riverfront Development (SRD) project in Ahmedabad; Lavasa, located near the city of Pune and advertised as the first planned post-independence hill station; and the ambitious Delhi-Mumbai Industrial Corridor (DMIC), stretching across seven states and involving the creation of nine new cities. These projects epitomize different strands of urban developmental action in different kinds of location and at varying scales. They are widely seen by the media, state, and market as a foretaste of an ideal urban future for an India that the middle classes can be proud of. SRD is inside a big city, Lavasa is a new township in the Sahyadri mountains near Pune, and DMIC is a massive intervention stretching over a 1,500 km length and affecting large regions at a national scale. Most importantly, all three have the strong backing of the state. Former Gujarat Chief Minister, now Prime Minister of India, Narendra Modi, had a personal commitment to the SRD project. Lavasa has received unprecedented support and facilitation by the state government, and Sharad Pawar, a former chief minister and current Union Minister is believed to have taken a personal interest in it.[2] DMIC, meanwhile, was a union government initiative, headed by a specially chosen bureaucrat, Amitabh Kant, who has a proven record of success in large state initiatives in different sectors.

The discussions of these emblematic projects are largely based on information available in the public domain. Central to all three is the phenomenon of greatest interest to this chapter: the production of real abstract spaces or non-places and what it tells us about how nature (and, to some extent, society) is understood by the developmental imagination. Two projects, SRD and Lavasa, actually leverage a unique ecological feature: a river in the case of SRD and a hilly landscape in the case of Lavasa. All three have a significant ecological impact as well as important implications for social equity. What makes these projects emblematic of the age is that all three are foundationally connected to the dynamic pressures and attractions of the global circuit of capital. In fact, each is ultimately a spatial strategy and product geared to attracting foreign investment into a city, a private profit-making enclave and a national scale region respectively. Each involves the production of real estate and will ultimately enable private profit and accumulation, through different pathways. Each also makes bold claims about the benefit to the public at large, though in each there is either a significant risk or an established set of losses and setbacks that poor and marginalized social groups face due to dispossession, dislocation or loss of ecological support systems related to their livelihood and survival. Finally, all three illustrate some common features of the developmental imagination's attitude toward natural systems and the socio-economically weaker social groups who directly depend on those systems.

Non-places in Auge's characterization are usually spaces of consumption, circulation and communication (1995, p. viii). They include infrastructural spaces like expressways and airports, or spaces of production and consumption like software parks, resorts, and theme parks, and even gated residential enclaves and integrated townships. As Lefebvre argues, referring to real abstract spaces (which, I suggest, are Auge's non-places) the form of these spaces is simultaneously an instrument of development and production as well as a product and commodity of the neocapitalist, or neoliberal, economy (Lefebvre, 1991, pp. 49–53, 336–42). Non-places might thus be produced for their own sake as well as to enable accumulation through economically productive activities they enable efficiently. While it is capital that ultimately seeks to drive the production of non-places, they are worthy of close attention on their own account in any discussion related to the way we see nature today. This is so for a number of reasons. To begin with, the production of these planned non-places can be easily seen as a proximate cause of significant social and ecological damage and destruction, whose impacts unfold across a larger than local space and time. This substantive impact derives partly from their energy intensive technological substance (as well as the mechanistic scientific knowledge system on which it is based) and partly from the political–administrative processes of their production that also echoes the Cartesian characteristics of expert knowledge. The other reason for paying attention to non-places relates to their impact on how we think about and relate to nature and society: as spaces with aspirational value, they promote a culture of abstraction and of alienation from nature as well as society.

Such alienation is clearly aligned with the twin tendencies that drive the production of non-places: the drive to accumulate capital on the one hand, and the core values and assumptions of the Cartesian way of knowing the world by cutting it up into discrete parts. Such a culture of alienation from nature and of fragmented knowing, this chapter assumes, is more significant than the immediate physical impacts of specific projects. Of course, the synergy between the two tendencies does not automatically mean that the real abstract space is destined to overrun "place" without resistance either from society (especially by people directly dependent on nature in a place) or the natural system itself. Lefebvre himself notes the tension between the tendency of capital (and a closely allied state, as increasingly in India) to dominate produced space, and the drive of the dominated to appropriate that very space for their own purposes (of survival or festival), to build back an originally pre-empted differentiation (Lefebvre, 1991, pp. 52–3) and relationality. We can thus take it as a given that while the ideology of non-places is increasingly gaining ground in India, it is also being met with social and natural resistance on the ground in multiple ways.

Place, Relationality, and Social Space

The concept of place has a large and lively four decades old literature devoted to it, especially in the West (Cresswell, 2004). This literature emerges from a critique of the loss of meaning, weakened connection with human life and nature, as well as the erosion of identity that Western urban development has brought in through planning and design. Most crucially, beginning with pioneering human geographers like Yi Fu Tuan (1997), the interconnections between bodily and social being, the natural world and the human production of the built environment have steadily gained more attention. Underlying this literature is a recognition that the values and methods organizing modern urban planning and development have tended to snip the very real, historical, emotional and ontological relationships that necessarily tie human life and the built environment to the natural world. A search for the basis of this "lost" relationality, as well as for the reasons for its loss marks this literature.

Relationality is a condition of *knowing* of a place as well as of its being. In a relational view, things do not exist, and are not considered to exist, independently of others. It is closely tied up with the idea of a totality and similar to how we understand the concept of ecology today (especially in its being an open process, and not a stable state) (Merrifield, 1993). In this regard, Merrifield quotes Ollman as saying that "each part is viewed as incorporating in what it is, all its relations with other parts up to and including everything that comes into the whole" (Ollman, 1990). A relational view of the built environment, a view that the discourse on place has striven to develop, thus looks at it as embedded in and emergent out of social and natural process. Place is thus conceived as a whole, parts of which are each defined as much by their own characteristics as by their relations with the others and with the whole. Seen like this, the built environment, social life and nature shape each other, for better or worse, at least partly through the medium of "place," itself considered as a totality always undergoing change. One implication is that in any discussion of the built environment, such a view makes it necessary to consider the way the process of "the production of space" conceives and impacts nature and society together, and to what social purpose.

This way of thinking about the built environment underlies Henri Lefebvre's eponymous discussion of "the production of space" (1991). His concept of "social space" (formulated before the initiation of the current discourse on place in human geography in the late 1970s) is clearly aligned with the way the idea and reality of "place" have been characterized in the literature. Relationality can be considered a central concern in the discussion of "place." Though Lefebvre does not use the term, it also underlies Lefebvre's conception of "social space," both in corporate nature (or "natural" space) and society necessarily into the phenomenon they describe. This is confirmed by the striking parallels between Lefebvre's discussion of "real abstract spaces" and Marc Auge's concept of "non-places." Both concepts describe a form of space that is the antithesis of "place," one with a significantly abstract, controlled, and reduced relationality.

A brief excursus into the idea of social space in Henri Lefebvre is necessary here to lay the ground for a fuller discussion of concepts like abstraction, abstract space and non-place. At the center of Lefebvre's "The Production of Space" is a simple assertion about the relationship between society and space: "(Social) space is a (social) product" (1991, p. 26). One implication of this statement is that every society, more specifically, every mode of production, produces (or secretes) its own specific space. One starting point for this production is the fact that the human body and society emerge and are sustained in nature. The historical inter-play of pressures exerted by the human body (need for shelter, security, and so on), society (modes of production, cultural values, and so on) and nature (landscape, climate, natural resources, and so on) has tended to produce highly differentiated spaces in nature. According to Lefebvre, this differentiated space is unlike the Cartesian space of expert disciplines (geometry, for instance), and of capitalism. The latter space is imagined (and sought to be produced) as a homogenous and neutral container of discrete objects, which is also separate from them.

For Lefebvre, pre-capitalist space surges forth out of the social act of dwelling in nature which embraces all human activities, including eco-nomic production. It is given its distinctive form by the relationships that organize everyday personal and social life in the ecological matrix we understand as nature. These relationships connect the exigencies of the human body (including its natural rhythms and gestures), the demands and promises of the natural environment, and a historically produced social life (including the acts of production in and through nature, as in primary activities) through the form of the space that the society produces. That space in turn helps reproduce those relationships, while always being subject to history, especially to direct human actions and natural events within it. Thus, coded into this space is an acknowledge-ment of the origin of people and place in nature, as in social history. We can assume that such coding is recognizable as the "sense of place" in vil-lages and old cities. This sense of place emerges from the relational char-acteristic of the built environment which, one could argue, also enables a more nurturing perspective on nature.

An important factor in the way this pre-capitalist space and its sense of place is produced is the character of the knowledge that helps produce and alter it. This is a lived knowledge, emerging from the social practices of dwelling in space, which also continually produces that space from "inside." It is a relational knowledge born of the relational experience of place, and therefore of nature and society. For Lefebvre, the space of capi-talism, by contrast, is produced out of a Cartesian inspired knowledge marked by a lack of relationality, and conceived from a vantage point "outside" any and every social (or socio-ecological) space.

This preliminary theoretical discussion is the broad frame through which we can examine the three cases that follow. Their discussion will try to show that they are each non-places in different ways. It will do so by calling attention to the different ways in which relationality is eroded in the process and the product of "non-place-making." In the discussion following the cases, I shall reflect on what the cases tell us about a number of things related to the rule of abstraction as a value and its impact on the way nature is imagined in the developmental imagination.

Sabarmati Riverfront, Ahmedabad

The Sabarmati Riverfront Project is a developmental intervention by the city government (with the direct encouragement of the state's chief minister), and an urban renewal project that focuses on creating public space and land for public amenities along the Sabarmati river that passes through the center of the city. The project was first proposed in the 1960s by the French architect Bernard Kohn, and again at other times in subsequent decades. However, it was only finally taken up in 1997 when the Sabarmati Riverfront Development Corporation Ltd (SRFDCL) was set up, though construction began in 2004.[3] Over a 10.5 km stretch, both the banks of the seasonal river have been re-profiled in section and plan to achieve a simplified geometry. About 185 hectares of land is expected to be created along the riverside, most of which is planned to be used either as public recreational space or for "world class" public amenities like museums, etc. About 15 percent of the land is intended to be sold as real estate to finance the project which is slated to cost about ₹1,500 crore (approx. US$300 million) (Mathur, 2012). The project was clearly visualized as part of the then Chief Minister (and now Prime Minister of India), Narendra Modi's broader commitment to a neoliberal economic vision that seeks to attract ever-increasing investment into the city and the state. It is thus the centerpiece of the desire for "first worlding" the fast growing city and competing for the attention of global capital. Through the project, Ahmedabad too stands to get its own world class riverfront complete with recreational facilities like theatres, museums, and promenades.

In concrete terms, the Sabarmati Riverfront Project seeks to literally *produce* usable space in the congested heart of Ahmedabad by modifying the natural slope of land as it descends to the bed of the seasonal Sabarmati, and by "rationalizing" the shape of the channel in plan. Its pivotal move is physical, filling up the natural slope of the river's edge to produce new land and hold it in place by reinforced concrete retaining walls. Bimal Patel, its architect, is quoted as having called this a strategy of "pinching the river" (D'Monte, 2011). The variable existing channel (average width, 382 meters) has been narrowed to a uniform 275 meters with an increased height of concrete embankments to compensate in depth for the loss of width, and ensure the same volume. The retaining walls are designed to channel and contain the flow of the river and protect low lying areas of the city from the occasional flood.

The river itself has been reengineered to overcome its seasonality, which has also displaced multiple informal uses to which it was put by the poor. The Sabarmati has traditionally had water only for four months in a year. For the rest of the time the riverbed has traditionally been put to multiple uses, especially by the thousands of poor people who live in decades-old slums along the river's edge and more than 4,000 families from among them are already displaced by the project (Desai, 2012; Mathur, 2012). The temporary land that the riverbed concedes for eight months of the year has been a playground, a venue for ceremonies, markets as well as the space where washermen launder clothes. However, those uses as well as the fact that the river runs dry for most of the year are presumably mismatched with the conceived riverfront as the future image center of an aspiring global city.

Discussion of SRD

Some things are immediately evident regarding the SRD project. Like in many other cities seeking to be linked into the global economic system, this state-run project seeks to produce recreational public space, especially at riverfronts where they are available, often replacing formal or informal land uses and activities related to production and subsistence. A rhetoric asserting the self-evident value of public space as well as of the environmental housekeeping that these projects promise always accompanies such projects. Many professionals involved in such projects often sincerely believe in the rhetoric themselves. However, like other such produced spaces, the Sabarmati riverfront is neither convincingly conceived as a space for all publics, nor is it willing to adjust to the contingencies of real nature, as we saw. Rather, it is oriented more decisively toward participating in the global competition for attracting investment. The profits from this investment tend to feed back into the global circuit of capital while some proportion remains with the local elite. The project is thus clearly addressed to the middle and upper classes of the city, who stand to benefit most from foreign investment. Not surprisingly, then, the project seeks to reproduce a Western vision of public space on the one hand that is attractive to the local elites, while also producing invaluable real estate to the extent of 28 ha (over 30 lakh, or 3 million, square feet which would yield a gross total built up area multiple times that number, depending on the Floor Space Index that will be allocated to this special project) at 15 percent of the total reclaimed extent of 185 ha.[4]

It is clear that the natural river was a social space defined by a relational web connecting natural processes, informal social activities, and meanings. The new riverfront, by contrast, is a spatial product. It is an urban space that privileges the lifestyle values of the elite and middle classes and simultaneously excludes the poor in multiple ways (see in this regard, Fernandes, 2004). Both these effects help the space to enable the larger process of accumulation of capital.

Here we recall again the similarity between Auge's concept of the "non-place" and Lefebvre's abstract space coming true. A lack of relationality is central to Auge's non-place. The Sabarmati of the *produced* riverfront is a non-relational ecological phenomenon. It is no more the seasonal river it was in its natural state. In that state its riverness in Ahmedabad—seasonal fullness, and a dry bed ecology out of season—was related to the larger riverine process it was part of, and which connected upstream socio-ecological implications to those downstream. The SRD project has expertly cut the space of the urban river out of that historically evolved socio-ecological web of relations to convert it into a "spatial product" (Easterling, 2005).

The attitude to the river is worth considering a little more closely. At one level, the riverfront project pivots on a conception of the river and its edge as a space of recreation. The conception of recreation, as well as of the chosen way of making the project feasible financially, however, lead to a figurative displacement of the very river that the project seeks to rescue and revivify.[5] That displacement and replacement by what is basically a long, artificial, open-ended tank in the site of the old river, are enabled by an abstract conception of the river that experts work with. That abstract river courses through controversies about how many "cusecs"[6] of water flows through the river at peak season (Sheth, 2007). Such a view, typical of the way technical professionals like architects and engineers conceive of the natural phenomena at the moment of design, allows Bimal Patel to explain the concept of the project as "pinching the river" slightly, to produce more usable space on its sides. This phrase deftly reduces the conceived river to a simple, fully understandable, docile, and nearly inconsequential trickle that is fully amenable to the control of the technician. The *conceived* river (as distinct from the real one) is revealed as an inert abstraction in that single phrase, one that may be re-engineered without significant consequence.

The monumental concrete embankments—symbols of control—also reveal another essential aspect of the way river and landscape tend to get conceptualized in the urban technical imagination. Like in the case of Mumbai, we see the imperatives of abstract categorization acting in synergy with the land fetish of developmental action, to clearly separate land and water from each other much more definitively than nature can (Burte and Krishnankutty, 2006; Mathur and Da Cunha, 2009, pp. 14–19). The water's edge with land is an ecologically complex zone in natural situations. Part of that complexity is the variable presence of water along the sides of the river which hosts many species specifically adapted to that environment. A physical complexity and temporal variability are necessary conditions for that biological complexity, as is the meeting of natural land and water. The concrete retaining walls of the new riverfront replace that complexity with the simplicity of a vertical plane of industrial material. That plane is the oversimplified physical embodiment of the conceptual partition between land and water in technocratic taxonomies. The project thus reveals a blindness, or perhaps an indifference, to the special ecological significance of the transition zone between land and water, a space made ambiguous because of its temporal variability.

Displacement, Resistance, Violence

An estimated 30,000 to 40,000 families will be affected by the SRD (Jadhav, 2011, as cited by Mathur, 2012; Our Inclusive Ahmadabad, 2010, p. 8). While its website claims that the project aims to create an "inclusive" public space, it has already displaced hundreds of families living in slums along the river, and sent them to relocation camps on poor and poorly serviced land at the outskirts of the city (Desai, 2012). They have thus been directly and actively excluded from the city in whose center they had lived for decades, offered cheap labor, and earned a meager living in return. That displacement has been resisted by the poor themselves (Desai, 2012, p. 54), as well as by other civil society initiatives such as Our Inclusive Ahmedabad, and violence and trickery has been allegedly used by the state's agents to accomplish it. Along with the poor, the river itself has been displaced and replaced by an artificial water body, a sort of aqueous spatial product. The river we see today is not, strictly speaking, the river that was, if you consider a river as necessarily integrated into a larger riverine process. Today water from a feeder canal of the Sardar Sarovar Project on the Narmada river is artificially fed into the new Sabarmati channel to keep water in the river all year long.

Between the three different ways in which it is viewed in the developmental imagination of the SRD—as a potentially pretty sight, a docile trickle, and an ensemble of inert components—the river is deftly converted from a relational and dynamic natural phenomenon to a real abstract space, that is, a non-place.

Lavasa

Lavasa is a new, under-construction hill-station 65 km from the big city of Pune, planned over 10,000 hectares of hilly landscape covering 18 villages. It is designed as a hospitality destination with well-developed leisure and conferencing facilities, as well as ownership second homes for nonresidents. It is meant to pull in over 2 million visitors annually (with an expected resident population of 300,000 and just under 100,000 jobs) (Lavasa Corporation Ltd, p. 2). The project is divided into four phases, which are like nodes built all along the hillsides embracing and overlooking a large artificial backwater originally a byproduct of the Tata power plant built nearby, early in the 20th century. Unusually, Lavasa Corporation Limited (LCL), a private company, has been given the status of a Special Planning Authority (SPA) that has usually been reserved for government organizations or para-statals like MMRDA and CIDCO.

Lavasa's business rationale is the demand that the globalized business class makes for leisure spaces within striking distance of a city on the international air traffic map, especially those that offer a safe, canned experience of "nature" (with the garnish of "culture" being especially welcome). The unique selling point of Lavasa is meant to be a combination of a peaceful and dramatic landscape, and an imitation Italian hill-town design by international architectural firm HoK.

Lavasa is in some ways a resort expanded to the size of a sprawling city (one fifth of Mumbai's footprint, ultimately), since it offers a range of residential, hospitality, event management, and conferencing facilities within a controlled faux urban environment. Most importantly, the so-called "city" is a business venture, profits from which go directly to LCL. This is very different from the manner of enabling capital accumulation in the Sabarmati Riverfront project. In the latter, there is an element of open-endedness since a real city is both the destination of investment and a part beneficiary.

There are a number of controversies Lavasa has been caught up in, based on allegations: that it has been granted undue favors from government in land allocation, as well as in the processing of its applications; about fraudulent or opportunistic take-over of land owned by tribal and dalit subsistence farmers by exploiting their illiteracy or lack of power, command over the bureaucratic record and business tactics; and about environmental damage and lack of appropriate environmental clearances from the sole state authority with the power to grant environmental sanctions, Ministry of Environment and Forests of the Government of India.

Discussion

Physically, Lavasa epitomizes the non-place disguised transparently as, what we may call a hyper-place. Non-places such as Sabarmati riverfront embody their abstract conception in a transparent aesthetic—of reinforced concrete in this case—one that promises to be impervious to time, weather and the impress of human life. Lavasa is the opposite kind of non-place. Committed to enabling consumption, it wears the disguise of an exaggerated place identity, and thus of an exaggerated promise of relationality. At the same time, it carefully lets the mask slip just enough so that the consumer is not distracted by the possible bite of either *real* nature or social relations.

Lavasa is, thus, deliberately designed like a theme-town or a large stage set. It plays the part of a hill-town, making a move toward relating sensitively to the hilly landscape in the way its buildings are arranged. This appears to institute a relationality into the produced space and built form with respect to the nature around. But that relationality is immediately revealed as being false by the aesthetics of the built form: a tacky imitation of an *Italian* hill town (apparently, Portofino, as declared on the website).[7] The real water in the valley, spreading naturally over its irregular shape, is also strangely artificial and will be more so in relation to its natural appearance, when the dams that Lavasa has got permission to build, are up. Its architecture and landscape design thus reinforces a culture of make-believe relationality, while actually having an instrumental attitude toward the socio-ecological context within which consumption occurs. This is of a piece with global trends that seek to produce "instant places" that pretend to a history and relationality and thereby to a local identity. The natural landscape is an important marker for such an identity. In such places, a historically evolved (and therefore "genuine") landscape "out there" is thus appropriated as part of the disguise of the place one stands inside. On the one hand, real local nature may be physically modified—with lawns, infinity pools, and yes, golf courses all altering natural processes—to the market's conceptions of places facilitating consumption. The make-believe world of the planned hill station infects the very real nature it looks out to. Look closely and the very real hills suddenly start appearing like they are part of the design.

Interestingly, large-scale unethicality has been alleged in a civil society investigation (Inquiry, 2009, pp. 9–17) in the land deals through which Lavasa corporation got possession of the lands. The modus operandi that the report outlines is fairly common in a lot of private and public developmental activity. Lavasa has countered that the deals were clean and has argued that, in fact, they were enacted through a market mechanism of direct negotiations with the owners and were ethically superior to projects where government forcibly acquired land and handed it over to private companies for development. Important though it is, the legality of the transfers is not the most interesting point here. Even if the transfers were legal on paper, it is the extreme abstraction of the modalities of the deal that is perhaps most crucial in determining the actual fate of the original landowners, as well as of the ecosystem they work closely with and presumably nurture.

Irrespective of the actual wrongs committed or not in the matter of land transfer to Lavasa, Lefebvre's notion of abstract space, the conceived space of experts and technocrats (whose "substance" is made up of numbers, data tables, and lines on a map), is a good lens through which to view the matter. It is worth emphasizing here that land was transferred from subsistence farmers eking out a living from the small parcels of land they personally till and its socio-ecological system they survive on, to a globally integrated business entity like Lavasa Corporation that sees this entire ecological system as an easily modifiable ingredient in a service industry "product" offered to a globalized customer base. From being the concrete center of a "community of land" (Leopold, 2009) for the subsistence farmer, land at Lavasa (as elsewhere, increasingly) is transformed into a concrete abstraction, as Stanek (forthcoming) explains the term: something not necessarily defined by the multiple relationships that were necessarily woven through it, but an isolated "piece of space" or terrain identified most closely by abstractions captured in the bureaucratic record.

The commoditization of land depends on the abstraction (and construction) of its potential as a commodity from the thick web of real socio-ecological relations that constitute it as a social space, that is, from the "community of land" (Leopold, 2009). In this commodity form, land is itself represented through extreme abstractions (survey numbers, tables, cadastral survey maps) and governed through even more abstract modes: registration documents, procedures, protocols of establishing title, and so on. These always involve complex and again abstract procedures for establishing validity or for legitimating transactions. The implications of these for ownership and possession continue to be fully understandable only to the literate, especially those with command over the bureaucratic process. Further the complexities of these procedures and the ambiguities within them ensure that only those with access to political power actually have command over the way the abstractions defining ownership, possession, developmental permissions, and so on, can be gamed for particular ends. They are also best positioned to know exactly what significant concrete leverage which abstractions can yield with respect to land, water or other resources. On the other hand, those who depend directly on the productive capacity of the land, the land workers (and "ecosystem people") whose command is much greater over the concrete processes of primary production, are routinely less conversant with the enormous concrete implications of these weightless abstractions. In most situations, they also have very little leverage within the bureaucratic system to ever be in a position to genuinely command the abstract bureaucratic procedures that actually determine the developmental process. In Lavasa, thus, we see, once more, the triumph of remotely controlled abstract process and space, over locally lived nature, and social life.

DMIC

The DMIC is a US$90 billion national scale project (involving significant Japanese investment) of industrial development organized around a new superfast Dedicated Freight Corridor whose primary purpose is to connect existing and proposed industrial clusters in and around New Delhi, as well as those on the route to Mumbai, to the largest port in the country, Jawaharlal Nehru Port Trust (JNPT), in the Mumbai Metropolitan Region. DMIC is conceived as an answer to a future problem and a present challenge: an anticipated explosion in demand for jobs and the felt need to maximize the general global competitiveness of the entire production-distribution cycle in the country, and specifically to compete better with China. The corridor passing through seven states is expected to reduce freight transit time between industries and JNPT to one tenth or one fifteenth of the current duration (15 days from Delhi to JNPT, today, will become 27 hours). Fifty-two percent of the FDI inflows of the country go to the seven states, and Mumbai and Delhi regions together, apparently, corner 92 percent of this share (which effectively means that the two city regions corner a little under half the FDI flowing into the country). To increase the return on investment on the high speed corridor (rail and road) and to house the population working in the new industrial facilities, nine new cities are planned either directly on the corridor or on its branches which extend eastward to Aurangabad in Maharashtra and westward to the new town of Dholera in Gujarat. As per the public statements of the MD of DMIC, Amitabh Kant, cutting edge urban planning and governance systems incorporating the latest information systems are being developed for each new city, and detailed planning work on these is underway at Dighi, the new port near Mumbai that is the southern terminus of DMIC.[8] What makes DMIC important to this chapter is that it is situated for the most part in the most water scarce belt of the country, a fact that becomes all the more important since it plans to host a large percentage of the national population when complete.

Discussion

DMIC's objectives are clearly "social" (or more narrowly, socioeconomic) alone. Predictably then, the natural simply does not figure in the foreground of the official story of the project except as a context to be managed. DMIC's website, for instance, has a lot of information about the way the project was conceived, the rationale for it, the business model, and so on.[9] However, there is no mention of the obvious challenges, prime among them the availability of water in the most arid zone of the country, which is the geographical heart of the project. There is an evident confidence in the feasibility of the project, based entirely on scenarios being developed and moulded in abstract space (the space of numbers, models, diagrams, flow charts) by technical experts whose interest would clearly be to serve the interests of the state as client. At the same time, a published critique of what presumably exists as a plan for water—including among other things, inter-basin transfers—suggests that it is not feasible since the rivers the plan seeks to tap into are already overharvested (Khosla and Soni, 2012).

Some general features common to the production of non-places are seen here. First, this abstract space (in other words, the conception of the proposed non-places) and the logic guiding it reveals a fragmented perspective: the social is completely separated from the ecological. No link is seen between the impact of creating new jobs—the social objective—through industrialization and production of non-places on the one hand, and the ecological consequences of this production. Second, the public representations of DMIC reveal a disinterest in *existing* socio-ecological wholes (in other words, "places" in human geography terms, and "social spaces" following Lefebvre). The fact that an EIA has not yet been completed and the lack of publicly available information about its terms and content, reinforces this tentative conclusion. This disinterest is typically complemented by intense attention the project appears to give to a centralized, control oriented, social and physical plan for *future* spaces that are currently the object of technocratic energies. The *fact* of nature and an existing society in place are considered less important than the *act* of producing new non-places in that very location.

Clearly, global, or globally connected local finance stands to profit the most from industrial production and tertiary economic activities that DMIC will directly and indirectly catalyze. A project of this size in a sensitive ecological terrain can be reasonably expected to have major socio-ecological costs, especially related to industrial pollution. Ecological degradation of large local landscapes and related damage to existing livelihoods and the local social fabric are after all common outcomes of industrialization in India, and in states like Gujarat that are heavily invested in DMIC (Hug, 2012).[10] These thus will most probably be borne locally (though some less visible part of the ecological cost might be borne globally through its carbon footprint and contribution to climate change) to a great extent especially by people "closer" to the ecosystem. Of course, the local catchment of the costs might extend across the country in proportion with the distance from which water will be carried into the DMIC area.

Discussion of the Cases

All three cases discussed above embody the transformation of unique and differentiated, socio-ecological spaces into different varieties and scales of non-places. It is clear that in each case the transformation is caused or proposed based on a way of seeing and valuing existing realities as well as specific future goals. The major benefits of these transformations will clearly go to national and international businesses though some would trickle down to local elites in every place. The major social and ecological costs of these transformations, meanwhile, will be borne first by the more vulnerable local people. In all three, the state has played an important facilitatory role.

The power and prestige of abstraction organize all three projects. Abstraction involves a separate consideration of realities, concepts and values that are interwoven in reality. When used as the basis of transformation, this abstract "map" reproduces, not the complexity of the existing reality, but its own oversimplifications. Real places are thus transformed into non-places through the instrument of expert knowledge. In all three cases, it is also possible to argue that this way of seeing and remaking is aligned more with the shared commitment of both market and state to capital accumulation than to the sustenance of existing ecologies or societies.

Abstraction as Fragmentation and Reduction of Place

It is worth examining the specific way in which abstraction works. Lukasz Stanek writes that the "distinction between the concrete, as embedded in a variety of relations, and the abstract, as impoverished, one-sided and isolated, can be applied to describe features of things, phenomena, thoughts, and experiences." Lefebvre, he notes, writes that "spaces considered in isolation are 'mere abstractions', while they 'attain real' existence by virtue of networks and pathways, by virtue of bunches or clusters of relationships" (Stanek, forthcoming). Thus, abstract space (that is, an abstract model of real social-natural space) is marked by a range of reductions and simplifications, and by fragmentations of mutually constitutive real-world phenomena in the minds and representations of experts, scientists, professionals and bureaucrats. This *conceived* space includes representations of nature and society and its abstract characteristics can be traced to the Cartesian model of analytic knowledge.

In the SRD we have seen that nature (in this case, the river) is reduced to an abstraction, by being separated from the built environment and society. It is viewed simply as a *measurable* volume of water flowing through the city within a defined physical channel. Such a view empties the river of any social and ecological content and implication. It also makes it easier to bracket it out of the changeful riverine system and process in expert representation. Together these moves allow us to believe that there can be no significant consequences of transforming the river radically, through physical intervention. From there it is a short step to propose that the complex social and ecological system of the river be transformed into a spatial product—a world-class riverfront—that is in reality an instrument of accumulation for the powerful classes. The widely asserted (but inadequately queried) need for cities to compete globally offers a powerful alibi related to "public interest" for this technical operation, which then clinches the argument.

Lavasa too separates nature from society, especially out of its historical centrality to the subsistence of long-settled communities. Nature emptied of society makes it easier to build a new consumption environment, one that is again global in its economic and aspirational associations, never mind that it is only for private profit and that the environmental and social impact are significant, with little public benefit. As a non-place of consumption, it also celebrates its "product" nature through advertised claims to being the first planned, post-Independence hill-station. DMIC, meanwhile, splits one kind of social concern (for new jobs at scale) away from the ecological as well as from another kind of social concern that it is silent about (the lives and livelihoods of long existing communities numbering in millions, presumably). It also establishes a hierarchy among these fragments, very clearly privileging the narrow aim of increasing big production (and accumulation) transparently lying under the concern for new jobs.

An important outcome of this procedure is that nature and society are both represented as being *inert* through abstraction and, therefore, much easier to ignore or modify in the conception and practice of development. An implicit hierarchy is also set up quietly, across and within each such isolated reality (nature, built environment, society) which devalues nature as well as the social groups closest to it.

Hierarchies within Abstract Space

The inertness imputed to nature and certain groups in society is related to a hierarchy between values and valued things that is always present in abstract representations. Abstract representations (whether maps, tables, or technical and scientific descriptions), thus, are not value neutral. They can be quite the opposite. Moreover, hierarchies of value help produce such representations, and such representations themselves reproduce the same or new hierarchies.

Let us recall James Scott's observation about the purposiveness of the state's representations. Scott suggests that representations of society or nature do not have to be complete or accurate; they merely have to aid the state's specific purposes in a given situation. Thus, he argues that a hierarchy often accompanies what appear to be neutral and descriptive representations. The privileging of one viewpoint is hidden by the apparent neutrality of analytic representations. However, Scott's point is precisely that the representation is actually prepared from a specific position "outside" a given situation, occupied by the state in his account. It is thus, not a truly neutral representation (Scott, 1998, p. 3).

The purposiveness of representation, thus, appears to determine what is represented and what is not, depending on the values, goals, habits, and convenience of those who produce them. In short, representations are tied to the agency of the makers of those representations. It is worth noting here that the conscious intentions of those producing representations, especially specialist technical experts, are often irrelevant. Disciplinary assumptions—regarding the nature of the object being represented, the practicability of constructing certain kinds of representations and not others and their utility, for instance—and available technical tools often themselves determine what is represented and how. Thus, independent of the immediate goals of those driving development—whether state or market players—the momentarily autonomous culture of expert action itself places limits on what is represented and how.[11] We can thus see that the contents and orientations of the full range of representations of any given space are shaped as much by political as by disciplinary ends. These twin drivers, perhaps, help account for commonly visible hierarchies that always seem to mark technical knowledge as well as state representations of social space.

As mentioned above, social space (or place) is separated in Cartesian representations into the built environment and natural environment.

Separate drawings and reports describe these two phenomena, and separate procedures govern their fates. As a result, the developmental purposes of both the state and technical expertise automatically value the built environment to be *produced* higher than the natural environment that simply exists in the background. For the expert and the developmentally oriented state (as obviously for the market) focused on what needs to be done, the *act* of building is in the foreground while the *fact* of nature is mere backdrop.[12] Representations, thus, favor the former over the other, often not even acknowledging the most stringent limits the latter places on the former.

The hierarchy between the built and the natural environment is both extended and paralleled in the representation of the social life of places including local populations. There is a hierarchy established between formally recognized spaces, parcels of land, built environments (those that are represented in the official record) and their recorded attributes on the one hand, and those that are not found in the bureaucratic record on the other. The formal and urban quite obviously ranks higher than the informal. Since according to Scott, the state is partial to stationary and legible places and populations (for their greater controllability), and since ownership is regarded as the most important index of the right to a space (including its "ecological services"), it is clear that such representations automatically weaken the claims and status of nomadic peoples, unauthorized layouts (including slums as with the SRD), and tenants. This also automatically reduces the representational status and bargaining power of social groups who might simply not be alert to the power of this record as with the subsistence farmers whose lands are now with Lavasa. They might thus be unable to defend their right to the sustainable yield of their socio-ecological spaces, against the perishable attractions of the market. This reinforces the implicit hierarchy underlying developmental agendas in urbanizing India that we can cast in terms of Gadgil and Guha's (1995) categories. The interests of social groups that profit from accumulation and who use up natural resources quickly and at a large scale (Gadgil and Guha's "omnivores") dominate over those of two other marginalized groups: on the one hand, those that nurture and depend entirely on the ecosystem (forest dwellers, agriculturists, etc., or "ecosystem people"), and on the other, those whose labor makes capital accumulation possible ("ecological refugees" including the urban poor who were once "ecosystem people").

Conclusion

Though they appear innocent, the abstractly conceived non-places that serve the purposes of capital accumulation, and that also define the new urban developmental paradigm in India today, are anything but. The appearance of harmony, order, and efficiency that marks their spatial and administrative form diverts attention away from the social and ecological degradation that is always necessary to achieve that appearance. Driven by the newly forged alliance between the market and state in India, this developmental paradigm is actually implemented by technical and managerial experts at an everyday level. Their abstract "scientific" knowledge and the impoverished representations it leads to in the work of experts like architects, engineers, economists, and bureaucrats among others, is an important ally of this paradigm. Of course, to go back to one of Lefebvre's starting points in *The Production of Space*, it is not simply the abstraction of this scientific knowledge or technical expertise that is the problem. It is rather that abstract knowledge (or *conceived* space), which is one "moment of space," is disconnected from the others—*lived* and *perceived* space respectively—and in fact dominates the other two to further the cause of accumulation.[13] In reality, as Lefebvre recognizes, the domination is only a project and not an accomplished fact. In the increasing socio-ecological contestations in cities and in the countryside, his perspective could lead us to recognize the return of the repressed moments: the lived socio-ecological space of peasants and forest dwellers (or their lived knowledge of *place*) as well as the perceived (or empirical) one of environmentalists and ecologists.

Notes

1. This chapter was originally to be written jointly with Malini Krishnankutty. I have benefitted greatly from many discussions with her throughout the writing, as well as her comments on more than one draft. Editorial comments from Kanchi Kohli and Manju Menon greatly helped streamline the argument. All errors are my responsibility.
2. See the following media reports, for instance: http://www.firstpost.com/politics/ is-lavasa-the-achilles-heel-of-the-mighty-sharad-pawar-495600.html (accessed on November 23, 2015), http://www.tehelka.com/realty-comes-back-to-bite-the-pawar-family/ (accessed on November 23, 2015). and http://www.indianexpress.com/news/ exips-officer-labels-sharad-pawar-ajit-supriya-corrupt-in-lavasa-case/1018679/ (accessed on November 23, 2015).

3. www.sabarmatiriverfront.com (accessed on May 6, 2013).

4. Calculated from information on the SRD website: http://www.sabarmatiriverfront. com/1/about-us (accessed on February 8, 2013).

5. Mathur (2012, p. 66) reports that Bimal Patel thinks of the project as one of offering respect to a disrespected river. The lack of water in it during the dry season is offered as evidence of such disrespect. A more substantive claim of protecting the river is based on the arrangement to treat sewage currently running into the water untreated. See http://www.sabarmatiriverfront.com/1/about-us (accessed on May 10, 2014).

6. Cubic feet per second.

7. This playacting is not an accident. The Lavasa website prominently announces that the design of Lavasa is based on New Urbanist principles. New Urbanism is a neotra-ditional (and neoconservative) architectural movement in the US that has sought to overcome the placelessness, or abstractness, of most 20th-century American develop-ment, through an architecture that restages a version of traditional American archi-tecture of "front porches" and variations on European styles. The difference is that the appeal in Lavasa is not to a local tradition of architecture, but to an imagined Mediterranean lifestyle.

8. Presentation at the 1st Built Environment Symposium on "Design as a Catalyst for Social Change" organized by the Aga Khan Planning and Building Service India at National Centre for the Performing Arts, Mumbai, on December 2, 2012. Also see for instance the focus on efficiency and the greater attention to the act of making new cities than to the fact of an existing socio-cultural landscape in this ecologically sensi-tive region in a recent interview Kant gave to Civil Society magazine, at http://www. civilsocietyonline.com/pages/Details.aspx?436 (accessed on November 23, 2015). Thanks to Kanchi Kohli for pointing me to this interview.

9. http://delhimumbaiindustrialcorridor.com/ (accessed on November 23, 2015).

10. Hug (2012) focuses on the poor record of the state of Gujarat in monitoring and con-trolling industrial pollution. Against this background, as he notes with concern, the fact that Gujarat is likely to attract the most industrial activity on the DMIC among all states involved, invites significant reflection.

11. Geographical Information Systems (GIS) is an interesting example in this regard. It is a software platform that seeks to integrate spatial and non-spatial (especially including social) data. It was anticipated by the change in assumptions about the object of repre-sentations that the pioneering environmental planner Ian McHarg made famous in his book *Design with Nature*. McHarg's Geddesian orientation led him to find ways of rep-resenting the ecological relationality of places on drawings that superimposed different processes and realities of a landscape. In the 1960s he pioneered a simple method of capturing ecological relationships on two dimensional drawings by overlaying tracing sheets documenting different ecological conditions and processes related to the same site to produce a complex picture of the site's ecological context. Non-spatial, including social, data was also integrated into different layers as appropriate. Proposed designs for freeways or campuses were then developed within the richer socio-ecological rep-resentation of the site. This logic is foundational to the workings of GIS today, though it allows computerized analysis integrating spatial and non-spatial data (see http://www. urisa.org/awards/ian-mcharg/, accessed January 12, 2016). GIS is thus a useful tool for a more relational representation of place, though procedures of using its logic and analyzing its outputs might still easily slide into analytic thinking.

12. "A strategy based on space, even if we leave military and political projects out of the picture, must be considered a very dangerous one indeed, for it sacrifices the future to immediate interests while simultaneously destroying the present in the name of a future at once programmed and utterly uncertain" (Lefebvre, 1991, p. 336).

13. Merrifield explains the politics that influences the power of different moments in the production of space, especially the role of capitalism, as Lefebvre sees it. "Relations between conceived-perceived-lived moments are never stable and exhibit historically defined qualities, attributes and interconnections. But the problem under capitalism is, according to Lefebvre, that primacy is given to the conceived; all which renders insignificant the 'unconscious' level of lived experience. What is lived and perceived is subsumed under what is conceived. The social space of lived experience is crushed, vanquished by what he calls an *abstract* conceived space which dances to the tune of the homogenizing forces of money, commodities, capital and the phallus" (Merrifield, 1993).

References

Auge, M. (1995). *Non-places: An Introduction to Supermodernity*. J. Howe (Trans.). London and New York: Verso.

Burte, H. and Krishnankutty, M. (2006). On the edge: Planning, describing and imagining the seaside edge of Mumbai. In *Peri-urban Dynamics: Case Studies in Chennai, Hyderabad and Mumbai* (pp. 87–109). New Delhi: French Research Institutes in India.

Choudhury, S. (2012, July 4). DMIC project right on track. *The Economic Times*. Retrieved November 23, 2015, from http://articles.economictimes.indiatimes.com/2012-07-04/news/32537212_1_dmic-project-ppp-model-delhi-mumbai-industrial-corridor-project.

Cresswell, T. (2004). *Place: A Short Introduction*. Malden, MA: Blackwell.

Desai, R. (2012, January 14). Governing the urban poor: Riverfront development, slum resettlement and the politics of inclusion in Ahmedabad. *Economic and Political Weekly*, XLVII(2), 49–56.

D'Monte, D. (2011, January 15–28). Sabarmati's sorrow. *Frontline, 28*(2). Retrieved May 13, 2013, from http://www.frontline.in/static/html/fl2802/stories/20110128280208500.htm (accessed on January 4, 2016).

Easterling, K. (2005). *Enduring Innocence: Global Architecture and Its Political Masquerades*. Cambridge: MIT Press.

Fernandes, L. (2004, November). The politics of forgetting: Class politics, state power and the restructuring of urban space in India. *Urban Studies, 41*(12), 2415–2430.

Gadgil, M. and Guha, R. (1995). *Ecology and Equity: The Use and Abuse of Nature in Contemporary India*. New Delhi: Penguin Books.

Guillen, M.F. (2006). *The Tayorized Beauty of the Mechanical: Scientific Management and the Rise of Modernist Architecture*. Princeton, NJ: Princeton University Press.

Hug, D.K. (2012). The Delhi–Mumbai industrial corridor and some issues of environmental governance. In N. Laine and T. Subba (Eds.), *Nature, Environment and Society: Conservation, Governance and Transformation in India* (pp. 170–191). New Delhi: Orient Blackswan.

Inquiry, P.C. (2009). *Report of the people's commission of inquiry*. Retrieved November 23, 2015, from http://www.indiaenvironmentportal.org.in/files/Interim%20Report%20Apr%2020-2009.pdf.

Jadhav, B. (2011). *A report on rehthan adhikar manch.* Ahmedabad.

Khosla, R. and Soni, V. (2012, March 10). Delhi–Mumbai corridor: A water disaster in the making? *Economic and Political Weekly, XLVII*(10), 15–17.

Lavasa Corporation Ltd. (n.d.). *City Guide January 2012.* Retrieved May 13, 2013, from http://www.lavasa.com/high/files/City_guide.pdf.

Lefebvre, H. (1991). *The Production of Space* (D. Nicholson-Smith, Trans.). Oxford and Cambridge: Blackwell.

Leopold, A. (2009). The land ethic. In S.M. Wheeler and T. Beatley (Eds.), *The Sustainable Urban Development Reader* (2nd ed., pp. 24–32). London and New York: Routledge.

Mathur, A. and Da Cunha, D. (2009). *Soak: Mumbai in an Estuary.* Mumbai: Rupa & Co.

Mathur, N. (2012, December 1). On the Sabarmati riverfront: Urban planning as totalitarian governance in Ahmedabad. *Economic and Political Weekly, XLVII*(47, 48), 64–75.

Merrifield, A. (1993). Place and space: A lefebvrian reconciliation. *Transactions of the Institute of British Geographers, 18*(4), 516–531.

Ollman, B. (1990). Putting dialectics to work: The process of abstraction in Marx. *Rethinking Marxism, 3*(1), 26–74.

Our Inclusive Ahmedabad. (2010). *Report of public hearing on habitat and livelihood displacements.* Ahmedabad: Our Inclusive Ahmedabad. Retrieved May 3, 2013, from http://www.spcept.ac.in/download/cuemisc/Public-Hearing-Report-2010.pdf.

Scott, J. (1998). *Seeing Like a State: How Certain Schemes to Improve the Human Condition Have Failed.* New Haven and London: Yale University Press.

Sheth, B.L. (2007, 15 April). Concerns over Sabarmati riverfront development project. *Down To Earth.* Retrieved March 1, 2013, from http://www.downtoearth.org.in/node/5786.

Stanek, L. (forthcoming). *Space as concrete abstraction: Hegel, Marx and modern urbanism in Henri Lefebvre.* Retrieved May 13, 2013, from http://www.henrilefebvre.org/text/Routledge_STANEK.pdf.

Tuan, Y.F. (1977). *Space and Place: The Perspective of Experience.* Minneapolis: University of Minnesota Press.

4

Coal Accounting: The Story of Fuel Kept Cheap

Vinuta Gopal

Coal remains the most used fuel to generate electricity today, globally. It is stated to be the cheapest form of power generation and therefore a valuable resource whose extraction, trade, and use in power generation are seen as essential to power the growth of economies across the world. The generation of power from coal is a technology that is mature and established in comparison to new forms of energy generation such as nuclear, solar, wind, and other technologies, and the price of coal has been lower and more stable than oil and gas prices. Coal in India currently accounts for almost 60 percent of the installed generating capacity of power, as of January 31, 2015, according to the Central Electricity Authority's (CEA) website.[1] India plans to continue its reliance on coal power for the future and projects coal to be a cheap energy choice in comparison to renewable and also believes in significant reserves available in the country (Planning Commission, 2006, 2012).

However, the impacts of coal on the environment at a local and global scale have increasingly occupied a lion's share of the climate change discourse as the science on climate change points to carbon emissions as the most significant contributor to global warming (CICERO, 2013; Greenpeace International, 2010). The assumptions on cost of coal and economically extractable reserves are areas that have not been examined closely and are issues that are likely to be the center of debates in the coming years.

This chapter attempts to look at what makes coal "cheap" and efficient for energy production. The chapter also looks at the various steps that have been taken by the government to trump coal as the nation's fuel even when the effects of such policy are gross environmental and social impacts, wastage of public funds, and blatant violations of laws. The costing of coal is a telling illustration of the politics of natural resource accounting.

Coal: A "Post Colony" Public Good

Mining during the British colonial rule in India was a private enterprise. Following India's passage into independence in 1947, the Government of India formed the National Coal Development Corporation in 1956 and also notified areas with substantial coal reserves under the Coal Bearing Areas Act of 1957. In national interest, these areas were allocated to public sector companies under the Ministry of Coal. Until 1972, some private mines continued to exist but after that all dormant and existing mines were transferred to public sector companies (PSUs). PSUs were awarded large tracts of "coal fields": forests with high grade, thick coal seams at surface levels which made open cast mining a profitable venture. Government policy and public companies kept the costs low with the sole interest of electrifying the nation—rural lighting, irrigation, and manufacturing being priority.[2] Since then, coal has been India's development fix.

Coal mining was entirely a central government enterprise for two decades until the Indian National Congress government's economic liberalization program. In 1993, under the Coal Mine Nationalisation (Amendment) Act, 1993 (No. 47 of 1993 gazette on June 9, 1993), state PSUs and private companies were allowed to take captive mines. This was an amendment to the clause of Section 3(3) of the legislation first enacted in 1973. By way of this amendment, the legislation allowed for any company engaged in generation of power, washing, or coal, or any other end use notified by the central government, to be able to carry out coal mining. Prior to this, it was only those companies engaged in iron and steel mining that were also allowed to carry out coal mining activity.

Though the legislation and subsequent executive orders paved the way for it, few allocations were made to private players. The 2013 Standing Committee on coal block allocations has referred to a Ministry of Coal submission which indicates that from 1993 to 2004 eligible companies would identify a coal block and apply to the Ministry of Coal. These applications would be looked into by the Screening Committee constituted on July 14, 1992 through an executive or administrative order of the Ministry. The submissions as recorded in the committee report states that, "since the applications were few and in some cases only one application against a block as identified by the applicant company were received, no such separate data was maintained in terms of number of applications received" (Lok Sabha Secretariat, 2013).

According to a 2012 report of the Comptroller and Auditor General (CAG) of India, coal assumed greater significance after 2003, which is when the Government of India (GOI) pronounced a mission "Power to all by 2012" (CAG, 2012). From 2004, over 194 coal allocations were rapidly made without any transparent assessment of financial capacity or technology (Lok Sabha Secretariat, 2013; Press Trust of India, 2012a). The loopholes and lack of transparency in the allocations procedures made being in the business of coal very profitable, as in many cases coal blocks were provided in excess of the coal required for the captive project or at higher grades (Dutta, 2014) and in cases the cheap coal acquired from allocated blocks were diverted to power plants that were selling at market rates (Bhaskar, 2014), not to mention cases where the company that was allotted the coal block had merely done so to acquire an asset with no intent of mining (Singh, 2012).

Corruption, Coal Allocations, and Profit-making

An important determinant of coal accounting in India was researched and brought out by the CAG in their explosive report in 2012 on the real reasons for coal inefficiencies (CAG, 2012). The CAG of India was set up under the Indian Constitution and has the task of auditing all receipts and expenditure of the Government of India and the state governments. This also includes those of bodies and authorities which are substantially financed by the government. This particular report of the CAG was a performance audit of "allocation of coal blocks and augmentation of coal production." It was set up to study the reasons for a shortage of domestic coal production against demand.

The report named 25 companies including Essar Power, Hindalco, Tata Steel and Power, Adani Group, Lanco, Vedanta Group, Arcelor Mittal, Jindal Steel and Power, and even smaller companies such as the Abhijeet Group or Bhusan Power and Steel who gained hugely in the private allocation process. The CAG report highlights that India's public exchequer also incurred loss of up to ₹311.81 crores. This is primarily because bank guarantees could not be recovered from the coal block developers that had acquired coal blocks but had not started mining (Chakravartty, 2012).

The report points out that way back in July 2004, the then Secretary, Ministry of Coal, prepared a note on "competitive bidding for allocation of coal blocks" in which he indicated that the allotment should be through a competitive bidding process as otherwise the person to whom the coal block is allotted would make a "windfall gain" on account of the difference in price of coal between that supplied by Coal India Limited and coal mined from a captive coal block.

The intent was to have a transparent and objective process for the allocation, and by auctioning the blocks, some part of the windfall gain would be tapped for public purposes. The CAG arrived at a figure of ₹1.86 lakh crore (US$37.2 billion) as financial gain to private players as being the difference between the average cost of production from a captive mine and the average sale price of opencast mines by CIL for the extractable reserves in the allocated coal blocks. The CAG said that a part of this gain should have gone to the national exchequer and instead went to the gain of private players. It also pointed out that out of 86 blocks that were supposed to start production in 2010–2011, only 28 blocks had started by March 31, 2011.

In the summer of 2012, "Coalgate," as it is popularly known, the largest scam in India to be exposed to date, hit the news headlines (Inamdar, 2013; Press Trust of India, 2012b). This shook the country and the Indian parliament as the coal ministry was headed by the Prime Minister, Dr Manmohan Singh, for most part of the period examined by the CAG. This scam exposed the corporate–political nexus and the real reason for coal shortages in the country. It also highlighted one of the largest subsidies that coal power was getting from the State—free access to land

and the fuel. The industry and government had been working hard to point to the environment regulatory process as the roadblock to the coal sector in the country. But "Coalgate" established that it was corruption at the highest level in the allocation process that was contributing to the problems faced by the sector as a whole (Bhattacharya and Colvin, 2012; Muthu, 2012).

Despite the convoluted explanations from the government, it has become clear that coal was being handed over on a platter, often to players who had no track record of good business practices. It was a land grab of massive scale and it was at the cost of the Indian tax payer and resulting in energy shortage in the country. The main contention of the CAG (2012) report was that by allocating coal blocks for free, and without a clear criteria and a transparent process for the allotment, the government was handing over limited national resources at a significant cost to the exchequer.

In a Public Interest Litigation filed by an NGO, Common Cause, in the Supreme Court, the petitioner, who is a former secretary in the Government of India, has called for cancellation of all the coal blocks allocated in the period examined by the CAG (IANS, 2012). Their plea is based (Anonymous, 2013) on the landmark Supreme Court judgment in the 2G spectrum case ((2012) 3 SCC 1), that clearly says that the "State, as a trustee, is legally bound to get the true value of a natural resource, and all arbitrary allocations of natural resources are illegal and void." The Supreme Court has further stated in a clarification on this judgment, in no uncertain terms that, "precious and scarce natural resources are alienated for commercial pursuits of profit maximizing private entrepreneurs, adoption of means other than those that are competitive and maximize revenue may be arbitrary and face the wrath of Article 14 of the Constitution."

In an important judgment,[3] the Supreme Court declared the allocations "illegal and arbitrary," and in their final order cancelled 214 coal blocks allocated between 1993 and 2010. This ruling was passed by a three-judge bench led by the then Chief Justice of India, R.M. Lodha. The stringent action taken by the courts showed that they were in no doubt that probity and legal processes had been flouted and they were not going to allow such travesty to take place (Supreme Court WP No. 120 of 2012—in the case of Manohar Lal Sharma Vs Principle Secretary and Ors).

This judgment established that allocating coal blocks at zero cost is akin to handing over precious national assets to private players. The government's position that it is being done to provide cheap power fell flat on its face. For example, the CAG pulled up the government for allowing Reliance Power to divert the coal mined from the coal blocks set aside for the Sasan UMPP to another of its power projects in Chitrangi. While the power purchase agreement Sasan had with the government for the UMPP was ₹1.19, the power it was selling from Chitrangi was ₹2.45 (Mishra, 2012). The CAG held that Reliance was reaping undue benefit from the coal blocks allocated to the UMPP.

In the Central Indian state of Chhattisgarh, the Adani Group has adopted the practice of integrated coal mine developer-cum-operator (MDO). Through this, a coal block owner contracts entire operations, including from land acquisition to developing and operating the mines. Following this, the developer supplies coal to the owner or to other parties at a tender-determined price. The Parsa East–Kente Basin mine allocated to a power generation utility from the state of Rajasthan, that is, the Rajasthan Rajya Vidyut Utpadan Nigam Ltd (RRVUNL). The contract for extracting and processing the coal was awarded to Adani Mining, which is a wholly owned subsidiary of Adani Enterprises. The washed coal will be sold back to the RRVUNL and the Adani–RRVUNL joint venture company (Pandey, 2013; Press Trust of India, 2013).

In the first auction of coal blocks after the cancellation, the country saw aggressive bidding by companies for blocks, and news reports estimated the auction amount and royalty payable to six mineral-rich states as likely to be a little more than ₹1 lakh crore over the next 30 years (Jai, 2015). This puts to rest any doubts about the CAG report figures of estimated losses.

The False Opposition of Energy Security versus Environment Clearances

As stated earlier, the coal sector which included private players, government ministries and knowledge institutions have held environment regulations responsible for "slowing down" the sector. If one was to examine the popular and official narrative on power shortages in the country and the challenges to India's growth dream, it is, more often than not, laid at the door of the Environment Ministry. In fact, in October 2012, a leading National magazine (Kumar and Bhuchar, 2012), *India Today,* carried a cover story titled "Green Terror" which argued that Jayanthi Natarajan, the current Environment Minister, and her predecessor, Jairam Ramesh, had "jinxed development in India." The article went on to point to the example of coal shortages and said that, "According to Coal India's annual report for the year 2011–12, as many as 179 coal blocks were awaiting clearances. Forestry clearances for diverting 28,771 hectares of land were yet to be granted, upsetting the government's power generation plans."

The Prime Minister, at the behest of the leaders of Indian industry, decided to propose a National Investment Board (NIB), which would be headed by the Finance Ministry, to address these "bottlenecks." In a strongly worded rebuttal to this proposal, Environment Minister, Ms Natarajan, expressed her considered opposition to any dilution of environmental processes. She also questioned abdication of the duties of her ministry in any way by this newly constituted body (Singh, 2012).

Her letter states that environment clearance had been granted to 181 coal mines with a total capacity of 583 million tons per annum during the 11th Plan Period, up to August 2011—doubling India's current capacity. This in turn meant that there were no roadblocks from the environment ministry for coal and attributed that the reasons for delays need to be found elsewhere. In addition, 113 coal mines had been granted permission to divert 26,000 hectares of forest land for industrial use. She asserted that clearances have been granted "far beyond what has been targeted in the current and future plans." The letter states that the "Ministry of Environment and Forests in the five years till August 2011 has granted environmental clearance to 210,000 MW of thermal power capacity. However, most of these projects have not been commissioned." She raises the question of why projects that have been accorded clearances are not commissioned and alleges that this "looks very similar to what we are finding in the case of coal allocation. Project proponents have sought and taken environmental clearance as this provides them with land and water allotment as well."

All officially available statistics point only to the fact that environment regulations have not stopped, or blocked, or slowed down, but have prioritized and pushed forward clearances of coal projects. In the last five years, the country has witnessed an unprecedented increase in new private coal mines and the establishment of coal-fired thermal power plants.

Table 4.1

Major reasons for slippage of power projects from the capacity addition target of 78,700 MW to 62,374 MW in the 11th five-year plan

Delay in placement of orders for main plant	6,660 MW
Delay in placement of orders for civil works	1,860 MW
Slow progress of civil works	900 MW
Poor geology	4,432 MW
Contractual dispute between project developer and contractor and their sub-vendors/sub-contractor	4,760 MW
Delay in land acquisition	810 MW
Environmental Concerns	**1,100 MW**
Law and order problem/local issues	580 MW
E&M work critical	600 MW
Difficult area and accessibility	100 MW
Total	**21,802 MW**

Source: Ministry of Power, 2012.

The statistics on forest diversions and environment clearances (issued under Environment Impact Assessment Notification, 2006) shows that coal projects, both mining and thermal power, account for large percentage of total approvals granted to projects by the Ministry of Environment and Forest (MoEF) clearances. Very few plants get rejected. For instance a fact sheet prepared by the Centre for Science and Environment in 2012 indicates that coal mining accounts for 65 percent of all the forestland officially diverted for mining under the Forest Conservation Act, 1980. It is by far, claims the study, the highest number of projects cleared in any of the five-year plan periods in the country since 1981 (CSE, 2012).

It also highlights that during India's 11th five-year plan period (until August 2011), 181 coal mines (including projects that applied for capacity expansion) were granted environment clearance (EC). The analysis indicates that the MoEF has granted approval to double the coal production capacity in the country within a period of five years (CSE, 2012).

In a report by the Prayas Energy Group released in 2011, "Thermal Power Plants on the Anvil—Implications and Need for Rationalisation" (Dharmadhikary and Dixit, 2011), the data from the MoEF was analyzed and the results showed that the ministry had accorded environmental clearances to coal and gas-based power plants whose capacity totaled 192,913 MW—almost double the planned addition in the current five-year plan period. It also showed that another 508,907 MW were at various stages in the environmental clearance cycle. Of these, coal-based plants accounted for an overwhelming 84 percent of the in-pipeline projects. The report went on to show that this was in fact more than six times the installed thermal capacity at the time and three times the capacity addition that would be required if India followed a high efficiency–high renewable energy plan. Environment clearances for coal projects stand in excess of the planned power addition in the next five-year plan (see Figure 4.1).

Figure 4.1
Current and in-pipeline thermal power capacity as of May 12, 2011

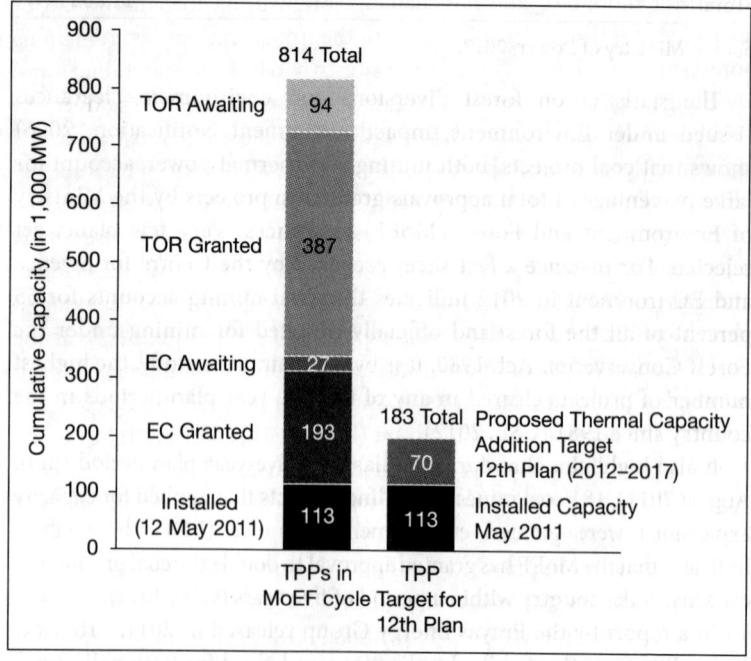

Source: Current Capacity-CEA, See footnote 1, In-pipeline Capacity-MOEFF.

From 2007 to 2011 alone, the coal mine lease area and coal production capacity have approximately doubled, compared to pre-2007 levels (CSE, 2011). Virtually all new coal mining and a significant number of the planned power plants are located in a region broadly referred to as Central India—covering the states of Madhya Pradesh, Chhattisgarh, Jharkhand, and parts of Odisha and eastern Maharashtra.

No-no to Moderate Licensing

In an attempt to provide direction to the coal industry on where mining would be more acceptable and clearances would be more likely to be given more easily, the former Environment Minister, Jairam Ramesh, through discussions with the Ministry of Coal and Coal India Limited, came up with the concept of "Go and No Go" areas in forests. It was, according to the Minister, an attempt to strike a balance between India's desire for more coal and the challenge of ensuring that this would be provided at a "lesser" cost in terms of the impact on our last remaining forests in Central India, home to a majority of tribal and traditional forest dwelling communities and the largest contiguous habitat of the tiger.

This zoning exercise, which was initiated by the Coal Ministry, created a furor with those who spoke about growth at any cost and civil society alike. While the Coal Ministry had only wanted easier access to virgin forests, they did not expect to hear that certain forest areas were totally out of bound for mining (Roychoudhury, 2011). In a note to the Cabinet Committee on Infrastructure, the minister indicated that making it almost compulsory for the forest clearance to be granted, even if the coal block was in pristine and unfragmented forests, would present a fait accompli situation to the ministry and would be against the spirit and intent of the Forest Conservation Act (FCA), 1980 (MoEF, 2011). On the other hand, civil society was concerned that this was merely a back door opening to dilute existing forest governance measures including the FCA and the Forest Rights Act (FRA).

The cabinet note prepared by the Environment Ministry to counter the Coal Ministry's note also argued that the area under consideration for "No Go" was merely 8.11 percent and 11.5 percent of the potential coal bearing and explored coal bearing areas respectively. However, the environment ministry also never indicated that no-go would be that for ever. These areas would be locked up as being critical energy reserves for the future, once again extending the reliance on coal into the future.

The entire saga on "No Go" was interesting in that it showed how the coal reserves in the forest were far more important to the government than the communities who lived in the forests over the coal or the habitat and ecology of the region. Though the state is vested with the responsibility of safeguarding the interests of the forest dwellers by law and also has a mandate to protect forests and endangered species like the tiger, all of these were not really of concern if what they were pitted against was resources that would directly further economic agendas.

Mahan and Chhatrasal are two adjoining coal blocs in Singrauli district of Madhya Pradesh where the above issue plays itself out. When the Go-No-Go was first released in 2010, both these and many other coal blocks in the Singrauli coalfields were categorized as "no-go." In the case of Mahan the Ministry's own Forest Advisory Committee (FAC) rejected the grant of approval to this project on the ground that rich forests and rights of forest dwelling communities will be impacted. This should not be allowed, especially since the coal is available in the Mahan coal block only for a period of fourteen years for the captive use of companies, Essar and Hindalco. However, many of these impacts were not borne in mind when approvals were granted, and the Minister of Environment herself went on record to say that permissions were granted on the insistence by an Empowered Group of Ministers (Kohli, 2013).

In a note to the cabinet in 2010, the Coal Ministry identified the need for accessing forest land for coal mining and stated that any "curtailment of energy source will ultimately result in the country missing growth opportunities." The Coal Ministry, supported by key infrastructure ministeries, the Planning Commission, and the Prime Minister's Office made the case for a reversal of the No Go areas as it held up investment.

This decision to reduce, even minimally, the coal reserves available for extraction and, in addition, to have to face a situation where coal blocks already allotted in "No Go' areas would not be allowed were considered to be bad signals to send to the investors in coal infrastructure. The exposure of banks that had lent to power projects which had been allocated coal blocks but had not got clearances was considered a serious issue and therefore the government sought to intervene and eliminate "No Go" zones. This was when the B.K. Chaturvedi Committee, Planning Commission member (Energy) was to make recommendations to the Group of

Ministers (GoM). The GoM was constituted in February 2011 with the mandate to suggest solutions on coal, regulatory hurdle for mining and industrial projects as well as other developmental issues (GoI, 2011).

The Chaturvedi Committeee, July 2011, was set up to examine and make recommendations considering the issue of environmental concerns and its impact on "developmental activities." The committee had two meetings in the first half of July and submitted its report on the 22nd of the month (GoI, 2011).

This committee came out with shocking recommendations that had the effect of recommending the dilution of both the FCA, 1980 and also the FRA. Reproduced below is one of the recommendations that in essence sums up the thinking of this committee which was to generally provide clearances except under extreme conditions—it however, reiterates that clearances will have to err on the side of generosity and not be too "restrictive" in nature.

...

(iv) Forest Clearance for coal mining should be given based on procedures under the Forest Conservation Act (FCA) and rules made thereunder. Coal bearing blocks should normally be taken up for mining and clearances given for it except where there is a strong case for rejection due to extremely dense forests and other ecological and environmental considerations of serious nature. Given the limited natural resources and international environment, it is not possible to be too restrictive.

The report of the B.K. Chaturvedi-led committee (GoI, 2011), which included secretaries of power, coal, finance, and environment and forest, is a document loaded in favor of coal mining. The constitution of the committee itself left a lot to be desired, as it did not include secretaries from the Ministry of Tribal Affairs and Ministry of Rural Development. Both these ministries should have had a say in this issue which would impact the implementation of the Scheduled Tribes and Other Traditional Forest Dwellers (Recognition of Forest Rights) Act, 2006 (in short, the FRA) and also had massive impact on displacement and rehabilitation of communities who have been living for generations in forest land that would be acquired for mining. There seemed to be a conscious effort to exclude them and isolate the environment ministry. The recommendations of the report focused entirely on a one-point agenda of increasing coal production. All the impacts of mining, whether on communities who will be displaced, habitat loss and impact on water bodies, health and environmental pollution, are categorically de-prioritized.

Coal against Development

The premise of the B.K. Chaturvedi-led committee report on "Solutions for coal and development issues" is the notion that "developmental activities" equals infrastructure creation and mining—not forest protection, or protection of the land and livelihood rights of communities, or not even the safeguarding of air and water quality. All of these are instead seen to be "environmental concerns." A deconstruction of this report highlights the context and manner in which natural resources and the associated common property regimes are viewed in the highest echelons of policymaking in the country. For example, the committee chose to look at regeneration of forests as the panacea for any impact that mining projects would have on forest habitats. The focus on increasing the "green cover" reflects the total lack of understanding of a forest as a complex ecological system.

The availability of coal in certain areas makes it appear a cheap fuel and its mining an inevitability. The report states quite simplistically that "Coal bearing blocks should normally be taken up for mining." It glosses over the concern that there are factors which add immensely to the cost of harvesting and using coal. And most of these costs are not borne by the company engaged in mining or power production but by the state, its tax payers, and its citizens.

The significant analysis by Prayas concludes that,

> these inputs involve critical common property resources and have significant externalities. A market based weeding out process will be littered with many incomplete projects which would have displaced people, impacted the environment and locked up huge amounts of financial resources, creating stranded assets of plant and transmission facilities. The costs of such weeding will be borne to a significant extent by the common people, the country and the environment. (Dharmadhikary and Dixit, 2011)

Contrary to allowing rational decisions to weed out high impact or high cost projects, domestic policy has promoted these projects at all costs. The perception that coal delivers development presupposes the fact that coal is abundant in India and it can be mined and burnt to generate power at cheaper costs than all other existing alternatives. Since large scale coal powered electricity generation has been historically twinned with development, coal imports have also increased by 20 percent to 105.8 million tons to cover the short supply of coal caused by the mismanagement of the mines and new thermal power plants being cleared without established coal linkages. In international coal markets, even though coal prices have fluctuated they remain much higher than domestic coal prices. The impression created by domestic policy that has aggressively pushed both coal mining and coal power projects is that this is the cheapest form of energy production despite its high costs. This is a classic example of faith that trumps market facts.

With regard to the moratorium on industrial activity in areas where the pollution index is extremely high and above acceptable limits, the Chaturvedi Committee recommends that these restrictions should be removed and only preventive measures should be prescribed. This ignores the fact that the high levels of pollution are already an indication that pollution control norms have been flouted and the carrying capacity of the region is reaching its limits. This is considered "acceptable" as the committee concludes that the availability of coal is geo-specific and hence, pollution is again a fall out that one will have to accept.

Pollution-related costs of coal increase with time as impacts get aggravated and concentrated in coal mining areas. With the large scale expansion of coal, India and many other parts of the world are only beginning to witness and experience the full range of "costs" of this expansion forced upon the industry from outside, a cost that until recently did not make it to the ledger on coal economics. The country is also waking up to the health impacts posed by these massive coal clusters that are being planned. A leading environmental voice, the Center for Science and Environment (CSE) (Narain, 2012), in a recent report pointed to shocking levels of mercury pollution in the Singrauli region spreading across the states of Uttar Pradesh and Madhya Pradesh. This region is also known as the energy capital of India.

In 2008, Greenpeace International commissioned the Dutch research institute CE Delft to conduct a preliminary analysis of the external costs of impacts to human health and the environment caused by coal mining and combustion. This study (Greenpeace International, 2008) examined the "cost" of the harm caused by mining and burning coal, which is not reflected in its price per ton or its costs for a kWh of electricity. This evaluation focused on the external costs in 2007 of damages attributable to climate change, human health impacts from air pollution and fatalities due to major mining accidents—factors for which reasonably reliable global data is currently available. Based on the factors examined, the analysis revealed that:

- Coal-fired power stations caused an estimated €356 billion worth of damage globally in 2007;
- Accidents in the global coal power chain cost at least €161 million in 2007; and
- Mining carries with it hidden damage costs, which came to at least €674 million in 2007.

Combining all the costs listed above, CE Delft arrived at a global figure of roughly €360 billion.

This is an indicative figure, and one that could be contested. However, what is becoming abundantly apparent is that the external costs of health, environmental degradation, climate disasters, and human displacement to name a few, are increasing as the unfettered growth of the coal sector continues unabated. Following "Coalgate," it also puts into serious doubt the question of whether the forest destruction and displacement of communities and livelihood loss that is part and parcel of the coal expansion is indeed for the "greater common good" or in fact quite the opposite and is for the good of a small group of corporate and political interests.

In India, there is growing concern and unrest brought on by the enormous scale of coal expansion leading to large scale displacement and livelihood loss, rampant pollution, and water conflicts in many regions where coal clusters are being proposed (Dharmadhikary, 2013). A Greenpeace commissioned study carried out by the Indian Institute of Technology, Delhi, released in 2012, examined the water availability of the Wardha and Wainganga rivers and the impact of thermal power plants on the rivers. The study revealed that the additional demand imposed by the large cluster of thermal power plants in Vidarbha reduces the future water availability for irrigation and other uses in the region by as much as 40 percent in Wardha and about 17 percent in Wainganga (Greenpeace India, 2012).

Examining the environment impact on the coal sector, the Carbon Tracker Initiative[4] published a study that shows that known fossil fuel reserves in the world today exceed what is considered the carbon budget available to us if we are to keep the world to a 2°C scenario by almost 5 times. 65 percent of these reserves are coal, with oil providing 22 percent and gas 13 percent. These fossil fuel reserves are currently accepted as assets for industry, while in reality, if we are to avert dangerous climate change, there is in fact no prospect of them being extracted and burnt. Stock markets ignore the risks of these assets turning out to be mere carbon bubbles and continue to trade without taking these risks into consideration. The report highlighted the following points:

- Already in 2011, the world has used over a third of its 50-year carbon budget of 886 $GtCO_2$, leaving 565 $GtCO_2$;
- All of the proven reserves owned by private and public companies and governments are equivalent to 2,795 $GtCO_2$;
- Fossil fuel reserves owned by the top 100 listed coal and top 100 listed oil and gas companies represent total emissions of 745 $GtCO_2$;
- *Only 20 percent of the total reserves can be burned unabated, leaving up to 80 percent of assets technically unburnable.*[5]

Most recently, at Warsaw, where the coal industry put up a show to challenge the ongoing UN Climate talks, Christiana Figueres, the UN Climate Chief (John and Readfern, 2013), challenged the industry to transform and categorically stated that to keep to the 2 degree limit, most of the coal available would have to be left in the ground.

Climate advocates believe that the writing on the wall cannot get clearer; however, the fossil fuel industry and the entire market economy, and the policy frameworks supporting this economy continue to operate in a bubble of climate change denial. The commodification of coal has ensured we perceive the resource through but one filter—that of a fuel source that powers the economy. All other considerations are collaterals that are viewed as necessary evils to further "growth."

A Policy Discourse That Protects Coal Interests

The B.K. Chaturvedi led committee succeeded in arming the GOM with reasons to do away with the "No Go" classification and opening up all areas for mining on the basis of a case-by-case clearance. The pressure on the MoEF was of course to clear as many coal mining projects as possible, as to be restrictive would be perceived as threatening the growth of the country.

In the meantime, the office of the Prime Minister, under his leadership and at the behest of top industry leaders, has set up the Cabinet Committee for Investment (CCI), which will steer clearances for large investment projects. It was set under the Government of India (Transaction of Business Rules), 1961, under the chairpersonship of the Prime Minister of India. The powers and functions body include identifying key industrial and infrastructure projects of ₹1,000 crore or more and any other "critical" projects, and expediting their approvals, especially when there are "undue" delays. It also prescribes time limits for decisions taken by various ministries and departments by regularly monitoring progress with respect to identified projects (Kohli, 2013).

The CCI was a rechristened version of the National Investment Board (NIB) whose mandate had been strongly questioned by Jayanthi Natarajan, back in October 2011 (Press Trust of India, 2012c). It was a clear indication that instead of approaching the issue of zoning, the industry tsars prefer the case-by-case clearance mechanism, as they can wield their power to circumvent and arm twist ministries into clearing projects. Reports indicate that coal has been high on the CCI's agenda ever since its first meeting (Sahu, 2013).

The current discourse is embedded in the view that coal equals development and, therefore, any limit to coal use is a threat to the country's economic ambitions and will negatively impact the "development" of its citizens. This view excludes from its understanding the impacts of coal extraction and burning, both in the present and in the future.

While climate change is viewed as an issue critical in developing India's future plans, as reflected in an entire chapter, "Sustainable Development and Climate Change," devoted to this in the 2012 economic survey, the approach, however, is to clearly put India's energy needs front and center. To quote from the survey, it says, "Managing energy needs for a rapidly growing economy will be at the heart of the response and India's voluntary endeavours toward climate change." Development is still entwined with carbon space, and the idea that a low cost, low carbon pathway could deliver energy security and address development needs is not on the table for consideration. A faithful but factually illogical emphasis on coal, by hiding its costs to citizens and to the environment, only obfuscates the best energy options waiting to be grabbed and creative routes to meaningful development.

Notes

1. http://www.cea.nic.in/installed_capacity.html (accessed on February 28, 2015).
2. Website of the Ministry of Coal, India, http://www.coal, has details of these developments as accessed on May 10, 2014.
3. http://supremecourtofindia.nic.in/outtoday/wr120.pdf (accessed on November 23, 2015).
4. http://www.carbontracker.org/wp-content/uploads/2014/09/Unburnable-Carbon-Full-rev2-1.pdf.
5. Extracted from the carbon tracker website. http://www.carbontracker.org/carbonbubble.

References

Anonymous. (2013, September 13). Similarities in 2G spectrum, coal block allocations: Bhushan to SC. *The Times of India*.

Bhaskar, U. (2014, May 1). The coal scam just got deeper. *The Mint*.

Bhattacharjya, S. and Colvin, R. (2012, August 23). 'Coalgate' corruption paralyses parliament. *Reuters*, New Delhi.

CAG. (2012). *Performance Audit: Allocation of Coal Blocks and Augmentation of Coal Production*. New Delhi: Government of India.

CICERO-Centre for International Climate and Environmental Research. (2013). Coal continues to dominate global carbon emissions. *Science Daily*, November 18, 2013. Retrieved November 23, 2015, from www.sciencedaily.com/releases/2013/11/131118193131.htm.

———. CSE (Centre for Science and Environment) (2012). *Overview (fact sheet on environment and forest clearances)*, Public Watch, Retrieved November 23, 2015, from http://www.cseindia.org/userfiles/GRP%20factsheet%20Full.pdf.

Chakravatty, A. (2012). Private firms made windfall gain of ₹1.86 lakh crore from coalblocks: CAG. *Down to Earth*, August 17.

Dharmadhikary, S. (2013, December 5). *Powerful forces get water for power. India Together.* www.indiatogether.org.

Dharmadhikary, S. and Dixit, S. (2011). *Thermal power plants on the anvil: Implications and need for rationalisation*. Prayas Energy Group, August 2011.

Dutta, S. (2014, May 1). CBI sniffs collusion between officials, Coalgate allottees. *The Times of India*.

GoI (Government of India). (2011). *Report of the committee constituted by group of ministers to suggest solutions on coal and other development issues*. Government of India, New Delhi, July 22, 2011.

Greenpeace India. (2012). *Water diversion to thermal power plants will reduce irrigation potential and worsen agrarian crisis in Vidarbha: Greenpeace*, Greenpeace.org., December 3, 2012.

Greenpeace International. (2008). *The true cost of coal*. Greenpeace. www.greenpeace.org, November 27, 2008.

———. (2010). *The case against coal*. Greenpeace. www.greenpeace.org, April 15, 2010.

IANS. (2012). Supreme Court issues notice to centre on coal block allocation. IANS, New Delhi, November 19, 2012.

Inamdar, N. (2013, October 15). 7 things you wanted to know about 'coalgate': A quick summary of the coal allocation scam. *Business Standard.*

Jai, S. (2015, 23 February). First coal block e-auction earns ₹1 lakh cr for states, *Business Standard.*

Kohli, K. (2013, October 30). *Is CCI a bypass lane for the laws?* www.indiatogether.org.

Kumar, D. and Bhuchar, P. (2012, October 5). Green terror. *India Today.*

Lok Sabha Secretariat. (2013). *Thirty-first report: Standing committee on coal and steel (2012-2013) on ministry of coal: Review of allotment, development and performance of coal/lignite locks.* New Delhi. April 2013.

Ministry of Power. (2012, January). *Report of the working group on power for twelfth plan (2012-17).* Government of India, New Delhi.

Mishra, R. (2012, August 17). Undue benefits to Reliance Power, says CAG Report on UMPPs. *The Hindu Business Line.*

Muthu, A. (2012, August 22). *Everything about the coal scam.* Greenpeace–India, Retrieved May 8, 2014, from http://www.greenpeace.org/india/en/Blog/everything-about-the-coal-scam/blog/41832/.

MoEF-Ministry of Environment & Forests. (2011). *Comments of MoEF on draft note for cabinet committee on infrastructure regarding making available more coal bearing areas for coal production,* February 1, 2011. Retrieved May 9, 2014, from http://www.indiaenvironmentportal.org.in/files/MoEF%20response%20to%20cab%20note.pdf.

Narain, S. (2012, November 15). Silence is the best policy. *Down to Earth.*

Pandey, P. (2013, April 8). Adani commences integrated coal MDO in India." *The Times of India.*

Planning Commission. (2006). *Integrated energy policy: Report of the expert committee.* Planning Commission, Government of India. Retrieved November 23, 2015, from http://planningcommission.nic.in/reports/genrep/rep_intengy.pdf.

———. (2012). *Recommendations on fuel made by the working group on power for the twelfth plan (2012-2017): Executive summary-Report of the working group for the twelfth plan (2012-2017).* Retrieved, May 9, 2012, from http://planningcommission.gov.in/aboutus/committee/wrkgrp12/wg_power1904.pdf.

Press Trust of India. (2012a September, 24) Coalgate: CBI to probe coal block allocations since 1993. *The Economics Times.*

———. (2012b, September 11). Coalgate a 'bigger scam' than 2G: SP. *Hindustan Times.*

———. (2012c, December 13). Cab nod for panel to clear mega projects, renames NIB as CCI. *Business Standard.*

———. (2013, April 8). Adani commences coal production at RRVUNL's Chhattisgarh mine. *The Economic Times.*

Roychowdhury, I. (2011, February 8). *Greens nixing growth, rues CIL chief. The Indian Express.*

Sahu, R.K. (2013, January 29). First meeting of cabinet committee of investment: coal, petroleum in focus. Retrieved May 10, 2014, from http://profit.ndtv.com/news/economy/article-first-meeting-of-cabinet-committee-of-investment-coal-petroleum-in-focus-316952.

Singh, R.R. (2012, September 17). Munda helped Abhijeet group grab 151 acres. *DNA India.*

Singh, S. (2012, October 10). Jayanthi assails investment super committee proposal. *The Hindu.*

Supreme Court of India. (2014). WP No. 120 of 2012 in the case of Manohar Lal Sharma Vs Principle Secretary & Ors, August 25, 2014.

Section II
Democratic Governance
of Nature

5

Value as a Justification in Water Resource Development

Shripad Dharmadhikary

Three time periods: the early 1950s, late 1970s, and early 2000s. Each separated by some 25 years. Time enough for new thinking to evolve on water, development, and environment. And yet, each one of them exhibits the same approach to rivers and water—the notion that any water that is not taken up directly for human use is a waste, has no value.

Water Resource Development in the Indus Basin

On August 15, 1947, India became independent from the British rule. At the same time, it was partitioned into two countries with Pakistan being separated out. While the horrors of the partition are well documented, less known, but equally significant, was the bitter dispute that arose between the two countries over the sharing of the waters of the Indus and its tributaries.

On the eve of partition, the Indus basin had one of the most extensive and well-developed irrigation systems in the world. Partition cut through this whole system and ruptured it, with many of the canals going in Pakistan, but the headworks remaining in India. Moreover, India was upstream of Pakistan on every river of the Indus basin. On April 1, 1948, India shut the gates on the main canals of the Upper Bari Doab Canal (UBDC), leading to cutting off of water supplies to the city of Lahore and large tracts of farmlands. This triggered the long-drawn dispute that was to take more than 12 years to resolve, with the signing of the Indus Basin Treaty.

The World Bank played a key role in mediating in the dispute resolution process. The Bank's involvement itself seems to have been initiated after the visit of David Lilienthal to the two countries.

David Lilienthal had been first a member, and then the chairperson of the famous Tennessee Valley Authority (TVA). The TVA had deep influence on dam building in India, with the Damodar Valley Corporation being modeled on it. The TVA was not just a technological model, but represented modernity, scientific temper and a nation on the move. The powerful appeal of this idea came from "the notion of science and technology operating through technical experts in interest of humankind, in particular in structures from which politicians and their vested interests had been banished" (Dharmadhikary, 2007). A particularly important part of this appeal came from the notion that with science and technology being employed to harness natural resources, there would be plenty for everyone, and thus, the vexed questions of equitable distribution would not arise.[1]

However, the most fundamental influence of the TVA is likely to be the idea that any water that is not wrung out of the river, any drop of water that is allowed to go down to the sea without being put to human use is "waste."

In 1951, David Lilienthal visited India and Pakistan. He had been sent here by the *Collier's* magazine to report on the happenings in India for them. But there is talk that he was in touch with the US government and was also acting informally as its eyes and ears in the region. Possibly for this reason, and also for his association with the TVA, Lilienthal commanded a lot of weight and during his visit had access to the highest political leadership on either side of the new boundary.

The Indus Valley dispute naturally commanded a lot of attention from him.[2] For him, it appeared to be one of the trouble spots between the two countries "where a solution could be reached" (Lilienthal, 1951). The way was, of course, to use the waters of the Indus that were "going waste." He wrote:

I suggest that this unnecessary controversy [the water dispute] can be solved by common sense and engineering...

Less than 20% of the water of the Indus basin is right now put to use for irrigation; most of the waters of the six life giving rivers of the Indus basin flow to the Arabian Sea unused. If this wasted water, or even a large fraction of it is put to use, both India's needs and Pakistan's needs could be met.

The urgent problem is how to store up now wasted waters, so that they can be fed down and distributed by engineering works and canals, and used by both countries, rather than permitted to flow to the sea unused.

Of course, India's own planning was not divorced from this notion of any water not used being considered as "waste." The first five-year plan document noted (Planning Commission, 1951):

A more recent appraisal of the water resources of the country...gives the total annual flow as equivalent to 1356 million acre-feet for the Indian Union. Of this only 76 million acre-feet or 5.6 percent are at present being used for purposes of irrigation; the rest flow waste to the sea.

Sometimes, it is said that this notion—of "water going waste to the sea"—should be seen in the context of the day and age when it was being used. We should not judge these statements by today's perspective. For example, if only 20 percent of the Indus basin water was being used, one could not blame the riparian population—who saw huge quantities in the river flowing by, even as their fields did not have water—if they thought this water was going waste.

In principle this is true, but we are *not* judging the statements by today's standards. Even if one looks at the context in which these statements were made, there are clear indications that "use" and its corollary, "waste" are not neutral terms. By definition, waste means something that does not have value, and value is not a neutral term.

The use of the water for irrigation is certainly an important and valued use. This is not being disputed. What is disputed is the notion that if the flowing water was not being used for irrigation (or some other specific uses like hydropower), then it was being wasted. This notion ignored the many other uses of water—some, like fisheries which benefitted humans, and others which served the purposes of other life forms and maintaining the ecology. In this way, value itself was not neutral, but privileged certain uses. What is crucial is that even in those times, these "other" uses were known, but it was just that they were not considered important or valuable enough.

Let us see in more detail how planners were aware of downstream uses of water allegedly going "waste" but only valued some of these uses.

The early 20th century started seeing a series of disputes over the sharing of the waters of the Indus Basin rivers, with conflicts escalating as diversions and damming increased. The dispute primarily arose between the (then British) provinces of Punjab[3] and Sind.[4] Punjab was upstream of Sind, and Sind was agitated that Punjab's irrigation diversions were affecting the water flowing in its region. Punjab on the other hand was protesting schemes in Sind fearing that they would create prior rights for Sind on the waters that were flowing through its (Punjab's) territory. This is of course the classic upstream–downstream conflict, the point we are trying to make here being that an awareness existed even in those days that water was not just flowing down "waste" but it was possibly being used or benefitting downstream areas.

When India's Bhakra project was being designed, it was well understood that large areas downstream would become dry as the water would all be stored behind the dam. Noted economist K.N. Raj mentions that "it was also clear that the river would almost dry up below Rupar" (Raj, 1960, p. 49). In fact, it was noted that certain pre-existing canals drawing water from the Sutluj river, the Grey Canals, would cease functioning as the river would become dry, and hence these areas were added to the Bhakra command with a special canal drawing water for these areas.[5]

In other words, there was recognition that prior to damming or diversion, the water that was flowing down was not going "waste," but it was meeting some needs. The real issue was whether all these needs and uses were given their due, whether all were valued or only some. To continue the Bhakra example, the planners of Bhakra acknowledged that water that was flowing in the Sutluj was meeting some irrigation needs (through the Grey canals) but did not recognize, or if they did recognize, did not put any value to the uses of this water for fishing, for navigation, for flood plain agriculture, and so on.

Some possible reasons why these uses were not recognized could be that the communities who were benefitting from these uses were economically or politically marginalized communities, or that these uses were not important enough in terms of the formal economy, that they did not generate or have potential to generate revenue.

It is very difficult to know what reactions these communities had to the attempts to dam and divert the waters of the Indus basin rivers, as the very fact that they were marginalized meant that their voices would not have been heard even at that time, let alone some 50 to 100 years later, today. But there are some indicators.

Historian Alice Albinia, writing in her travelogue-history of the Indus basin, says the following (Albinia, 2008, pp. 48, 50):

> Some Cassandra-like Sindhis looked in alarm upon both the irrigation projects under way upstream in the Punjab, and those planned for Sindh. (If the level of water went down, they feared, navigation would be harmed; the impact of fishing and agriculture was not even considered.) But the British dismissed these concerns, believing there was enough water to go round...

> The Sukkur barrage [in Sind, on the Indus, completed 1932] changed Sindhi society for ever. Huge areas of wasteland were turned into fertile agricultural regions.... Landowners and administrators lavished praise upon this, the biggest irrigation project in the world.... Only the farmers of the Delta looked upon Sukkur with askance.

> By enabling the storage of huge amounts of river water, and viewing each drop that went out to the sea as "wastage," what the engineers had ignored was the need of plenty of fresh water downstream in the Delta, in order to maintain a healthy balance with the salt water from the sea, and thus to safeguard the unique ecosystem of mangroves, shrimp beds, fish and farmers...

> "The farmers here voted against the Sukkur barrage," Baboo says.... The old men at Karochan agree: "After Sukkur opened, farmers became fishermen," says the doctor. "And with Kotri [another barrage on Indus, downstream of Sukkur, completed 1955], then all the rice fields went saline.... But nobody would listen to us that the Delta needs more water."

Albinia also indicates how culture and commerce decide what is considered valuable and what is waste. She discusses how the delta, once the richest of all lands in Pakistan, was seen and documented by the British as being harsh and barren. And since its agricultural practices were very different due to its peculiar hydrology and soil characteristics, its "frequently flooded paddies, shifting settlements and semi-nomadic farmers" did not fit the picture of a "able or desirable agricultural model" (Albinia, 2008, p. 48) And,

> for the British, who wished to transport grain quickly into northern India, it made better economic sense to develop Punjab and upper Sindh than to defend the strange agrarian culture of the mangroves. (Albinia, 2008, p. 48)

No wonder, the waters of the Indus that were running down to the rich and fertile Delta were seen as going "waste" and this became the justification of many large dams and diversions.

Another indication that the planners, even in the 1950s, were aware of the many different roles played by flowing waters comes from this statement in India's first five-year plan. The chapter on irrigation and power states:[6]

...

12. The total quantity of water flowing in the rivers, a rough quantitative indication of which has been given in paragraph 8 above, is not wholly available or needed for irrigation.

This is due mainly to the following reasons:—

...

iv. Certain quantities of water must be allowed to flow in rivers for hydro-electric development, for purposes of navigation, conservancy and water-supply for towns and villages.

In spite of this, many such uses, particularly conservancy, did not merit much consideration, and river basin development proceeded on the basis that any water going to the sea was a waste, and with plans to extract the very last drop. The Narmada project is an excellent example of this.

The Narmada Project

The Narmada river flows through the three states of M.P., Maharashtra, and Gujarat. It has been at the heart of an intense water dispute concerning the sharing of the waters between the three states and the height of the Sardar Sarovar Dam (SSD), the terminal dam on the river before it meets the sea. The SSD is being built in Gujarat, but its submergence also includes areas in the other two states. The dispute resulted in the appointment, by the Government of India, of the Narmada Water Disputes Tribunal (NWDT) in 1969, under the Interstate Water Disputes Act, 1956. The tribunal gave its final award in 1979. This was 28 years after Lilienthal's or the first five-year plan's reference to waters being wasted. Yet, the language, and more important, the substance of the Tribunal Award was little different.

The Narmada river is about 1,300 km long, and it flows for about 150 km after the SSD site before it meets the sea. The Narmada estuary is extremely rich in fisheries, particularly the Hilsa.

The tribunal assessed the annual availability of waters at the SSD site to be 28 Million Acre Feet (MAF) at 75 percent dependability.[7] What is important is that in allocating the shares to each of the states, the tribunal distributed all of the 28 MAF amongst the three riparian states and Rajasthan.[8] While in principle, this water was to be used by the states as they pleased in their territory,[9] it was clear that this "use" or "allocation" was essentially for irrigation, and domestic and industrial water supply. No other use was really considered. This is clear from the method of measuring the utilization of each state given by the Tribunal, which essentially consists of measuring the discharge of the canals or the pumps.[10]

In other words, each and every drop of water was distributed for these specified uses upstream of the SSD. The 150 km or so of the river downstream was almost forgotten,[11] and any water that went down the SSD was labeled as wasted.

The SSD has a power house at the toe of the dam, called the River Bed Power House (RBPH). The RBPH is envisaged to play a meaningful role only till the "full development" along the entire length of the river upstream, that is, till all the water is eventually used or extracted upstream. Till such a time, water will go down the SSD without being used, and hence, the RBPH is expected to be active (only) till such a time, generating power from this water which otherwise would be wasted. The tribunal order states that:[12]

...

(5) It may be mentioned that in many years there will be surplus water in the filling period after meeting the storage requirements and withdrawals during the period. This will flow down to sea. Only portion of it will be utilisable for generating power at Sardar Sarovar River-Bed Power-House and the rest will go waste. It is desirable that water which would go waste without even generating power at the last River-Bed Power-House should be allowed to be utilised by the party States to the extent they can.

Thus, any water that actually flowed down below the dam (without generating power) was considered waste.

That the Narmada project involved extracting every last drop of water from the river has in some ways been acknowledged years later by Yoginder Alagh, former Chair of the Gujarat Government's Narmada Planning Group, which had done detailed planning for the project. Writing in the Indian Express on May 30, 2009, Alagh says,[13] for the Narmada project,

> So we modelled ten daily flows in four reservoirs and modelled groundwater
> aquifers.... The modelling was so good that we very accurately used up all
> the water for the crops, the trees and for drinking. We all forgot the obvious.
> Rivers also need water.

Of course, strictly speaking, this was not true. The planners had not
"forgotten" all of the river, and the needs for its ecological and other
functions. They had just sacrificed these needs for extracting maximum
in terms of other use.[14] When the matter was being argued in front of
the tribunal, Gujarat had requested the tribunal to allocate water to it for
releasing downstream of the dam to meet the downstream need. It had
quantified this need to be 0.7 MAF. The tribunal had disallowed this, but
had told Gujarat that any water needed for the downstream areas can
be let down the dam by Gujarat from its own share of nine MAF. This
is also recorded in the formal order of the tribunal.[15] However, Gujarat
has chosen not to do this, and its entire share of nine MAF is planned
for being diverted out of the river at the dam.

Thus, the Narmada experience also shows that "waste" is not a term
born out of ignorance of other uses and functions of the river, but it is an
expression of the low or no value assigned to these needs.[16]

Interlinking of Rivers

This project, otherwise known as the National Perspective Plan, is a
massive project that will link many rivers and involve the construction
of large number of big storage dams, diversion structures, canals, tunnels, etc. It has two components: the Himalayan component involving
14 links and the Peninsular component having 16 links. The plan was
developed by the (then) Ministry of Irrigation and the Central Water
Commission in the 1980s.[17] However, it came into limelight some ten
years back, in 2002, when the Supreme Court of India, in an order,
pushed for its accelerated implementation.

The project has many serious problems and has been facing tremendous
opposition. This chapter does not go into the issues with the project. What
it highlights is the basis of the whole project, which is the same notion of
water going waste.

The National Water Development Agency (NWDA) is the agency that
has been tasked with carrying out various studies and giving a concrete

shape to the whole project. According to the NWDA, the rationale of the project is the "interbasin transfer of water from surplus basins to deficit ones with a view to minimize the regional imbalances and optimally utilize the available water resources."[18]

At the heart of the project is the notion that some river basins are having surplus water. This notion is highly problematic, as a river basin can be considered surplus only if one discounts the ecological and other roles of the river and considers only a narrowly limited range of (human) uses and functions of the rivers. The NWDA tries to preempt criticism by saying that "only surplus flood water after meeting all in-basin requirements in foreseeable future has been planned for transfer to water deficit areas."[19] But even this notion that flood water is surplus is a mistaken notion. The ecology of the river (and the basin) has evolved based on its historical natural flows, and this includes the seasonal pattern of high and low flows. Thus, any part of the flow, including the floods, can be considered surplus only by discounting the ecological functions. Often, maintaining the ecological integrity of the river is essential to support a range of livelihoods like fisheries and river bank agriculture. Thus, in discounting the ecological functions, often even the benefits accruing to large human communities are discounted.

In this manner, we see that the notion of surplus—that is fundamental to the interlinking of rivers program—can operate only by privileging certain uses of the river flow over others. In other words, surplus water is that water which is otherwise going waste. Indeed, one does not need to dig very deep in the National Perspective Plan to see that the notion of surplus is the same as "water going waste to sea."

In giving more information about the project, the NWDA website presents a document giving details of the river linking scheme. Among other things, this document says[20]:

> The initiative taken by the Government of India in preparing the scheme benefiting various regions was welcomed by the States. The general consensus emerged that the monsoon flood waters which otherwise run waste into the sea should be conserved in various storage reservoirs, big and small. The water so conserved could then be utilized for irrigation, power generation etc.

Thus, the floods water that are "going waste" to the sea, become the surplus. Apart from the privileging of certain uses over others, the conversion of "waste" into "surplus" also becomes possible due to technology that makes possible the transfer water from one basin to the other.

From the Indus basin development to the modern day program of "interlinking of rivers," the notion of value has been used to propose and justify massive dams and diversion projects. On the one hand, irrigation and other uses are proposed as having high value, and hence the projects that deliver these benefits are justified for the positive value they are supposed to create; on the other hand, there is the negative value if they are not built, that is, the water is going waste. This negative value is the other side of the coin of justification of these large projects. Here, it is important to stress that the water flowing to the sea is "waste," not because it does not serve any purposes, nor because these purposes served are not known. This water is waste because the "other" purposes, these "other" functions—which are often known and understood—are not considered important enough by the mainstream, by the politically powerful, that is, they do not have any value for the powers that be.

By all standards, the Indian state's program of extracting every drop of water from the rivers has been extremely successful, the success being evident from the fact that several rivers no longer meet the sea. The 12th five-year plan document notes this, saying (Planning Commission, 2012, p. 145):

> [A] study by the International Water Management Institute (IWMI) shows that Krishna and Kaveri have reached full or partial closure. Another IWMI study shows that in the Krishna river basin, the storage capacity of major and medium reservoirs has reached total water yield, with virtually no water reaching the sea in low rainfall years.[21]

It must be mentioned that this notion of waste has been increasingly challenged, especially as the communities whose voices were not heard have gathered strength and expression. One of the responses of the mainstream (including economics) has been to attribute value to some of the hitherto non-recognized uses and functions. These have included monetizing values of non-monetary costs and benefits for use in decision making tools such as cost–benefit analysis, or governance and compensation mechanisms such a "payment for ecological services."

There has been an attempt in the recent years to introduce in India one such mechanism, a mechanism that has the notion of value much more explicitly at its core, though its method of operation is somewhat different. We now turn to look at this mechanism, as it can have far reaching implications. This mechanism can be referred to in brief as "a market of tradable water entitlements or rights."

Tradable Water Entitlements

Conceptually, the mechanism is simple. First, create and allocate to everyone a right to water. This appears to make the method progressive, even radical. Then, create a market where these rights can be freely traded, bought, or sold. Such a market will ensure that soon water will be allocated to those who extract maximum value from it (which is how they will be able to pay for and buy all the rights from others). An underlying assumption is that maximum value extracted by anyone from water is equivalent to the largest societal benefit, since the societal resource of water has been used to deliver highest value. Such a method, it is argued, will be the most efficient method of optimal inter-sectoral allocation of water. One of the biggest advantages of this method is that all allocation (and diversion) will be voluntary.

Like many such market mechanisms, the push for its introduction in India has come from the World Bank and the Asian Development Bank.

In the late 1990s, the World Bank began a comprehensive and wide-ranging review of India's water sector, which was called India Water Resources Management Sector Review. This review resulted in the publication of six reports in 1998, one each on the aspects (and with the titles) of Intersectoral Water Allocation, Planning and Management, Groundwater Regulation and Management, Irrigation, Rural Water Supply and Sanitation, Urban Water Supply and Sanitation and one synthesis report. Though this process was called a "sector-wide program undertaken in partnership between the Government of India and the World Bank, also with contributions from the governments of U.K., Denmark and the Netherlands" (World Bank, 1999a, p. ix), it was clearly initiated and led by the World Bank.[22]

This World Bank-led review argued for introducing tradable water rights as an important mechanism of inter-sectoral water allocation in India. The bank was also promoting this at the global level. The bank's Water Sector Resources Strategy, adopted in 2003, says (World Bank, 2004, p. 16):

> Recognizing and managing water rights is as essential for managing irrigation systems as for managing river basins or aquifers…. The essence of this change is that water rights (of individuals and communities, including traditional users) enjoy the same legal certainty as land and other property rights. Once established, such rights give rise to a series of fundamental and healthy

changes. First, those requiring additional resources (such as growing cities) will frequently be able to meet their needs by acquiring the rights of those who are using water for low value purposes. Second, there are strong incentives for low-value water users to voluntarily desist, making reallocation both politically attractive and practical.

The report on inter-sectoral allocation of water from the 1998 review makes clear what the implementation of the mechanism would look like, giving the example of Chennai (World Bank, 1999b, pp. 133–134).

> As in all parts of the world, the value of water for irrigated foodcrops is a fraction of the value for urban and domestic purposes. Rough calculations suggest that the value of water in irrigation in Tamil Nadu is less than ₹0.5/cubic meter. Even if Metrowater [Water Supply Company for Chennai] could pay several times this amount, it could obtain additional water…

> The potential for voluntary inter-sectoral transfer of water to urban users from irrigation provide a promising low cost alternative.

While the above example deals with the diversion of water from agriculture to urban use, the same mechanism would also be used for diverting waters from agriculture (and other "low valued") uses, to industry and high value entertainment activities like tourism, golf courses, and so on.

On similar lines, the water policy of the Asian Development Bank[23], adopted on January 16, 2001, also says (ADB, 2001, p. 30) that "The allocation of water to high-value uses is a matter of economic accountability" and that "It will support the evolution of water allocation through markets of transferable water rights" (ADB, 2001, p. 18).

An interesting point here is that ADB and the World Bank talk about allocation of water to highest value uses and users, with an aim to maximize the economic impact of water. We can also look at this process as one where water itself becomes a valuable commodity by attaching itself to a high value use. If one looks at the use of the notions of waste (and value) of water in the context of river basin planning, dams, and irrigation, one see this process taking place. Water, which is low-value and waste when it is running into the sea, becomes a high-value item when it is used (or attached to a use) like irrigation or hydropower. The tradable water rights mechanism only makes this "valuation" explicit. In fact, a more accurate description would be that the tradable water rights mechanism explicitly commodifies water.

In the 2000s, the World Bank and ADB, driven by their respective water strategies and policies, initiated large-scale reforms of India's water sector through a series of water sector improvement and restructuring loans. These reforms essentially constituted a package of privatization, commodification and marketization of the water sector. Albeit, the progress of these changes has been much slower than envisaged due to large scale protests, resistance, and informed critique of these measures. One of the measures that was a part of these reforms was the introduction of the tradable water entitlements mechanism.

Maharashtra was the first (and till date, the only) state to move in this direction. In 2005, the Maharashtra Assembly passed the Maharashtra Water Resources Regulatory Authority Act 2005 (MWRRA Act). This act created the MWRRA (or Authority), an independent regulatory authority on the lines of the Electricity Regulatory Commissions that were put into place some years earlier. The many functions and powers of MWRRA include

1. "to determine the distribution of Entitlements for various Categories of Use and the equitable distribution of Entitlements of water within each Category of Use" (Clause 11 (a) of the MWRRA Act),

2. "to fix the criteria for trading of water Entitlements or Quotas on the annual or seasonal basis" (Clause 11 (i) of the MWRRA Act)

Together these constitute the mandate and the direction for the MWRRA to set up a market of tradable water entitlements. And while the MWRRA Act talks of trading on annual or season basis, the Authority's power to affect "permanent transfer of Entitlements" (Clause 11 (l) of the MWRRA Act), means that these trades can also result in a permanent purchase/transfer of water rights.

On June 7, 2011, the MWRRA put out on its website a "Draft Approach Paper on Trading in Water Entitlements."[24] The paper talks about such trading being in the interest of increasing overall water use efficiency, but is fairly circumspect regarding the extent of trading envisaged. This is possibly due to the strong criticism that has been made of the attempts to introduce such trading and the apprehensions voiced at its serious implications.

For example, the World Bank and even the MWRRA have referred to the beneficial experiences of Chile, where similar trading arrangements are supposed to have led to many efficiency gains. The World Bank, in its 1998 Water Sector Review, justifies the introduction of tradable entitlements saying (World Bank, 1999b, p. 134):

> In terms of practice, formal, managed water markets have come into use in a number of countries (e.g., Chile, USA, Australia). These experiences show that markets offer a practical, tested alternative for the voluntary reallocation of water.

Talking particularly about the Chile experience, the bank mentions substantial economic gains being produced (World Bank, 1999b, p. 138) and how in Chile, "regulated water markets, based on an explicit water rights system, exist and have reportedly proven to be effective as a means of allocating water resources to their most productive use."

However, elsewhere (World Bank, 1999c, p. 108), the bank itself has recorded that:

> The main disadvantage, or risk, of the new system is monopolization of water rights. A couple of power companies and a single individual have been accused of accumulating some 70% of all water rights in Chile.

However, the bank just mentions this, and leaves it at that. The bank has been pushing for the tradable rights mechanism essentially ignoring this and other problems. There is other information from Chile as well. In September 2010, an abridged, English version of a report on Chile's water markets was published by several organizations (Larrain and Schaeffer, 2010). The report documented how just 3 companies own 90 percent of the water rights for hydropower generation in the country, with just one company Endesa owning 80.4 percent. Interestingly, it also documents how Endesa was initially a state-owned company, which was bought by a private national company and is now owned by an Italian conglomerate. Thus, the water rights have now gone into the hands of foreign players. The report also brings out many other problems with the market system.

With this and other critiques in place, the MWRRA has chosen to be cautious on the introduction of the tradable water entitlements regime. First, it is calling this effort a pilot project. Moreover, in a bid to allay apprehensions that the trading will divert water from agriculture to industry, the MWRRA has said that the trading will be only intrasectoral, that is, within the irrigation sector.

Of course, this is not likely to really dispel the fears, because MWRRA's Revised Approach Paper[25] lets the cat out of the bag when it says that it is only the irrigation sector that has any surplus water to trade, the industry and domestic sector are not only drawing their full quota but their demands are increasing, and "Non-irrigation users do not have surplus quota to transfer." Therefore, says the Revised Approach Paper, "inter sectoral trading is not advised *at this stage*"[26] [Emphasis added].

Diversion of Water for Industries in Maharashtra

There is another reason for the caution shown by the MWWRA. In the last several years, Maharashtra has witnessed the diversion of huge amounts of water from irrigation to industry. In the last 10 years (from 2002 to 2012), the total water diverted annually from irrigation allocation for industry and urban areas[27] is close to 1,900 million cubic meters.[28] According to the government itself, this water could irrigate 2.85 lakh ha of land every year. These diversions have been at the center of massive protests in the last several years.

One of the points of controversy has been that a significant part of the diversion has been in the area of Vidarbha. Vidarbha has been much in the news due to the large scale suicides of farmers who have been pushed into debt due to repeated crop failures. One of the main reasons for the crop failure has been the scarcity of water. Another reason for the intensity of the protests has been that lot of the diversions have been for thermal power projects, many owned by private companies. With these projects leading to massive pollution and displacement, a feeling has been created that not only has the water of the poorer farmers been diverted and they have been left to bear the brunt of pollution and other impacts, but that this water has been diverted to serve the interests and profits of big business and corporate houses.

The reaction of the government to the strong protests over these diversions has been to amend the MWRRA Act, with retrospective effect. One of the issues raised by the protests was that the diversions from irrigation and the allocation to specific industries and urban bodies were being approved by a High Power Committee (HPC) consisting of various state ministers, whereas the MWRRA Act gave the powers to the Authority to do this. In essence, the HPC did not have the powers to divert the waters, and all the approvals by it were illegal. The government responded to this by amending the act to make all the approvals by the HPC legal, with retrospective effect, barred them being challenged in any court, and took away the powers of the Authority to allocate water and gave them to the state cabinet. However, it did not in any way address the core of the issue, that is, the diversion from agriculture to industry of large quantities of water. Hence, the concern and the anger amongst the people remain.

It is against this background that the trading of water entitlements as introduced by the MWRRA needs to be seen. Notwithstanding all the disclaimers by MWRRA that the trading will be only within the irrigation sector, the reality is that the main purpose of trading is to enable allocations to highest value-added users, and these are the industry and urban users. MWRRA has already indicated the future direction by saying that inter-sectoral trading is not to be taken at this stage. So it is likely to be taken up at a later stage. The most important advantage of the trading regime, already pointed out previously, is, as the World Bank says (World Bank, 2004, p. 16), it makes "reallocation both politically attractive and practical." This is because the players agree to give up their rights voluntarily, in lieu of money.

Given the situation in Maharashtra, with many large industries lined up, with thermal power capacity of around 90,000 MW in the pipeline, it is clear that the thirst for water is going to grow. Thus, in the future, the intensity of the conflict is only likely to increase. In such a situation, it's not surprising that trading in water entitlement would have a special appeal to the political leadership and to industry. If farmers are willing to sell their water rights for use in industry, then there would be no protests! Of course, the long term consequences would be serious, and many. These include the possible concentration of water rights in the hands of few, the marginalization of farmers (with water sold away, land may not be of much use for agriculture, so land itself may be sold off too), the loss of food security, and so on.[29] But in the short term, it may offer a seemingly easy and convenient way out for the political and economic elites.

The Value of Water

The above examples show how value has been central to the justifica-tion of and decision making in large water projects. Value was often used qualitatively, and not quantified. For example, when irrigation was presented as a justification to build a dam, it was considered valuable in itself. It also got value because in the absence of water being put to this use (or a few other uses), water was considered to have no value, or as waste. It was almost as if the myriad other roles, uses, and functions of the water were invisible, or when visible, of negligible value.

The cost benefit calculations were more in the nature of costs of building projects versus the revenues they would generate. But the intrinsic higher value of the purpose they were to serve was not doubted. In fact, this notion of the higher value (of irrigation, or power uses) and the waste have been powerful tools in creating public acceptance of projects in the eyes of society at large—whether it is the decades old projects of the Indus basin or the most modern, proposed projects of the Interlinking of Rivers program.

There were serious consequences of this approach. Essentially, all the functions that were not valued—the invisible or glossed over uses and roles—were undermined. The communities associated with these functions suffered.

By consistently invoking the notion that water was (is) going waste to the sea, the planners dismissed these other roles and functions of water, and in turn downplayed, or masked, or even suppressed the impacts, and hence the real costs of these projects. Was this done deliberately, with intent to conceal the negative impacts, or was it just a manifestation of the mindset of those controlling the decisions who genuinely believed they were doing the best for society? There is enough evidence to show that at least many of the negative impacts were not unknown and were glossed over; that the notion of value and waste were conveniently used to justify the path suited to those who were powerful. Even if this is doubted for the projects in the decades gone by, it is almost certainly true in today's time, where there is ample recognition of the many roles and functions played by water that is labeled as going "waste."

Over the years, there have been attempts to give a place to the aspects which were neglected (considered a waste) till then, by introducing some form of valuation of these—whether for the aspects that could be quantified or those that are essentially non-quantifiable. In theory, if one can provide a valuation for each and every use and function of water, then we can say that the decision could be taken in a scientific and rational manner, as each aspect would be given its due consideration. In such a scenario, water not being used would not be considered going waste, but would be considered as providing certain services whose utility would be valued in some quantitative terms and then balanced with the valuation of the benefits. But in practice, this does not seem to have happened.

Apart from possible refinements to the cost–benefit analysis, such valuations have also been used for conservation and environmental governance. These include measures like "payment for ecological services," or the "clean development mechanism" with the trading in carbon credits emanating from projects that save carbon emissions. The mechanism of "tradable water entitlements" can also be said to be one such mechanism where valuation of a resource or its use is used for governance; in this case, allocation of water to specific activities.

The efficacy of such mechanisms remains questionable, both in terms of their being able to bring recognition to aspects being ignored till now or in terms of influencing the final shapes of project, programs, and in general the broad trend of unrestrained exploitation of resources.[30]

What are the reasons that the use of valuation based mechanisms in governance have not led to significantly improved outcomes? Or that the attempts to ascribe value to uses which so far have been deemed a waste have not led to better projects or better resource-use with more holistic and rounded approach?

There are several important issues here. The first is the difficulty of putting a value to every use and function of water. The issue here is essentially of who is putting these values? With whose eyes is the river, the water being seen? As we have seen, one of the reasons what water flowing down to the sea is considered waste is because many of its uses and functions are invisible to the eyes that reckon these values. In other words, the establishment that plans and pushes such large projects, the powerful interests behind them, are blind to the other uses. It is only when the communities who "live with" the "wasted" water are involved in the planning and decision-making will all the roles and functions become visible. So long as this does not happen, many uses of the river and water will remain invisible.

When the rehabilitation policies for the tribal communities to be displaced by the Narmada (Sardar Sarovar) dam were designed, they were said to be very progressive as they talked about giving land for land. While this was a significant provision, it was not enough. The tribal life was sustained by numerous things they drew from the environment, like fish from the river, use of the river water for bathing, washing, and water for cattle, the wood, fruits, fodder and other produce from the forest, and so on. In the rehabilitation policy, while the loss of livelihood due to loss of land was acknowledged, there was no policy for the replacement of other things. One of the results was that most people who shifted to the resettlement sites had to give up their cattle: a most valuable resource that provided milk, fertilizer, and cash income also. The reason for such lacunae in the rehabilitation policies was because they were designed by people who lived an entirely different kind of life, in entirely different surroundings; they had little recognition for what is of value for the communities that were to be displaced.

Taking another example, if the communities who lived in the Indus basin Delta, or those who live in the Narmada estuary were to be involved in the planning of the Indus basin projects or the Narmada project, the fisheries of the delta or the estuary would have figured (and figured far more prominently) in the whole process. They would most certainly have allocated and reserved flows in the river for protecting their fish and their livelihoods.

The second issue is that even when certain uses are recognized and ultimately valued, they are still not taken into consideration for project design. Consider the Indus basin. One of the major storage projects on the Indus is the Tarbela dam. The IUCN carried out a study to estimate the impacts of the upstream projects on the Indus Delta. One of the points made by the study was (IUCN, undated, p. 3):

> From an *economic* perspective the natural resources used in the Indus Delta have an estimated value of 120 million US$. This excludes the unquantifiable value of environmental aspects such as biodiversity, habitat provision and coastal protection. In comparison, releasing 25 percent of the Tarbela Dam water for floods, thus making it unavailable for irrigation or power generation, would cost 38 million US$. Any loss of irrigation or hydroelectric power, therefore, is likely to be more than offset by financial benefits remaining with communities in the Delta from natural-resource use. [Emphasis in original]

Yet, there is no move to change the operation of the Tarbela Dam to release the suggested water. The reason is clear; the benefits of the Tarbela Dam accrue to the more powerful section of the society, such as the famers in the plains of Punjab (and Sindh) and the users of the electricity generated—mainly the urban and industrial sectors. These are the economically and politically dominant sections; the ones that controls the decision-making. Releasing water from the Tarbela for floods may create more benefits for the delta inhabitants, but the voices of these communities are not strong enough, so the operation of the dam is unlikely to be changed. Thus, it's not just a question of "how much value" that will determine the decisions on water resource use, what is equally critical is the question of "of value to whom."

Where the marginalized communities can mobilize sufficient strength, we can see how what they value can be given priority. One of the most important examples of this is the Pak Mun dam in Thailand, on the Mun river—the largest tributary of the magnificent Mekong. The 134 MW hydropower project was completed in 1994 and become hugely controversial due to the impacts on the rich fisheries of the Mun river. A strong people's movement emerged, leading to long protests and an occupation of the dam site with a demand to decommission the dam. As the strength of the movement grew, the Thai government agreed to open (and keep open) the gates of the dam while the Ubon Ratchathani University conducted studies of the fisheries. Even though the study recommended keeping the gates open for five years, the government decided to keep them closed for 8 months in a year, and shut them in November 2002.[31] While the victory was brief, it showed that if the communities have the political strength, what they value can get primacy.

Similar examples can be found in struggles closer to home in the Narmada and other valleys.

The third important point is that even when the ignored aspects are valued, the question arises as to who assigns values to these aspects. For example, what is the value to be attributed to the fish catch of a tribal person? Would it be the market price of that fish? It could be, if the value is given by say an official of the government. But for the person himself/herself, it probably represents much different things—nutritional value, the value of self-reliance, the availability when he/she needs it. If this person was to put a value, it could be very different from the value ascribed to the fish by an outsider. Take another example: if the river provides the water for the cattle of a tribal household, how is it to be valued? There is no market value for this. The crucial point here is that the correct meaning of value can only be the value as attributed by the person who is using the water. A value attributed by someone else would not only not capture the real "value" to the user but would also be biased by the different world view and perspective.

In this context, the tradable water entitlements can claim for themselves a superior feature—that the value (price) can be determined by the person holding the right to use that water, who could be a small farmer or a marginalized person. But this is specious advantage. In reality, since the mechanism will operate in the existing market framework, the price will be determined by the dynamics of this market. The prices in the mechanism will have to align with the contours of the existing market framework, which means they will end up replicating the value structure of that market. In other words, no matter what, in this mechanism, the value of water for growing crops for a small farmer is always likely to be lesser than the value of water for an urban conglomeration, or a thermal power plant, or a golf course. In such circumstances, the mechanism will end up strengthening this value structure and in fact help in imposing it more strongly. In this manner, putting water into an economic-market system can become a trap. Thus, the framework in which the values are judged and valuation is done is crucial to what values get precedence over others.

This issue becomes more important when we talk about attributing valuation to things that essentially have not been (or cannot be) valued so far by the market system. There have been suggestions to do such value attribution to many things—to the ecological services of water, of forests, to the social functions of a river, to the sufferings of the displaced people. This is suggested as a means to ensure that these aspects are given space and consideration in water resource planning. Unfortunately, attempts to assign monetary values to such elements are doomed to failure, as they push these aspects into the very framework (financial/monetary) that has little capacity to value them. This is because the (existing) monetary and financial framework represents precisely the set of values of the establishment and the elites.

Consider the example of Vedanta's proposed bauxite mining in Niyamgiri hill in Odisha. The rich bauxite deposits in the mountain-top represent millions, possibly several billion dollars' worth of aluminium. For the Dongria Kondh people who live there, the mountain is sacred, and they revere it as their Niyam Raja. Vedanta wants to mine the mountain. The Dongria Kondh people want the mountain not to be touched. The moment you try and attribute some valuation to the mountain, it is transferred to the mainstream global economy framework. In this framework, the mountain, its many ecological services, and its sacredness, even taken together, is not likely to be able to compete with several billion dollars. It will stand defeated even before the game has begun. Thus, there are two frameworks of valuation. In one, aluminium is important; important enough to fetch billions of dollars for its owners. In the other framework, the Niyam Raja is beyond value. Aluminium has little use in that world (at least as of now), and the place of bauxite is inside the mountain. In deciding whether to mine or not, the actual values one attributes are secondary; the decision is already made the moment one chooses which framework is to be used. Naturally, which framework is to be used really depends on who is going to make decisions.

Democratizing Value

Undoubtedly, value has been a key driver and a justification of water resource development historically, and continues to be so even now. But as the above discussion has shown, this value is not neutral.

First of all, value essentially has meant value for humans. Value as has been used has inherently meant that unless water is put for human use, there is no value. Thus, at one stroke, it has reduced the rights of all other life forms, of the environment, of the ecology over water, and has nullified the crucial role played by water in the entire planet. In practice, this has meant that human value has come at the cost of the value for other inhabitants and other elements of the planet, even at the cost of grave damages to them.

But even when we talk of value for human beings at the exclusion of others, it is not value for just for any human use, but only for the use of some sections of humans. Thus, value has been loaded in favor of the powerful and the elite. Delivering value has essentially meant delivering value for the powerful.

Thus, water that is not delivering value to this select group of humans is by definition "waste." A result has been the justification and subsequent implementation of huge projects, dams, and diversions that have benefitted a few at the cost of many others, and at the cost of the destruction of the very environment in which water is located.

Indeed, this is the reason why the use of this notion of "waste" persists even today, in context of projects like the interlinking of rivers, in spite of the increasing recognition of other uses. Without such a notion of waters running waste to sea, grand projects and diversions are becoming increasingly difficult to justify.

The increasing difficulty in maintaining the credibility of this notion of waste is one of the reasons for the introduction of schemes like tradable water permit. For, in absence of a higher value, the only way of reallocating water to the needs of high money producing activities is to bring water into the economic-financial setup.

Thus, value has become an instrument in water resource appropriation. The key to address this problem is to democratize the concept and practice of "value," as the prior discussions show.

This means that there should be the involvement of all communities in planning for water resource development (thus, making visible all values, nor just the values that are useful to a select few) and the meaningful involvement of all communities in decision-making around water resource development (thus ensuring that all values get due consideration and no one set of values dominates at the cost of others). However, what is of overarching importance is the selection of a proper framework in which to locate the values and valuation, for the selection of the existing global financial economic framework virtually predetermines the outcome by privileging certain values and consigning others as waste. It is essential that the framework that is selected to locate the discussions and decision-making on water resource development be a framework that can value outputs like irrigation and power, but also value fisheries and riverbed farming; that can value the use of water for manufacturing goods, but can also value the flowing river, the sacred river, the swim in the river; that can find the river useful for humans but not consider as waste its roles and functions for nonhumans, even nonliving entities on the planet. It may be emphasized that when one talks of valuation here—in the context of valuing the flowing river, valuing the sacred river, or several others—it is not a valuation in terms of money or value in terms of reducing these to a commodity. One would like to stress that the very essence of the framework being advocated is that it would move away from commodification, and value various things in the more generic meaning of the word, namely, to estimate the significance, the importance, the desirability, and the ethics of something.

It is crucial that such democratization be at the heart of any methods and mechanisms that are used for water resource planning and development—whether the traditional cost–benefit analysis or the more modern environmental-flows[32] methodology. In other words, the crucial determinants of moving toward a more just, sustainable, and equitable water resource development are the twin questions and the democratization of their answers—Whose Voices? Whose Values?

Annexure

Monetizing Non-tangibles in Cost–Benefit Analysis and Payment for Ecosystem Services

CBA is one of the important tools to evaluate and compare various options for economic activities and projects like dams, power stations, and so on. However, one of the criticisms against the CBA has been that it would include only those costs (and benefits) that can be directly measured in monetary units. To address this issue, various people have tried to assign monetary values to such intangibles. One of the well-known methods is to carry out a "willingness to pay" survey, which would assess how much people are willing to pay to preserve that particular (intangible aspect)—for example, the opportunity to enjoy a free flowing river. Alternatively, one can assess how much compensation they would need to accept the loss of the said benefit.

For example, a study (Muller, Mendelsohn, and Nordhaus, 2009) that estimates the damages due to air pollution in the USA and compares it with the conventionally measured value added by the same industry, finds that "the largest single industrial contributor to external costs is coal-fired electric generation, whose damages range from 1.4 to 3.5 times value added depending upon modeling assumptions." In calculating the damages due to the coal-fired electric generation, the study measures the health impacts, with value of human life based on studies that survey "premium required by workers to assume additional mortality risks in the workplace," and "their willingness to pay to avoid additional mortality risks." The study then takes Value of Statistical Life as US$6 million per premature mortality.

In another example, Dr Bharat Jhunjhunwala, an economist and an activist working on economics of large dams, has come out with a CBA for the Kotli Behl 1B hydropower project in Uttarakhand. He uses a variety of assumptions and methods to work out the costs for aspects that would be affected by the construction of the dam including quality of water, biodiversity, river rafting, aesthetic value of free-flowing water, etc.

Note that these examples are given only to illustrate the concepts and methods for assigning costs to various intangibles.

Ecosystem services, as the name suggests, are services provided by (a healthy) ecosystem. The Millennium Ecosystem Assessment classifies ecosystem services into four categories, namely supporting, provisioning, regulating, and cultural (Millennium Ecosystem Assessment, 2005, vi). With many ecosystems facing over-exploitation and degradation, the services provided by them are seriously impacted. Amongst the many measures to preserve the ecosystems is a set of measures that can be classified as "payment for ecosystem services." In such a mechanism, the users of these services pay the resources owners to provide this service. In other words, it's an economic incentive to the resource owners to preserve the resource and continue the provisioning of the service. An example noted by the Millennium Ecosystem Assessment is that of Costa Rica, which in 1996:

> [E]stablished a nationwide system of conservation payments to induce landowners to provide ecosystem services. Under this program, the government brokers contracts between international and domestic "buyers" and local "sellers" of sequestered carbon, biodiversity, watershed services, and scenic beauty. By 2001, more than 280,000 hectares of forests had been incorporated into the program at a cost of about $30 million, with pending applications covering an additional 800,000 hectares. (Millennium Ecosystem Assessment, 2005, p. 96)

Notes

1. For an extensive analysis of this "idea of the TVA" and its influence on Indian dam building and river basin management, see Klingensmith (2007), and also a review of the same by this author in *Biblio: A Review of Books*, November–December 2007 (Dharmadhikary, 2007).
2. Though his main concern—and the focus of his writing—seemed to be to prevent India from going Communist. The titles of his two pieces at that time are telling: *Another Korea in the Making*, and *Are We Losing India*, in the *Collier's*, August 4, 1951 and June 23, 1951.
3. The undivided Punjab then consisted of today's Indian Punjab (except areas that were under PEPSU), today's Haryana, parts of today's Himachal, and today's Pakistani Punjab.
4. In the initial years, Sind was a part of Bombay province, and later was an independent province by itself.
5. This was essentially replacement irrigation and was the so-called Zone 2 of the command. See Dharmadhikary (2005, p. 196) for details.
6. Chapter 26: *Irrigation and Power*; First Five Year Plan, URL: http://planningcommission.nic.in/plans/planrel/fiveyr/1st/1planch26.html (accessed November 25, 2002).

7. Final Order and Decision of the NWDT, Gazetted on December 12, 1979, Clause II. Available at http://www.sardarsarovardam.org/assets/SitepagesDocument/SPD__Userid2_20100402_104848.pdf.

8. Gujarat got 9 MAF, MP 18.25 MAF, Maharashtra 0.25 MAF, and Rajasthan 0.5 MAF. The yearly surplus or deficit was to be shared by the states in the same proportion.

9. Final Order and Decision of the NWDT, Clause III (3).

10. Final Order and Decision of the NWDT, Clause IX (vi).

11. We will come to this later.

12. Final Order and Decision of the NWDT, Clause IV (5). It may also be mentioned that when eventually "full development" had taken place upstream, the RBPH would not generate any power, but there is provision for it to be used as a pumped storage scheme with an additional weir 16 km downstream at Garudeshwar. Of course, this arrangement does not detract, rather it supports the notion that any water that flowed down below the dam was wasted.

13. Yoginder Alagh, *Drained of All Sense*, Indian Express, May 30, 2009 http://www.indianexpress.com/news/drained-of-all-sense/468356.

14. In any case, the Narmada Bachao Andolan, the struggle of the people affected by the dams on the Narmada had been reminding the powers that be, from the mid-1980s at least, that they had not left any water for the river, nor for the thousands of fisher people and other communities downstream of the dam.

15. Final Order and Decision of the NWDT, Clause IX (vii).

16. It may be mentioned that the impacts on this are already being seen in the regions downstream of the dam with greatly diminishing yields of hilsa being reported, and increased pollution as the dilution effect of the flowing waters on the effluents discharged into the river is reduced. See for example reports in the *Indian Express*, July 24, 2009, *As rains stay away, hilsa catch drops to new low* (http://www.indianexpress.com/news/as-rains-stay-away-hilsa-catch-drops-to-new-low/493332) and, *The Economic Times*, August 8, 2012, *Hilsa prices soar to Rs 1,000 per kg as shrinking Narmada and Hooghly make breeding difficult* (http://articles.economictimes.indiatimes.com/2012-08-08/news/33100832_1_hilsa-catch-utpal-bhaumik-hilsa-prices).

17. Website of the National Water Development Agency http://nwda.gov.in/index2.asp?slid=108&sublinkid=14&langid=1.

18. http://nwda.gov.in/index2.asp?slid=108&sublinkid=14&langid=1.

19. http://nwda.gov.in/index2.asp?slid=108&sublinkid=14&langid=1.

20. http://nwda.gov.in/writereaddata/linkimages/2175421921.pdf.

21. River "closure" is a term meaning that the river no longer meets the sea. Of course, this does not mean that the approach is being discarded. The 12th Plan document in fact remarks that "This does not mean that the Twelfth Plan should reduce allocations to this vitally important sector of the Indian economy.... The only implication is that we need to seriously reconsider our priorities here.... We also have many large projects underway that need to be expeditiously completed" (Planning Commission, 2012, p. 147).

22. How this was a World Bank initiative and what was the implication have been detailed in Dharmadhikary (2008), which also discussed some of the issues of the tradable water rights mechanism. This chapter also draws from that report.

23. http://www.adb.org/documents/water-all-water-policy-asian-development-bank?ref=sectors/water/publications.

24. On website of MWRRA, at http://mwrra.org/3)%20AP%20Entitlement%20Trading%20English.pdf (accessed on August 24, 2012).

25. The Revised Approach Paper was prepared by the MWRRA after getting comments and feedback on the original discussion paper of June 2011. However, this revised paper is not on the MWRRA website. It was sent by the MWRRA to the *Lokabhimukh Pani Dhoran Sangharsh Manch* (People Oriented Water Policy Struggle Platform) of Maharashtra, of which this author is a member.

26. Even the first Draft Approach Paper says, in Sec 4, page 3, that "inter-sectoral trading cannot be considered at this stage."

27. It should be noted that diversions to urban areas are not only for meeting domestic water needs. A significant part of urban demand is for commercial uses.

28. White Paper on Irrigation of Government of Maharashtra. Government of Maharashtra (2012), p. 95.

29. We will not go into these here as that is not the main thrust of this chapter.

30. See, for example, Muradian et al. (2013).

31. Website of International Rivers, http://www.internationalrivers.org/campaigns/pak-mun-dam-0 (accessed on February 23, 2013).

32. A more accurate and better description would be ecological-livelihood-cultural-social flows.

References

ADB (2001). *Water for all water policy of the Asian Development Bank,* Asian Development Bank, Manila. Retrieved from http://www.adb.org/sites/default/files/pub/2003/water-policy.pdf (accessed on September 15, 2006).

Albinia, A. (2008). *Empires of the Indus: The story of a river.* London: John Murray.

Anand, R.L. (1956). *Punjab agriculture facts & figures,* Economic and Statistical Organisation, Government of Punjab.

Dharmadhikary, S. (2005). *Unravelling Bhakra, Manthan Adhyayan Kendra, Badwani, India.* Retrieved from http://www.manthan-india.org/wp-content/uploads/2015/04/Unravelling-Bhakra.pdf (accessed on October 15, 2015).

Dharmadhikary, S. (2007). Damning India's big dam policies: New books by Rohan D'Souza and Daniel Klingensmith. *Biblio: A Review of Books, XII*(11–12, Nov–Dec): 23–24.

_____. (2008). *The World Bank as a knowledge producer: How the bank uses flawed processes to generate unsound knowledge for promoting disastrous policies,* Manthan Adhyayan Kendra, Badwani, India. Retrieved November 25, 2015, from http://www.manthan-india.org/spip.php?article34.

IUCN (undated). *The lower Indus river: Balancing development And maintenance of wetland ecosystems and dependent livelihoods,* IUCN. Retrieved from http://www.waterandnature.org/flow/cases/Indus.pdf (accessed on October 2, 2004).

Klingensmith, D. (2007). *"One valley and a thousand": Dams, nationalism, and development.* Oxford University Press: New Delhi.

Larrain, S. and Schaeffer, C. (Eds.). (2010). *Conflicts over water in Chile: Between human rights And market rules,* Chile Sustainable, Heinrich Boll Stiftung, Council of Canadians. Retrieved from http://www.blueplanetproject.net/resources/reports/ChileWaterReport-0411.pdf (accessed on May 25, 2011).

Lilienthal, D. (1951). *Another Korea in the making,* In Collier's, August 4, 1951.

Maharashtra, Government (2012). *Rajyatil Sinchanachi Pragati va Bhavishyatil Vatchal: Shweta Patrika, Khanda 1, Jal Sampada Vibhag (Progress of irrigation in the state and future path, White Paper, Vol. 1, Water Resource Department, in Marathi)*, Water Resources Department, Government of Maharashtra, Mumbai.

Millennium Ecosystem Assessment (2005). *Ecosystems and human well-being: synthesis* Washington, DC: Island Press. Retrieved fromhttp://www.millenniumassessment.org/documents/document.356.aspx.pdf (accessed on May 25, 2015).

Muller, N., Mendelsohn, R., and Nordhaus, W. (2009). *Environmental accounting for pollution: Methods with an Application to the United States economy*. Retrieved from http://nordhaus.econ.yale.edu/documents/Env_Accounts_052609.pdf (accessed on November 9, 2011).

Muradian, R., Arsel, M., Pellegrini, L., Adaman, F., Aguilar, B., Agarwal, B., Corbera, E., et al. (2013). Payments for ecosystem services and the fatal attraction of win-win solutions. *Conservation Letters, 00*(2013), 1–6.

Planning Commission (1951). *First Five Year Plan: Chapter 26: Irrigation and Power*. New Delhi: Planning Commission, Government of India. Retrieved November 25, 2002, from http://planningcommission.nic.in/plans/fiveyr/1st/1planch26.html

———. (2012). *Twelfth Five Year Plan, Faster, More Inclusive and Sustainable Growth Volume 1*. New Delhi: Planning Commission, Government of India. Retrieved from http://planningcommission.nic.in/plans/planrel/12thplan/pdf/vol_1.pdf (accessed on January 5, 2015).

Raj, K.N. (1960). *'Some Economic Aspects of Bhakra Nangal Project: A Preliminary Analysis of Selected Investment Criteria.'* Mumbai: Asia Publishing House.

Rangachari, R., Sengupta, N., Iyer, R., Banerji, R.P., and Singh, S. (2000). *Large Dams: India's Experience, a WCD Case Study Prepared as an Input to the World Commission on Dams*. Cape Town: World Commission on Dams. www.dams.org.

World Bank. (1999a). *Initiating and Sustaining Water Sector Reforms: A Synthesis*. World Bank, Washington D.C. and Allied Publishers Limited, Mumbai.

———. (1999b). *Inter-Sectoral Water Allocation, Planning and Management*. World Bank, Washington D.C. and Allied Publishers Limited, Mumbai.

———. (1999c). *The Irrigation Sector*. World Bank, Washington D.C. and Allied Publishers Limited, Mumbai.

World Bank. (2004). *Water Resources Sector Strategy: Strategic Directions for World Bank Engagement*. The World Bank, Washington D.C. (Publication No. 28114), Retrieved on November 25, 2015, from http://www-wds.worldbank.org/external/default/WDSContentServer/WDSP/IB/2004/06/01/000090341_20040601150257/Rendered/PDF/28114.pdf.

6

The Effectiveness and Equity of Payments for Reducing Forest Loss

Simone Lovera

Introduction: The Role of Forests in Climate Change Mitigation

Deforestation is widely recognized as one of the most important environmental crises humankind is facing. According to the 2010 State of the Forest report of the UN Food and Agricultural Organization, which is the lead UN specialized agency in the field of forest policy, an average of 13 million hectares of forests was lost annually in the period between 2000 and 2010 (FAO, 2010). Forest ecosystems represent near to 90 percent of the earth's terrestrial biodiversity (World Bank, 2004) so forest loss is one of the key causes of global biodiversity loss. 350 million of the world's poorest people, including an estimated 60 million indigenous people, depend almost entirely for their subsistence and survival on forests (World Commission on Forests and Sustainable Development, 1999). For many indigenous peoples, forests are more than their home and livelihood; they see themselves as part of the forest, and the forest as part of their biocultural heritage (IPCCA, 2011). Forests also provide a wide range of wood and non-wood products that support the livelihoods of an estimated one billion people (FAO, 2010; World Bank, 2004).

Moreover, forests have an important function in climate change mitigation and climate stabilization. An estimated 289 gigatonnes of carbon is stored in forest biomass, which represents some 86 percent of the earth's above ground carbon (FAO, 2010). In 2006, when discussions on a new global scheme to conserve forests as part of the climate regime started, it was estimated that deforestation and forest degradation contributed an estimated 17 percent of the world's annual human-induced greenhouse gas emissions (Intergovernmental Panel on Climate Change, 2007; Stern, 2006). Thanks to successful national efforts to reduce forest loss, this percentage has declined significantly, but forest loss is still estimated to contribute some 10 percent of global human-induced greenhouse gas emissions.[1] Forests also play an important role in regulating hydrological flows and rain patterns, both locally and regionally (Stern, 2006).

The first international agreements that urged countries to conserve forests and other ecosystems were signed in the 1960s. Since then, a large number of legally binding and non-legally binding commitments have been made by governments to manage forest sustainably and/or reduce forest loss.

The role of forests in climate regulation was already recognized before the UN Framework Convention on Climate Change (UNFCCC) and was adopted at the UN Conference on Environment and Development (UNCED) in 1992. At the Ministerial Conference on Atmospheric Pollution and Climate Change in Noordwijk, the Netherlands, in 1989, a conference that played a key role in building the political momentum for a legally binding instrument to address climate change, a provisional target for net forest growth was adopted (Gupta et al., 2013).[2] Subsequently, a commitment was included in the UNFCCC to promote sustainable management and to promote and cooperate in the conservation and enhancement of forests and other so-called sinks and reservoirs of greenhouse gases.[3] The Convention also stipulated that developed countries were to provide new and additional financial resources to support developing countries in their efforts to implement this commitment. This combination of a global commitment to contribute to environmental protection and a complementary commitment by developed countries to provide new and additional[4] financial resources to enable developing countries to do so, formed a red threat in many agreements at the 1992 Earth Summit. The idea behind this combination was that environmental protection benefited the planet as a whole, and developing countries needed to prioritize poverty reduction, so the costs of environmental action should be borne by those countries that could afford it. As the Malaysian prime minister, Mahathir bin Mohamad stated shortly before the UNCED, "*If it is in the interests of the rich that we do not cut down our trees then they must compensate us for the loss of income*" (Humphrey, 2008).

This concept was embedded in the principle of common but differentiated responsibilities, which was incorporated in the UNFCCC as well.[5] The Global Environment Facility (GEF), which was established by the World Bank, the UN Environment Programme and the UN Development Programme in 1991 and subsequently adopted as the financial mechanism of the UNFCCC, further refined the principle by elaborating a system in which the full incremental costs of activities that contributed to global environmental goals would be funded through the facility. Simply said, these incremental costs are the costs of the project implemented minus the benefits the project is expected to provide to the country itself, for example, in terms of local watershed protection or provision of fuelwood and timber. Since its establishment, GEF has funded over 300 medium and large-scale projects focusing on forest conservation, totalling more than US$1.6 billion.[6]

From Trade as a Problem to Trade as a "Solution"

At the time of the UNCED conference, in 1992, environmental policy-making was still a relatively new discipline that was heavily influenced by the altruistic discourse of the World Commission on Environment and Development, which had emphasized the distributional dimensions of sustainable development, including impacts on future generations (United Nations, 1987). As a result, UNCED was clearly dominated by a progressive, social-democratic political discourse (Arts et al., 2010). The results of the UNCED conference include a strong focus on public policies and measures financed through public funding.[7] The role of business and industry in sustainable development was recognized, but only as one of nine so-called "major groups," a rather awkward late-night compromise concept that also covers social sectors and groupings as diverse as indigenous peoples, women, trade unions, and nongovernmental organizations.

In the last decade of the 20th century, environmental organizations were gradually becoming more aware that economic policymaking was a key underlying driver of environmental degradation. In particular, there was a rapidly increasing awareness of the mutual impacts of trade and environmental policymaking prior to and at the UNCED conference. As a result, both the threats of trade liberalization for environmental policymaking and the threats of "unilateral trade measures" to protect the environment for trade liberalization were recognized in the UNCED agreements.[8] In response, organizations like the World Conservation Union started to hire economists to advise them on the linkages between economic policymaking and nature conservation.

Market-based conservation mechanisms, on the other hand, are hardly found in the original UNCED agreements. Most environmentalists saw the market as a problem rather than a solution to environmental challenges. Initial attempts were made to regulate and/or influence markets and consumer choices through certification systems like the Forest Stewardship Council, but those who saw the market as a possible environmental solution formed a clear minority.

Only in the US, the cradle of free market ideologies, there were some first experiments with market-based approaches to address environmental challenges. The most well-known experiment was the Clean Air Act,[9] which included the first so-called cap and trade system. Through this system, companies were assigned a certain amount of pollution they could cause. If they succeeded to reduce pollution even further, they could sell the remainder as a credit to companies that failed to meet their pollution target. The Clean Air Act has been considered a success in terms of reducing pollution, but there is little convincing evidence that the possibility to trade pollution permissions was the key factor in this success. It is more likely that the sharp and mandatory pollution reduction targets were the main success factor, the trading possibility just made these targets palatable to industry (Carbontrade Watch, 2003; Lohmann, 2006).

Despite this lack of evidence, US policymakers and US-based NGOs started to promote cap and trade mechanisms as a possible solution to global warming (Lohmann, 2006). In the first years after the UNCED summit, they met with little enthusiasm in other countries. There was broad consensus amongst countries that there was a need for mandatory reduction targets of greenhouse gas emissions for different countries based on a global assessment of the total reductions required. But few countries were enthusiastic about the idea of a trading system (Lohmann, 2006). The US was a very dominant player in the climate negotiations, though, as it was by far the largest per capita polluter, its participation was considered indispensable for an effective climate regime. In the chaotic last days of the negotiations for the Kyoto Protocol in 1997, the protocol that established a system of mandatory country emission-reduction targets, the US succeeded in finding sufficient political support for including a complicated emissions trading system in the Kyoto Protocol. Ironically, even though it achieved almost everything it wanted, the US administration subsequently did not obtain sufficient national support to actually sign the Protocol:

> Its environmentalist backers ... were left in the odd position of having to champion an agreement largely written by the US for US purposes based on the US experience and US economic thinking, but which no longer had US support ... a little tested idea spearheaded by a small US-elite was now perceived as a global consensus and the "only show in town." (Lohmann, 2006)

Despite the little support it originally received, the idea of a cap and trade system for environmental pollution rapidly gained political support, especially in the EU. The reasons were not so much based on the success of the Kyoto Protocol, which entered into force only in 2005. Rather, it was the increased mainstreaming of conservative if not neoliberal policy approaches in environmental policymaking that created the ground for market-based mechanisms (Arts et al., 2010; Humphrey, 2008). Integration of environmental policymaking into mainstream politics had always been a key ambition of the small elite of progressive thinkers that started the environmental movement, but few realized this also implied that politically mainstream decision-makers would start taking the lead in environmental policymaking. Moreover, the economic specialists that had been hired to cross the bridge between economic and environmental policymaking started to introduce market-based approaches in environmental policies. At the same time, environmental sciences became more and more popular amongst more conservative students and scholars, who started to experiment with neoliberal, market-based approaches to environmental challenges, and close collaboration with industry. As a result, the 10 years celebration of UNCED, the World Summit on Sustainable Development in 2002, was marked by the enthusiastic promotion of public–private partnerships with corporate actors, who gained significant influence in international environmental policymaking (Arts et al., 2010).

Payments for Environmental Services: Old Schemes with a New Name

The earliest "payments for environmental services" (PES) schemes' date from the 1930s. In 1936, the US Government established the Agricultural Conservation Program, which was reformed into the Conservation Reserve Program by the US Agriculture Act in 1954. The latter is still one of the largest schemes in the world, providing almost US$2 billion per year in payments to US farmers that agree to remove lands at risk from erosion from agricultural production and restore or plant permanent vegetation on those areas.[10] Since it was reformed by the 1985 Farm Bill, the scheme has gradually expanded (Cain and Lovejoy, 2004). In 2010, it covered some 31.3 million acres.[11]

The EU followed some 50 years later. In 1985 it introduced regulation ECC/797/85, which permitted member states to give agro-environmental incentives to farmers in environmentally sensitive areas who were willing to apply a rather broad range of (presumably) environmentally sound practices. This triggered various national incentive schemes, amongst others in the UK and Germany (Latacz-Lohmann and Hodge, 2003). The agro-environmental regulation ECC 2078/92 of 1992 greatly expanded the scheme by making it mandatory for EU member states to implement an agro-environmental program, by expanding the scheme to all agricultural land and by introducing a financial contribution for these schemes from the EU budget itself. At the same time, the Environmental Cross Compliance was introduced, which imposes environmental conditions on farmers receiving general EU agricultural subsidies. The agro-environmental measures have expanded significantly in the past decade. For the period 2007–2013, the EU spent no less than 20 billion euros in contributions to these schemes—this is on top of the expenditures by national governments, which carry the main financial burden of the scheme (Latacz-Lohmann and Hodge, 2003).

Only in the 1990s, the term "payments for environmental services" started to be used for these, often much older, schemes that provide subsidies or similar financial incentives for actions that contribute to environmental goals. A broadly accepted definition of "payments for environmental services" was more or less absent from the literature until 2005, when Sven Wunder, a chief scientist at the Centre for International Forestry Research, proposed the following definition:

"A PES is:

a voluntary transaction where

a well-defined ES (or a land-use likely to secure that service)

is being "bought" by a (minimum one) ES buyer

from a (minimum one) ES provider

if and only if the ES provider secures ES provision (conditionality)."
(Wunder, 2005)

It is noteworthy that many scholars (e.g., Engel et al., 2008) concluded from this definition that PES was a market-based conservation mechanism. However, as Milder et al. (2010) discovered, no less than 98 percent of all payments for environmental services are actually made by Governments, often State Governments. The apostrophes placed by Wunder around the term "bought" were not accidental in this respect. Moreover, the term "voluntary" in the definition does not so much indicate a free market in which environmental services can be bought and sold by anyone, but rather that the individuals or institutions who decide to "sell" or "buy" an environmental service are free to choose whether they want to do so. And even this is not always the case, as the Government institutions providing the payments are seldom allowed to freely choose which environmental services they buy and from whom— in most schemes this is strictly regulated in the policy instrument establishing the scheme. For that reason, Vatn et al. (2011) point out that:
"PES, as defined by Wunder (2005) seems more like a theoretical concept than reflecting what is found in practice."

In fact, Wunder himself already wrote in another paper in 2005:

Except for the emerging carbon markets—it seems incorrect to constantly refer to some of these schemes as "markets for environmental services." After all, they are seldom true markets, since spatial specificities usually restrict or eliminate any of the competitive forces so fundamental to the proper functioning of markets. (Wunder and Vargas, 2005)

The question is: why did these schemes have to be redefined as PES? Wunder and Vargas (2005) suggest that it was mainly the neoliberal trend amongst Northern donors that triggered environmental institutions to call their incentive schemes a payment for, or even market in, environmental services. However, they also point out:

Yet in most of the developing world, "markets"—like other labels with a clear monetary association—may not be considered "sexy" at all; they may actually turn people off. Indeed, we have found that the notion of "reciprocal solidarity arrangements" and similar terms are seen as much more culturally acceptable in many parts of the developing world. In Pimampiro (Northern Ecuador), for example, a pilot watershed payments scheme recently changed name from "payment for environmental services" to "retribución" (recompense) for these services because that term was deemed more politically palatable to the urban water users who finance the monetary payment to upstream farmers. (Wunder and Vargas, 2005)

The authors also tell a story about a PES project by Fundacion Natura in Bolivia that met with a lot of resistance:

Natura staff are convinced that if they had started the dialogue using terms other than "markets" or "payments," progress towards project sustainability would have been faster and far easier.... It also has become evident that referring to these mechanisms as "markets" is likely to be highly counterproductive in places like Bolivia.... And, just as we package some non-market transactions, calling them "markets" to sell them to a donor in the North, we also need to show a similar sensitivity to local perceptions when these projects take place in developing countries. (Wunder and Vargas, 2005)

While pressure of northern donors has triggered a gradual expansion of PES schemes in developing countries, they have expanded less rapidly than originally expected. Already in 2005, Wunder pointed out:

[T]here remains much doubt, particularly in the Southern Hemisphere, about the ultimate desirability of markets. Such market skepticism may at times be conveniently coupled with hostile attitudes towards globalization, US foreign policy, the World Bank and other Bretton Woods institutions. And, while many in the North continue to insist religiously on markets as the universal remedy, this discourse—often led by economists—frequently ends up fostering more resistance than persuasion in developing countries. (Wunder and Vargas, 2005)

REDD+: A New Neoliberal Approach to Forest Policy

As described above, forest conservation was included in the international climate regime from the start. When the Kyoto Protocol was negotiated, the role of so-called Land Use, Land Use Change and Forestry

(LULUCF) in mitigating climate change was recognized as well.[12] A set of complicated rules was developed that allowed the developed countries that took up mandatory emission reduction commitments to take into account some of the reduction caused by carbon sequestration through reforestation and afforestation activities as well. They could even opt for including sustainable forest management activities. However, trading forest-related credits through the Clean Development Mechanism (CDM), through which northern polluters could offset their emissions with projects in developing countries, was considered more complicated, as developing countries had not taken up emission reduction commitments. So emissions could only be offset through specific projects, but it was (and remains) hard to estimate the additional value of one specific forest conservation project. To compensate for increased emissions, a project actually has to reduce emissions, that is, the emissions should be less than they would have been in a so-called business as usual situation (additionality), and they should not be undone by a damaging activity simply being replaced to another forest (leakage). Both issues are very hard to address (see also Fry, 2008). Estimating what would have happened to a certain forest in the absence of a conservation project is, and remains, a speculation (Karsenty, 2008). Historical deforestation rates do not necessarily form an indication for the future, as most countries go through a forest transition curve once their services sectors and other economic sectors that do not depend on wood or expansion of agricultural land grow (Karsenty, 2008; Rudel et al., 2005). Improved overall governance in combination with increased environmental awareness has also triggered improved forest management in many countries. In fact, by 2015, forest cover loss has already been halted or even reversed in 124 countries (FAO, 2015).[13]

Leakage, the phenomenon of replacement of forest loss from one area to another, is even harder to address. It has been suggested by REDD proponents that leakage could be addressed through a so-called nested approach, in which REDD+ projects are embedded in national REDD+ programs (Angelsen et al., 2009). But leakage also crosses borders. Countries with a high stake in an effective climate regime[14] have pointed out that leakage will always be prevalent to project-based forest conservation as long as the demand for commodities that trigger forest loss, such as palm oil and meat, is not addressed. As Boucher et al. (2011) point out, "leakage is not an accident; it is the inevitable result of economically driven deforestation in a globalized world."

Due to the above-mentioned problems, which remain largely unresolved, there was, and remains, a serious concern that the inclusion of forests in carbon markets will undermine the effectiveness of the climate regime, or, as it is called in the negotiations, the "environmental integrity" of the regime. After all, if a polluter can avoid reducing a ton of carbon by buying a ton of carbon offsets from a REDD+ project that does not reduce emissions in reality, because the project is not additional, not permanent, not well-calculated, or leads to increased emissions elsewhere, the main damages are with the climate regime itself (Fry, 2008; IPCCA, 2011).

Due to these concerns, countries decided to include afforestation and reforestation projects in the CDM only (see also Backstrand and Lovbrand, 2006). Moreover, to address the permanence issue, reforestation and afforestation projects provided temporary credits, which turned them into relatively unattractive carbon offset opportunities. The EU went even further: it decided to exclude the possibility of buying forest-related credits from the CDM from its own internal emission trading system, which at that moment represented 97 percent of all formal carbon trade (EC, 2008).[15] As a result, in 2011, reforestation and afforestation projects represented no more than 0.73 percent of all CDM registered projects.[16]

A number of countries were highly disappointed by the exclusion of forest conservation from the CDM. Costa Rica, which had set up its expensive PES scheme in 2007, had done so in anticipation of being able to receive significant amounts of carbon offset finance for the scheme (Lovera, 2012). The scheme was partially financed through a national tax on gasoline, but it would not have survived financially if Costa Rica had not been able to conquer a total of 70 million dollars in loans from the World Bank—which it received in anticipation of a potential international funding scheme for forest conservation that would have created the revenue to pay back the loan. In 2005, they found an unlikely ally in the Government of Papua New Guinea (PNG), which had been confronted with strict forest conservation related conditionalities in a World Bank loan.[17] Incidental links, through a senior advisor, between the Prime Minister of PNG and a group of North American and Brazilian scholars that had been promoting the idea of compensated reductions (e.g., Santilli et al., 2005), triggered the enthusiasm of the PNG Government for REDD+ as a way to profit economically from conservation. The idea was similar to PES: countries would be compensated financially for the "environmental service" of conserving forests.

The original advocates of REDD+ promoted the scheme with the argument that "forests had been excluded from the climate regime" (Santilli et al., 2005).[18] This was legally incorrect, as the UNFCCC included a commitment to manage forests sustainably and forest conservation projects were already receiving millions of dollars of financial support from the UNFCCC's financial mechanism, the GEF. The proponents of compensation for avoided deforestation expected more substantial financial flows though. The influential Eliasch review (Eliasch, 2008), for example, had calculated that inclusion of forests in mandatory global carbon markets could generate between US$17 and 33 billion per year.[19] It should be noted that this figure was based on the potential supply of carbon credits by forest conservation rather than the potential demand for those credits. In reality, demand for such credits never rose above US$178 million,[20] due to the absence of ambitious emission reduction targets and the absence of possibilities to use forests to compensate mandatory emission reductions, especially in the EU.

The Governments of Costa Rica and PNG invited a number of other forest countries to form a Coalition for Rainforest Nations, which launched a formal proposal for a scheme that would provide financial compensation for developing countries that reduced their deforestation in 2005.[21] It should be noted that the actual membership of the coalition is very unclear. The original submission was made on behalf of 10 countries only, but on its website, in 2013,[22] the coalition lists no less than 41 countries, including countries like Uruguay and Paraguay that do not possess any rainforests. The website does not clarify that a country like Paraguay suspended its membership of the coalition in 2008.[23] There also have been frequent contradictions between the positions taken during the negotiations by the Coalition for Rainforest Nations and its presumed member groups.[24]

Despite this lack of clarity about which countries the coalition actually represents, its proposal rapidly received broad support from both developing and developed countries. As Gupta et al. (2013) point out:

The basic premise of REDD is simple: incentivizing developing countries to reduce their deforestation rates, and in the event they succeed, to compensate them financially. This concept appeals to both developed and developing countries. The former are attracted by its proclaimed cost-effectiveness and its potential to help them meet their emission reduction targets; the latter are drawn by the prospects of funding and view REDD as their opportunity to participate meaningfully in the global climate change regime.

This concept fitted well within the new ideologies of market-based approaches to environmental challenges:

> The AD proposal is an approach to forest and carbon sink conservation that fits comfortably into the logic of environmental economics and neoliberalism. (Humphrey, 2008)

The political momentum for the Reducing Emissions from Deforestation proposal was greatly increased by the timely initiatives of two donors at the 13th Conference of the Parties of the UNFCCC, which took place in 2007 in Bali, Indonesia. The Norwegian government, inspired by an open letter of two Norwegian conservation groups, announced a contribution of approximately 3 billion dollars to the scheme.[25] Moreover, the World Bank launched its Forest Carbon Partnership Facility, which was to channel an average contribution of 3.6 million dollars to countries that wanted to get "ready" for REDD.[26] As a result of this political momentum, the Bali Conference agreed to start negotiations on policies and incentives to reduce emissions from deforestation as part of the so-called Bali Action Plan that was to agree on "long-term cooperative action" as well as a successor agreement to the Kyoto Protocol in 2009.

The Bali Action Plan itself subsequently missed this deadline due to a dramatic collapse of the negotiations in Copenhagen in 2009, but the negotiations on the forest scheme progressed relatively well. In 2010, at the 16th Conference of the parties, the UNFCCC adopted (with reservations from Bolivia) a series of decisions that included a decision on:

> policy approaches and positive incentives on issues relating to reducing emissions from deforestation and forest degradation in developing countries; and the role of conservation, sustainable management of forests and enhancement of forest carbon stocks in developing countries.[27]

It should be noted that the abbreviation REDD+ was popularized by a number of countries, including Norway, and a large number of scholars, but never formally adopted. In fact, when the negotiations in REDD+ ended up in more sturdy waters in 2012, a number of countries suddenly started to question the legal status of the abbreviation, and it was deleted from the final outcomes of the Rio+20 Summit and the 11th Conference of the Parties of the Convention on Biodiversity.[28]

REDD+ itself rapidly gained popularity, though, especially due to the strategic deployment of the 3 billion dollars investment of the Norwegian government. Through the World Bank, and the UN–REDD program, which was established by the UN Food and Agricultural Organization, UNEP and UNDP in 2008, these funds were matched with far more modest contributions by other governments and distributed over at least 45 countries, who were offered the money to develop so-called "readiness" programs. The suggestion that this was just a first contribution of a scheme that might deliver up to US$30 billion in forest funding per year took away a lot of initial resistance. Most countries saw the contribution as welcome support for their underfunded forestry sector. It was not until the financial expectations significantly lowered, in 2011, that opposition against REDD+ started to gain ground.

NGOs and Indigenous Peoples' Organizations (IPOs) were divided from the start, especially northern NGOs and the few IPOs that received funding from the Norwegian government emphasized the potential benefits of REDD+. Climate Action Network, whose REDD+ working group consisted virtually of northern members only, stated in its submission in 2007, "deforestation and degradation should be addressed as part of the evolving global climate change regime most effectively and quickly."[29] North American NGOs like Conservation International provided even stronger support to Papua New Guinea and Costa Rica's proposal to consider incentives for developing countries in favor of REDD.[30] Indigenous peoples emphasized that it was up to indigenous peoples themselves to support REDD or not. As the International Indigenous Forum on Climate Change stated in a submission in 2009, "IIPFCC's should not be seen as an endorsement for REDD per se and communities, based on their own experiences, can and should be allowed to make their own determination on REDD."[31]

Many southern NGOs and social movements were more sceptic, if not entirely against REDD+. The climate justice movement especially, which had established an informal network called Climate Justice Now! in Bali, rejected REDD+ with ever stronger terms, leading to the rejection of REDD+ by massive "peoples" summits' like the Cochabamba Peoples' Summit on Climate Justice and the Rights of Mother Earth, which gathered 18,000 people,[32] and the Rio+20 Peoples' Summit, which gathered no less than 40,000 people.[33]

The reasons for these rejections were varied. The Cochabamba declaration puts a stronger emphasis on the right to free prior and informed consent (FPIC), emphasizing REDD+ had violated it.

> We condemn market mechanisms such as REDD (Reducing Emissions from Deforestation and Forest Degradation) and its versions + and ++, which are violating the sovereignty of peoples and their right to prior free and informed consent as well as the sovereignty of national States, the customs of Peoples, and the Rights of Nature.[34]

This is technically correct, as REDD+ was developed virtually without the participation of indigenous peoples. Indigenous peoples are not even allowed to observe the REDD+ negotiations, which mainly take place in closed "informal" negotiation meetings. So per definition, they have not given any "prior" consent to this policy that will impact significantly on their lands (FAO, 2009). The declaration also clearly rejects carbon markets: "We demand that countries stop actions on local forests based on market mechanisms."[35]

The Cochabamba Summit also played a significant role in influencing the position of its host country Bolivia. Despite the fact that it had just accepted a REDD readiness grant from UN–REDD,[36] and that it still promoted REDD as part of the Coalition for Rainforest Nations in 2007[37] the country felt obliged to support the outcomes of the Cochabamba Summit, which it submitted formally to the UNFCCC secretariat.[38] It subsequently developed its own joint mitigation and adaptation proposal for forest conservation,[39] in a clear attempt to be able to use the UN–REDD support for its forest policy, without the necessity to formally support REDD+. In subsequent submissions the Plurinational State of Bolivia questioned the linking of forests to global carbon markets and only to mitigation, since this authorizes the commodification of the environmental functions of Mother Earth, considered sacred by Bolivian society, into a commercial commodity, thus allowing the transfer of responsibilities for mitigation of climate change from developed to developing countries, fostering the latter to continue subsidizing the former.[40]

Concerns about REDD+ and Equity

The main reasons why climate justice groups and some governments rejected REDD+ were multiple:[41] The concept of payments for environmental services was seen as a way to privatize, commodify, and commercialize nature, which was considered morally unacceptable, especially in the eyes of indigenous groups that fostered nature as sacred.[42] Groups were also concerned about the definition of forests that had been adopted in the Marrakesh Accords, which reduced the concept of "forest" to any random collection of trees, thus including monoculture tree plantations. Their fear that this would lead to climate funding being invested in the establishment and/or expansion of monoculture tree plantations was not unfounded—the few afforestation and reforestation projects that were financed by the CDM or the, entirely unregulated, voluntary forest carbon offset market include a high number of monoculture tree plantations, often with devastating impacts on local communities.[43]

An even larger number of NGOs and IPOs[44] were concerned about the possible inclusion of REDD+ projects in carbon markets. They shared and reiterated the original concerns about permanence, additionality, and leakage that triggered countries to exclude REDD+ as a carbon offset opportunity in the first place. Moreover, there was a broadly shared concern amongst climate justice groups that the inclusion of REDD+ in carbon markets would have significant negative impacts on indigenous peoples and other forest-dependent peoples, as it would trigger land grabbing by more powerful actors interested to benefit from such offset opportunities (see also, Global Forest Coalition, 2008). These concerns are shared by many academics, and even by most of the institutions financing REDD+ (Angelsen, 2008; Chhatre and Agrawal, 2009; Peskett et al., 2008; Vatn et al., 2011).

It should be noted that it is not yet decided whether REDD+ will be financed through mandatory carbon markets: At the 17th Conference of the Parties, countries decided that activities to reduce emissions from deforestation "could" be financed through public funding or private funding,[45] but this was merely a confirmation of the actual situation, in which some US$7.7 billion of commitments in public funding, mainly for REDD readiness,[46] were matched with some US$178 million in investments by the private sector in voluntary forest carbon offset markets (Forest Trends, 2011). As mentioned above, the recently adopted Paris Agreement opens up an opportunity for a future forest carbon offset market, but the rules and conditions of this market are still to be developed.[47] Currently, 95 percent of all REDD funding is public, and it is unlikely this situation will change before a possible new regime will be in place, which will be by 2020 the very earliest. Yet, there is a strong tendency in most countries that are preparing their REDD+ program to include large-scale if not nation-wide PES schemes in their national REDD+ program. The main donors to REDD+, the World Bank, UN–REDD, and the Norwegian government, are clearly pressuring countries to design their REDD+ programs in such a manner that they could eventually be financed through carbon offset markets.[48]

The basic underlying assumption of REDD+ is that forests are being destroyed because they are considered of less economic value than alternative uses of land. REDD+ responds to this by attributing a clear economic value to forests, or at least to the carbon stored in forest. But an increased economic value also inherently increases the risk of elite resource capture, as it makes it attractive for economically and politically powerful actors to seize control over the forest and exploit the economic opportunities created by REDD+ (Karsenty, 2012; Peskett et al., 2008; World Bank, 2008). This risk is exacerbated by the fact that the majority of the world's forests are historically inhabited by people who are economically and politically marginalized, like indigenous peoples and peasants without formal tenure rights (FAO, 2009; WCFSD, 1999; World Bank, 2008): Because forests were considered of minor economic value, actors who could chose normally opted to acquire and convert more fertile, accessible, or otherwise economically attractive areas into agriculture, so these more attractive areas have been concentrated into the hands of relatively rich farmers and subsequently deforested (Angelsen and Kaimowitz, 2001). For that reason, most of the large remaining forest areas can be found in areas that are remote from urban centers and/or infrastructure, mountainous, wet, hot, or otherwise unattractive for commercial exploitation. Economically and politically less powerful actors were often forced to move to less attractive areas, which were mountainous, wet, hot, remote, or otherwise less attractive for commercial agriculture. Many of these economically marginalized actors also lack the capacity to deforest large tracks of land, and because their labor and investment capacity is limited, they are not able to keep large tracks of land under production. Even if tracks of forests were converted, it was normally on a small-scale and/or rotational basis only (Hall, 2010). This has occasionally caused forest degradation, but there is significant evidence of such small-scale interactions having a positive effect on the forest biodiversity as well (World Bank, 2008).

In the case of indigenous peoples and traditional communities, cultural value systems have played an important role in forest conservation and restoration as well. Especially for communities that depend on hunting and gathering for all or a significant part of their livelihood, an ecologically viable forest is more than an economic opportunity, it is their livelihood. This awareness of the socio-economic value of forests has, in most traditional communities, also contributed to a strong and often culturally inspired conservation spirit, including cultural taboos on the exploitation of certain areas and species. Up to 1.5 billion people depend on forest resources for part of their livelihood, including, in particular, fuelwood and building materials, medicinal plants and edible plants, fruits, animals, mushrooms, and other "forest foods."[49] Most of these goods are gathered from the forest for free, which means they never enter formal economic statistics. As the people who depend on these free products are economically marginalized, the relative welfare impact if they lose access to these resources is significant (IPCCA, 2011; World Bank, 2008).

For many indigenous peoples, the forests they live in form an important part of their cultural identity as well. If forests are lost, or if they lose control over their own forest, it has significant impacts on their cultural identity and self-esteem, and thus their overall well-being (IPCCA, 2011). Payments for the "environmental service" of curtailing traditional forest management and/or shifting cultivation practices can also lead to the loss of traditional forest-related knowledge and other biocultural practices (IPCCA, 2011). The Asian Indigenous Peoples Pact, for example, has expressed strong concerns that REDD might be used to discourage or even ban shifting cultivation practices.[50] There also is a particular concern that women's needs in terms of having free access to forest resources like fuelwood and medicinal plants might be overlooked (IPCCA, 2011; Lovera, 2008a). The majority of PES schemes pay people for refraining from certain forest extraction activities (Vatn et al., 2011). As a result, there has been a growing tendency amongst, especially, indigenous young people to accept a PES payment and leave the community for the city, as they are not allowed to practice any of their traditional land management practices anymore. Such rural–urban migration can form a significant threat to the cultural survival of numerically small and even larger indigenous peoples (Lovera, 2012). So PES schemes can add to already existing challenges of urban migration and cultural alienation of young indigenous people and resulting ageing of the remaining community (Jonas et al., 2012).

Increased economic value of forest areas can also frustrate land reform, and the recognition of outstanding land claims by indigenous peoples. By increasing the (potential) value of the forested areas in their estates, large landholders will be less inclined to agree to land reform policies—and in countries like Paraguay and Brazil the political power of these actors is significant (GFC, 2008; IPCCA, 2011). Many REDD proponents have argued that land tenure should be "clarified" before REDD+ or PES initiatives can be successfully implemented (e.g., Angelsen, 2008; Peskett et al., 2008). But in most developing countries with a colonial history, there are millions of hectares of disputed lands and the historical land claims of indigenous peoples especially are far from being settled (Jonas et al., 2012). In the absence of full settlement, there is a strong risk that REDD+ will reinforce historical injustices by providing payments for environmental services to land owners who have obtained their land through colonial occupation, abuse of land reform schemes, or even more blunt land allocations that took place during colonial and/or dictatorial regimes. There also is a significant risk that the "clarification" of land rights under REDD will be used by neoliberal actors to promote privatization of land, which subsequently makes it easier for carbon brokers or other actors who want to exploit forest land to buy up small plots, thus triggering land concentration.

Attempts to Make PES and REDD+ More Equitable

Triggered by wide-spread concerns (Peskett et al., 2008; Vatn et al., 2011; Wunder, 2008) about the equity impacts of REDD+, and PES in general, significant efforts have been made to develop "pro-poor" REDD+ and PES schemes, especially by institutions like the World Bank and the UN that are assumed to have poverty eradication as their primary mandate. Intense advocacy campaigns by NGOs, social movements and, especially, IPOs at the UNFCCC meetings played a significant role in raising the attention on the possible negative impacts of REDD+ as well. As a result, both the UNFCCC negotiators, and donors like the World Bank and UN–REDD, decided to develop safeguards to protect the rights and needs of indigenous peoples and local communities. These safeguards are deliberately silent on the question of commodification though, which was not seen as a problem by these neoliberal actors at all.

The adoption, in 2007, of the UN Declaration on the Rights of Indigenous Peoples (UNDRIP),[51] has given a significant impetus to the elaboration of safeguards in the field of REDD+. UNDRIP spells out the biocultural rights of indigenous peoples regarding their lands and forests. It states amongst others that:

- Indigenous peoples have the right to own, use, develop and control the lands, territories and resources that they possess by reason of traditional ownership or other traditional occupation or use, as well as those which they have otherwise acquired. (Art. 26.2)
- States shall give legal recognition and protection to these lands, territories and resources. Such recognition shall be conducted with due respect to the customs, traditions and land tenure systems of the indigenous peoples concerned (Art. 26.3)

The political momentum created by the adoption of UNDRIP was used by IPOs who implemented a successful advocacy campaign to seek recognition for the rights enshrined in this, formally nonbinding, UN declaration. The UN–REDD program formally committed itself to respecting the rights enshrined in UNDRIP[52] and the 17th Conference of the parties of the UNFCCC adopted a set of nonbinding safeguards[53] that included the following:

> Respect for the knowledge and rights of indigenous peoples and members of local communities, by taking into account relevant international obligations, national circumstances and laws, and noting that the United Nations General Assembly has adopted the United Nations Declaration on the Rights of Indigenous Peoples.

Other REDD+ donors like the World Bank and the Norwegian government have adopted similar although slightly less explicit safeguards.[54] Especially the recognition of the right to FPIC is considered of significant value by indigenous peoples, although there is little evidence this right has been respected anywhere in the way the UN itself has recommended.[55]

Despite these significant efforts to establish safeguards that will lead to more equitable outcomes of REDD+ projects and programs, many remain concerned that the bias in favor of economically and politically actors of REDD+ is inherent to the scheme and thus cannot be addressed through safeguards. An analysis of the Global Forest Coalition of the impact of market-based conservation in five different communities revealed that,

The use of market-based mechanisms inevitably means that the odds are stacked against those in a weaker initial negotiating position. This includes people with no legal land tenure and those unable to afford the considerable expense involved in the preparation of environmental impact assessments, the delivery of environmental services, the fulfillment of a range of quantifiable qualification criteria and the provision of upfront and operational finance, including insurance against project failure. This implies that market-based conservation mechanisms will inevitably lead to increased corporate governance over biodiversity conservation, and erode the governance systems of (monetary) poor communities and social groups including indigenous peoples and women. (Global Forest Coalition, 2008)

As these tendencies are inherent to REDD+ as a neoliberal forest conservation scheme, they cannot be addressed by greater participation of indigenous peoples, respect for FPIC (which has already been violated by REDD in the first place, as previously explained) or even respect for land rights. Even in schemes where the territorial and other rights of indigenous peoples were formally respected and the benefits are presumably "shared" with them, forest carbon offset schemes still lead to a concentration of wealth in the hands of a few powerful carbon brokers as indigenous peoples are simply unable to access the carbon market by themselves.[56] There are no known cases of forest carbon offset schemes initiated and run by indigenous peoples themselves.

The Munden Project, a consultancy firm with expertise in international commodity markets, points out that the inherent complexities of calculating the amount of carbon a REDD+ initiative sequesters,

[A]lmost certainly requires a multinational organization, one that is well-capitalized and capable of managing many clients at once.... Will these organizations be numerous? Unlikely. Will they be domiciled in developing countries? It seems improbable.... Forest carbon is likely to behave as any commodities market would, which implies that producers will derive only marginal benefits from the market as a whole. (The Munden Project, 2011)

Additionally, Broughton and Pirard (2011) caution that the presumed efficiency of market-based instruments is based on the assumption that local actors would have access to comprehensive information about the opportunity costs of conservation. However, in reality, few REDD+ actors can be expected to have such access, especially because opportunity costs are dependent on very volatile commodity markets in products that trigger forest conversion, such as meat, vegetable oils and, increasingly, bioenergy.

Similar conclusions were reached by a major report on the poverty impact of REDD prepared by Peskett et al. (2008) for the Poverty and Environment Partnership, a partnership of a large number of UN agencies and REDD+ donors. The report cautions that REDD+ might have significant negative impacts on the poor, also because it might lead to higher food and land prices. The report cautions that poor communities are likely to be excluded from REDD benefits due to a bias toward more visible activities such as protected areas instead of community forestry, and due to the high compliance costs of REDD+. These costs include possible liabilities, for example, when trees planted are lost due to fires or storms.[57] Also, while communities are certainly able to obtain some financial benefits from PES and REDD+ projects, these benefits tend to be marginal in comparison to the benefits PES and REDD+ project developers obtain. A comparison by the World Rainforest Movement, of the per capita benefits of local communities and project managers involved in the Juma forest carbon offset project in the Brazilian Amazon, revealed that an average community member received US$0.18 per day as a benefit from the project, while the project managers were paid approximately US$830 per day.[58]

The most significant impact reported in the GFC analysis on market-based conservation mechanism was the sense of disempowerment felt by many community members. In all cases in the study, local residents reported that their control over their forests and livelihoods had decreased because, "the main decisions were now taken by other actors" (Global Forest Coalition, 2008).

Thus, communities that had their own governance systems promoting collective sustainable management of biodiversity became, under the impact of market-based mechanisms, more likely to act individually (deliberately or otherwise) and pursue individual economic interests such as jobs, profits, and financial rewards. Traditional biodiversity-related knowledge was less likely to be shared, communal lands were more at risk of being privatized and sold off, and biodiversity-friendly economic activities such as bee-keeping were likely to be substituted by monoculture timber plantations. The position of women within the communities was also affected, as women's interests are more likely to be overlooked in commercial transactions (Global Forest Coalition, 2008).

Alternative Incentives for Forest Conservation

There is very broad support for the notion that recognizing and strengthening the rights of indigenous peoples and local communities to manage and control their forests is an important strategy to conserve forests (Agrawal, 2001; Nagendra, 2008; Nepstad et al., 2006; Pfaff et al., 2010; Porter-Bolland et al., 2012; World Bank, 2008). However, considering the significant amount of the literature that has been produced on the technical aspects of REDD+, there has been remarkably little research on the success factors that have triggered forest conservation. A comprehensive research by Kuchli on the historical patterns leading to forest restoration in 12 different countries found that effective community governance over forests played a key role in most of these success stories.

> Local empowerment, rather than central control, is the first step towards long-term preservation of natural resources and the environment. (Kuchli, 1997)

As one of the key motivations for forest conservation for local communities he identifies the fact that

> the forests is their home and not merely one of the many places they have chosen to exploit for profit. (Kuchli, 1997)

This conclusion is very much in line with the motivations identified by indigenous peoples and local community representatives themselves, for example, in a participatory analysis of the drivers of community forest restoration that was undertaken by national Global Forest Coalition members in seven different countries (Hall, 2010). During the workshops that were organized during this analysis, local people pointed out that forests are not considered in a reductive, mechanical way by indigenous peoples. Rather they are an integral part of peoples' and communities' existence and identity, intrinsic to life itself, both practically and spiritually: the forests are central to many indigenous peoples' traditions and culture, and are a source of food, medicines, and building materials. For some, the forest is also home to their gods, and of great spiritual importance (Hall, 2010). Many indigenous peoples identify themselves as custodians of Mother Earth.

Territories and areas conserved by indigenous peoples and local communities (ICCAs) cover an estimated 22 percent of the earth's terrestrial surface (World Bank, 2008). There is significant evidence that ICCAs are not only beneficial from a perspective of human rights and social welfare, but that they are at least as effective as a conservation policy as conventional protected areas (ICCA Consortium, 2010). An elaborate research by Porter-Bolland et al. (2012) concluded that forest areas managed and governed by local communities showed lower deforestation rates than formal protected areas, which is remarkable, as protected areas are often established in areas that are relatively less attractive for agriculture or other forms of land use, such as mountains, deserts, and large unfragmented forests (Nagendra, 2008).

In-depth research on the most effective ways to support community conservation is remarkably scarce. The ICCA consortium has itself performed an analysis of the best ways to support ICCAs (Borrini-Feyerabend, 2008). It concluded that by far the most important forms of support are the legal and political recognition of ICCAs, and the rights and governance systems of the ICCAs that conserve them. A preliminary analysis by the Global Forest Coalition, the ICCA Consortium, and the Commission on Environmental, Economic and Social policy of the World Conservation Union on the most effective ways to support forest conservation and restoration by ICCAs led to similar conclusions (Global Forest Coalition et al., 2012), as did a more elaborate legal review of policies and laws to support ICCAs (Jonas et al., 2012). Here again, PES systems were not amongst the schemes mentioned by the different authors of these legal reviews. Rather, laws and policies that formally recognized ICCAs and the rights of indigenous peoples and communities to manage these areas autonomously were seen as the most effective ways to promote them.

Discussion: The Equity and Effectiveness of PES vis-à-vis Alternative Incentive Schemes

The fact that PES schemes were not highlighted amongst the policies and mechanisms that could promote community conservation in the above-mentioned studies on ICCAs does not imply that they do not play a role in stimulating community action at all. There are a number of cases in which carefully designed PES schemes, in combination with other policies and measures, have contributed to the overall success of forest conservation schemes that involve (members of) local communities (Landell-Mills and Porras, 2002). However, it is often unclear whether the PES mechanism has been the main factor in the success of the overall scheme, or whether other factors like existing community management traditions, accompanying deforestation bans, or reduced demand for commodities like beef or timber, were the main driver of conservation (Pfaff et al., 2008). In an analysis of PES schemes in Mexico, Alix-Garcia et al. (2005) found that the payments had had very modest impacts on existing conservation practices only, also because few of the participating communities actually understood that the payments were made for forest conservation activities. Moreover, a significant part of the payments ended up in the hands of loggers with established links to the main implementing agency, which allowed them "to exert pressure on the way the agency implements its programs." In many cases, the payments ended up replacing existing command and control measures. Similarly, Pfaff et al. (2008) concluded that the PES scheme in Costa Rica had not had significant success as far as reducing deforestation was concerned, as most of the payments went to landholders that would not have destroyed their forests anyhow.

It is important to realize that PES schemes do not necessarily target communities. Some of the newer schemes, which were developed with the explicit intention to contribute to the reduction of poverty in rural communities as well, include both payments to the community and individual payments,[59] or even payments to the community only.[60] But most schemes, especially the larger and older schemes in the US and EU, target individual farmers and other land owners. This implies that they do not contribute to strengthening the communal traditional and/or cultural value systems that were identified by scholars like Agrawal (2001), coalitions like the ICCA Consortium (Borrini-Feyerabend, 2008), and individual indigenous representatives (Global Forest Coalition et al., 2012) as the cornerstone of community conservation, which is arguably one of the most equitable and cost-effective forms of forest conservation.

Rather, these "classic" PES schemes are based on the assumption of a "homo economicus," that is, the assumption that financial gains are by far the main motivation for human action. REDD+ is based on a similar assumption that financial contributions are the only incentive that would trigger action to conserve forests (Angelsen, 2008). As the original submission by

Papua New Guinea and Costa Rica states: "Nevertheless, in the absence of revenues streams from standing forests, communities, and governments [i]n many developing nations have little incentive to prevent deforestation."[61] Eric Solheim, former Minister of Environment of Norway, put it even more bluntly: "Tropical deforestation happens because it is more profitable to cut down forests than to look after them" (Bond et al., 2009).

By establishing an entitlement to financial compensation for an "environmental service" like reducing deforestation, the proponents of REDD+ create the assumption that deforestation by itself is a right, a free option of the forest owner—or a country in the case of REDD+— and that reducing it is a "service" to outsiders (Karsenty, 2008; Wunder, 2007). Such a vision may fit well into the original 1992 discourse of the Malaysian government, but at country level it seems at odds with legislation in most countries, which requires a specific permission from the government in the form of a license or logging concession whenever a significant area of forests is converted. In fact, an estimated 86 percent of the world's forests is state property.[62] In continents like Africa and Asia, almost all forests belong to the state. So national governments in these continents have the right to prohibit or permit deforestation, without any legal need for compensatory payments.

Even at an international level, it can be questioned whether countries have a right to destroy their forests in the absence of any financial compensation. While customary international law, and key legally binding instruments like the Convention on Biodiversity, have embraced the principle of sovereignty of nations over their natural resources, this principle is always combined with the caution that States also have *"the responsibility to ensure that activities within their jurisdiction or control do not cause damage to the environment of other States or of areas beyond the limits of national jurisdiction."*[63] By contributing to global warming, and by disturbing regional rain patterns, large-scale deforestation definitely causes damage to the environment of neighboring states.

Several researchers (e.g., Alix-Garcia et al., 2005) have identified the risk that PES payments to individuals might actually lead to an erosion of community values. Kuchli (1997) highlights the conflict between what he calls "the short-sightedness of individuals versus the long-term needs of the community," embracing the latter as the cornerstone for successful forest restoration. Karsenty (2012) also highlights the risk that PES or REDD+ payments might lead to so-called "opportunistic behaviors" by countries:

Using incentives to prevent highly lucrative activities could not only prove to be ineffective: it could also generate opportunistic behaviours and raises issues of equity.... As pointed out by Gregersen et al. (2010), using incentives systematically within such a REDD+ framework would encourage potential oil palm developers to ask for plantation permits in the primary forests (turning the baseline scenario into a self-fulfilling prophecy), with the expectation of receiving financial compensation to develop lands elsewhere. A regulation prohibiting the development of large-scale agricultural plantations on densely forested land would be much less costly than using incentives, and would prevent "rent-seeking behaviours" of powerful players.... Effective combinations between regulation and incentives will need to be designed in order to avoid important drifting of the costs and capture of the bulk of the funds by opportunistic and powerful players.

A related, significant risk of PES programs is that conservation activities will be undone once contracts run out and payments stop, also because they are top-down schemes that do not create community ownership over forest conservation. While most PES schemes foresee the possibility of renewal of contracts, land owners might not be interested to do so if commodity prices have improved in the meantime and the payments are no longer sufficient to compensate for the resulting higher opportunity costs. The largest and oldest PES scheme in the world, the US Conservation reserve program, provides a quite dramatic example in this respect. When wheat prices rose dramatically in the 1970s, some 26 percent of the lands that had been set aside as part of the Great Plains Conservation Program were put into production again (Cain and Lovejoy, 2004).

Conclusion

While significant efforts have been made the past years to design PES and REDD+ schemes that are more equitable and socially just, these schemes are based on the rather simplistic assumption that individual actions are mainly driven by financial incentives. This argument is based on a theoretical assumption embedded in a neoliberal environmental discourse rather than a profound analysis of the success factors behind existing examples of forest conservation and restoration.

Research by enlightened economists like the late Elinor Ostrom and Nagendra (2006) has demonstrated that social pressures and community values play a significant role in motivating individual economic actions. According to representatives of IPLCs engaged in forest conservation and other area-based conservation activities themselves, such pressure and value systems form the cornerstone of their motivation. In their testimonies on why their communities were motivated to conserve their forests rather than destroy it, indigenous peoples seldom mention financial motives. Rather, they highlight traditional value systems:

> Indigenous People have always considered that this land is sacred and that the welfare and health of the planet depend on their health and conservation. This is the vision that has and is still motivating our communities to maintain the conservation and restoration of our territories. We are seeking to recover usurped ancestral lands, and to restore their vitality, to recreate the forests as they once were, before the expansion of Western agriculture and deforestation. (Geodisio castello, an Indigenous legal expert from Guna Yala, Panama, during the 2010 national workshop on the underlying causes of forest restoration in Panama, in Hall, 2010)

Representatives of traditional communities in India, Tanzania, Nepal, Colombia, and Brazil have given similar clarifications for their conservation efforts (Hall, 2010).

Analysis of the effectiveness of existing PES schemes in Costa Rica and Mexico has demonstrated that the schemes have relatively limited added value to existing community conservation practices and/or command and control measures such as deforestation bans. Most schemes became effective when combined with regulations banning or at least strictly regulating forest conversion only and/or when they were accompanied with policies that recognized community rights over their forests (Asquith et al., 2002; Karsenty, 2012). Arguably, these projects might have been a success without any compensatory payments as well.

There is an undisputable argument that compensatory payments might have made these regulations politically more palatable. As most payments for environmental services schemes are in fact renamed subsidy schemes (Broughton and Pirard, 2011; see also Corbera et al., 2007), such a trend would fit within a long and established tradition of policy-makers buying public support for potentially unpopular measures through lavish subsidy schemes. However, one might wonder whether this is an effective use of the still very limited resources that are available for environmental policy implementation. Most countries that embraced large-scale PES schemes have been faced with significant challenges of how to obtain long-term financing for such schemes, which have added to existing budgetary challenges in the US and EU, as well as disproportionally high loans in small countries such as Costa Rica (Lovera, 2012; Vatn et al., 2011).

In fact, as the history of REDD+ explains, the financial unsustainability of its own PES scheme formed the key motivation for one of the two countries that originally proposed the REDD+ scheme: Costa Rica. REDD+ itself is based on an international interpretation of the same assumption that motivated PES schemes: countries will only be willing to conserve their forests if financially compensated to do so. However, it has become clear in the course of 2011 and 2012 that it will be a tremendous challenge to mobilize sufficient financial resources to compensate developing countries for the full opportunity costs of maintaining forest cover, especially when REDD+ schemes go hand in hand with (partly subsidized) rapidly increasing demand for commodities like palm oil, soy, and wood that make it more attractive than ever to convert forests into agricultural (or tree) monocultures.

It should be emphasized that some form of financial reward to forest countries is defendable in light of the principle of common but differentiated responsibilities and the overall assumption enshrined in the UNFCCC (and CBD) that developing countries are entitled to some form of financial support for their efforts to contribute to address global environmental challenges such as climate change and biodiversity loss. But reward and compensation are two different concepts. The concept of reward, which was embraced as a foundation for the original financial mechanism of the UNFCCC, the GEF, assumes that forest conservation mainly benefits countries themselves, but that developing countries are entitled to some international support as well in light of the global benefits of forest conservation.

The concept of compensation assumes that forest conservation would not benefit countries at all, and that they should thus be fully compensated for any efforts made. This does not only overlook ample evidence on the local and national benefits of forest conservation, including economic benefits (TEEB, 2009), but also the lack of historical evidence that such payments are needed or even helpful to convince countries to conserve their forests.

There is clearly a need for more scientific research on the success factors that triggered countries to halt or even revert their forest cover loss, and the success factors that triggered IPLCs to conserve forests in their territories and areas. Initial analysis indicates that financial support played only a modest role in these successes. Rather, there are indications that financial support schemes might actually aggravate conflict at the community level (Alix-Garcia et al., 2005; Global Forest Coalition, 2011) as they trigger elite resources capture and provide an incentive for illegal land grabbing. More in general, REDD+ and PES schemes tend to create an entitlement to compensation for forest conservation, which is at odds with more successful forest policies and community norms that simply prohibit forest conversion, without any need for compensatory payments. As Broughton and Pirard (2011) state:

> [T]he rapid and wide-ranging implementation of [market-based instruments] to address environmental issues rests on a fragile justification: the presumed inappropriateness of regulatory instruments in certain contexts. Despite the limitations of such an argument, it is followed by many decision-makers in a context where the virtues and efficiency of economic liberalism are often taken for granted.

It is broadly acknowledged that PES and REDD+ schemes can have serious equity implications. Aside from the many inherent issues with these schemes from an equity, social justice, moral, and environmental effectiveness point of view that were already raised above, from a purely financial point of view, they are a highly inefficient forest conservation policy as they create a need for permanent funding flows in a time when there is significant insecurity about future forest funding. It is clear these policy mechanisms also need a serious reconsideration in light of the emerging evidence that alternative policies like recognizing community and indigenous peoples' governance over forests have proven to be far more effective, equitable, and economically efficient.

In its essence, REDD+ is a neoliberal conservation policy based on the narrow assumption that human beings are only motivated by purely financial motives, and that forests should thus be commodified, privatized, and commercialized so as to capture all their values. This assumption is not only unfounded as there is ample evidence that human beings have conserved many forest areas for a multiple of nonfinancial motivations, but it also forms the basis for a system that will, per definition, further marginalize the people that are most dependent on forests for their livelihoods, no matter how many safeguards and other theoretical standards are being adopted.

Notes

1. http://news.mongabay.com/2012/1231-year-in-rainforests-2012.html?utm_source=People+and+Forests+E-News&utm_campaign=bf6871d2c1-People_and_Forests_E_News_JAN_2013&utm_medium=email, last accessed on January 12, 2012.
2. The Noordwijk Declaration on Climate Change, 1989, Article 21. The target was net forest growth of 12 million hectares annually in the 21st century.
3. Article 4.1 (b) of the 1992 UN Framework Convention on Climate Change, Rio de Janeiro, 1992, http://unfccc.int/resource/docs/convkp/conveng.pdf.
4. New and additional funding means funding that is additional to existing official development aid.
5. Articles 3.1, 4.1, 12.1, and preamble of the UN Framework Convention on Climate Change, 1992. Article 4.7 emphasizes the need for financial support.
6. http://www.thegef.org/gef/SFM.
7. Report of the United Nations Conference on Environment and Development, Rio de Janeiro, 3–14 June 1992, vol. I, Resolutions Adopted by the Conference (United Nations publication, Sales No. E.93.I.8 and corrigendum), resolution 1, annex II.
8. Article 3.5 of the UN Framework Convention on Climate Change, 1992.
9. Clean Air Act, 42 U.S.C. #7401 et seq. (1970), http://www.epa.gov/regulations/laws/caa.html.
10. http://crs.ncseonline.org/nle/crsreports/10Oct/RS21613.pdf.
11. http://crs.ncseonline.org/nle/crsreports/10Oct/RS21613.pdf.
12. FCCC/CP/2001/13/Add.1.
13. Please note that the definition of "forests" used by the FAO includes monoculture tree plantations, and in many countries there is an ongoing replacement of old-growth forests by monoculture tree plantations, which is not counted as forest cover loss.
14. http://unfccc.int/resource/docs/2007/sbsta/eng/misc14a03.pdf.
15. http://carboncapitalist.com/state-of-the-market-reports-released-at-carbon-expo/ last accessed on 24 August 2011 and http://siteresources.worldbank.org/INTCARBONFINANCE/Resources/StateAndTrend_LowRes.pdf, last accessed on February 27, 2012.
16. http://cdm.unfccc.int/Statistics/Registration/RegisteredProjByScopePieChart.html, last accessed on August 24, 2011.
17. See http://www-wds.worldbank.org/external/default/WDSContentServer/WDSP/IB/2004/03/25/000265513_20040325144148/additional/820140748_200404147051155.pdf for more information on the loan and the conditionalities.
18. Please note the official submission by PNG and Costa Rica that introduced the REDD+ proposal also claims that "The UNFCCC by itself, however, provides neither a mandate nor an incentive for reducing emissions from tropical deforestation," despite quoting that very mandate. FCCC/CP/2005/MISC.1, http://unfccc.int/resource/docs/2005/cop11/eng/misc01.pdf.
19. Similar supply-based calculations were published by Chomitz et al. (2007), Dutschke et al. (2008), Peskett et al. (2008), Peskett and Harkin (2007), and Richards and Jenkins (2007).
20. Forest Trends, 2011. State of the Forest Carbon Markets 2011. http://www.forest-trends.org/publication_details.php?publicationID=2963. It should be noted that demand for forest carbon offsets might rise again as a result of the 2015 Paris Agreement, which opens the door for a possible mandatory forest carbon offset market.

21. FCCC/CP/2005/MISC.1, http://unfccc.int/resource/docs/2005/cop11/eng/misc01.pdf.
22. http://www.rainforestcoalition.org/nations.aspx, last accessed on January 11, 2013.
23. Personal communication with Dr. Miguel Lovera, former UNFCCC focal point and Arq. Oscar Rivas, former Minister of the Environment of the Republic of Paraguay, January 10, 2013. Please note that institutional data on the UNFCCC focal point and Minister of Environment from Paraguay listed on the Coalition's website in 2013 were at least 3 years old. Mexico faced similar complications: It was initially listed as member, but requested to be removed from the list as it had never confirmed its membership in the first place (Lovera, 2012).
24. See, for example, the contradictions between the positions of the Coalition for Rainforest Nations, which includes 11 least developed countries, and the positions of the least developed countries themselves in FCCC/TP/2012/3 (http://unfccc.int/resource/docs/2012/tp/03.pdf).
25. http://www.regjeringen.no/en/dep/md/Selected-topics/climate/the-government-of-norways-international-.html?id=548491.
26. http://www.forestcarbonpartnership.org/fcp/.
27. Decision FCCC/CP/2010/Add.1.
28. Decision XI/19, Convention on Biodiversity. http://www.cbd.int/doc/decisions/cop-11/full/cop-11-dec-en.pdf.
29. http://unfccc.int/resource/docs/2007/smsn/ngo/013.pdf.
30. http://unfccc.int/resource/docs/2007/smsn/ngo/003.pdf.
31. http://unfccc.int/resource/docs/2009/smsn/ngo/108.pdf.
32. http://www.accionecologica.org/servicios-ambientes/declaraciones-internacionales/1625-conferencia-mundial-de-los-pueblos-sobre-el-cambio-climatico-y-los-derechos-de-la-madre-tierra.
33. http://cupuladospovos.org.br/wp-content/uploads/2012/07/FinalDeclaration-ENG.pdf.
34. http://www.accionecologica.org/servicios-ambientes/declaraciones-internacionales/1625-conferencia-mundial-de-los-pueblos-sobre-el-cambio-climatico-y-los-derechos-de-la-madre-tierra.
35. http://www.accionecologica.org/servicios-ambientes/declaraciones-internacionales/1625-conferencia-mundial-de-los-pueblos-sobre-el-cambio-climatico-y-los-derechos-de-la-madre-tierra.
36. http://www.un-redd.org/UNREDDProgramme/CountryActions/Bolivia/tabid/976/language/en-US/Default.aspx.
37. http://unfccc.int/resource/docs/2007/sbsta/eng/misc14.pdf.
38. http://unfccc.int/resource/docs/2010/awg13/eng/misc05.pdf.
39. http://unfccc.int/files/bodies/awg-lca/application/pdf/3_bolivia_ws_redd+__bkk_august_2012.pdf.
40. FCCC/SBSTA/2013/MISC.12.
41. See, for example, Global Forest Coalition (2008), Lovera (2008b), and http://www.redd-monitor.org/2012/11/14/guest-post-redd-resistance-around-the-world/.
42. See above and for example http://www.redd-monitor.org/2012/06/20/kari-oca-ii-declaration-indigenous-peoples-at-rio-20-reject-the-green-economy-and-redd/.
43. See for example http://vh-gfc.dpi.nl/paginas/view/152, http://www.timberwatch.org.za/index.php?id=53 and http://www.wrm.org.uy/countries/Ecuador/face.pdf.
44. http://www.redd-monitor.org/2008/12/08/accra-caucus-statement-on-forests-and-climate-change/.

45. FCCC/CP/2011/9/Add.1, http://unfccc.int/resource/docs/2011/cop17/eng/09a01.pdf, last accessed on January 10, 2013.
46. REDD+ Partnership, 2011. REDD+ Partnership Voluntary REDD+ Database Updated Progress Report, June 11, 2011, page 6, table 1. See http://reddplusdatabase.org/.
47. https://unfccc.int/resource/docs/2015/cop21/eng/l09r01.pdf, last accessed on January 8, 2015.
48. See for example http://peopleforestsrights.wordpress.com/2012/12/04/doha-updates-mrv-as-a-trojan-horse-for-carbon-markets/.
49. http://www.fao.org/forestry/livelihoods/en/.
50. http://unfccc.int/resource/docs/2012/smsn/ngo/235.pdf.
51. http://www.un.org/esa/socdev/unpfii/en/drip.html.
52. UN Collaborative Programme on Reducing Emissions from Deforestation and Forest Degradation in Developing Countries, 2008. FAO, UNDP UNEP Framework Document, June 20, 2008, http://www.un-redd.org/LinkClick.aspx?fileticket=gDmNy DdmEI0%3d&tabid=587&language=en-US, last accessed on August 25, 2011.
53. Decision FCCC/CP/2010/Add.1.
54. http://www.regjeringen.no/en/dep/md/Selected-topics/climate/the-government-of-norways-international-/why-a-climate-and-forest-initiative.html?id=547202, World Bank, 2009. Design Document for the Forest Investment Program, a targeted program under the SCF Trust Fund. World Bank Group Washington. http://www.climateinvestmentfunds.org/cif/sites/climateinvestmentfunds.org/files/FIP_Final_Design_Document_July_7.pdf. Please note the operation policy 4.10 on Indigenous Peoples of the World Bank would apply to REDD+ activities as well, even though the World Bank has denied it applies to readiness programs. http://web.worldbank.org/WBSITE/EXTERNAL/PROJECTS/EXTPOLICIES/EXTOPMANUAL/0,,contentMDK:20553653~menuPK:64701637~pagePK:64709096~piPK:64709108~theSitePK:502184,00.html and http://www.forestcarbonpartnership.org/fcp/sites/forestcarbonpartnership.org/files/Documents/PDF/Oct2009/FCPF_en_soc_guidelines_10-15-09.pdf.
55. UN Permanent Forum on Indigenous Issues, 2005. Report of the International Workshop on Methodologies regarding Free, Prior and Informed Consent and Indigenous Peoples E/C.19/2005/3, available at: http://daccess-dds-ny.un.org/doc/UNDOC/GEN/N05/243/26/PDF/N0524326.pdf?OpenElement.
56. See, for example, http://www.redd-monitor.org/2010/08/02/juma-reserve-project-in-brazil-fundacao-amazonas-sustentavel-responds-to-criticism/.
57. http://www.wrm.org.uy/countries/Ecuador/face.pdf.
58. http://www.redd-monitor.org/2010/08/02/juma-reserve-project-in-brazil-fundacao-amazonas-sustentavel-responds-to-criticism/#more-5287.
59. http://fas-amazonas.org/programa-bolsa-floresta/.
60. http://sociobosque.ambiente.gob.ec/.
61. FCCC/CP/2005/MISC.1, see http://unfccc.int/resource/docs/2005/cop11/eng/misc01.pdf.
62. FAO (2009). Please note this state ownership is often vehemently challenged by forest-dependent Indigenous peoples and local communities, who tend to foster long-standing land claims over these forest areas.
63. Article 3, Convention on Biological Diversity, 1992.

References

Agrawal, A. (2001). Common property institutions and sustainable governance of resources. *World Development, 29*(10), 1649–1672.

Alix-Garcia, J., de Janvry, A., Sadoulet, E., and Torres, J. (2005). *An Assessment of Mexico's Payment for Environmental Services Program*. University of California at Berkeley and CIDE for the FAO Comparative Studies Service Agricultural and Development Economics Division. Rome, Italy, p. 79.

Alvarado, L.X.R. and Wertz-Kanounnikoff, S. (2007). *Why Are We Seeing "REDD"? An Analysis of the International Debate on Reducing Emissions from Deforestation and Degradation in Developing Countries*, Analyses. Institut du développement durable et des relations internationales. Paris, France, p. 28.

Angelsen, A. (Ed.). (2008). *Moving Ahead with REDD: Issues, Options and Implications*. Bogor, Indonesia: CIFOR.

Angelsen, A. and Kaimowitz, D. (Eds.). (2001). *Agricultural Technologies and Tropical Deforestation*. Wallingford, United Kingdom: CAB International.

Angelsen, A., Borckhous, M., Kanninen, M., Sills, E., Sunderlin, W.D., and Wertz-Kanounnikoff, S. (Eds.). (2009). *Realising REDD +: National Strategy and Policy Options*. Bogor, Indonesia: CIFOR.

Arts, B., Appelstrand, M., Kleinschmit, D., Pulzl, H., and Visseren-Hamakers, I. (2010). Discourses, actors and instruments in international forest governance. In J. Rayner, A. Buck, and P. Katila (Eds.), *Embracing Complexity: Meeting the Challenges of International Forest Governance*, A global assessment report. Prepared by the Global Forest Expert Panel on the International Forest Regime. IUFRO World Series Volume 28, Vienna.

Asquith, N.M., Vargas Ríos, M.T., and Smith. J. (2002). Can forest-protection carbon projects improve rural livelihoods? Analysis of the Noel Kempff Mercado Climate Action Project, Bolivia. *Mitigation and Adaptation Strategies for Global Change, 7*(4), 323–337.

Backstrand, K. and Lovbrand, E. (2006). Planting trees to mitigate climate change: Contested discourses of ecological modernization, green governmentality and civic environmentalism. *Global Environmental Politics, 6* (1), 50–75.

Bond, I., Grieg-Gran, M., Wertz-Kanounnikoff, S., Hazlewood, P., Wunder, S., and Angelsen, A. (2009). *Incentives to Sustain Forest Ecosystem Services: A Review and Lessons for REDD*. Natural Resources Issues No. 16. International Institute for Environment and Development, London with CIFOR, Bogor, Indonesia and World Resources Institute, Washington, DC, p. 47.

Borrini-Feyerabend, G. (2008). *Recognising and Supporting Indigenous & Community Conservation: Ideas & Experiences from the Grassroots*. CEESP Briefing Note No. 9, September 2008. IUCN, Gland, Switzerland.

Boucher, D., Elias, P., Lininger, K., May-Tobin, C., Roquemore, S., and Saxon, E. (2011). *The Root of the Problem, What's Driving Tropical Deforestation Today?* Cambridge, MA: Union of Concerned Scientists.

Broughton, E. and Pirard, R. (2011). *What's in a Name? Market-based Instruments for Biodiversity*. Health and Environment Reports No. 8, May 2011, IFRI, France.

Cain, Z. and Lovejoy, S. (2004). History and outlook for Farm Bill Conservation Programs. *Choices*, 4th Quarter, 37–42, American Agricultural Economics Association.

Carbontrade Watch. (2003). *The Sky Is Not the Limit*. Amsterdam, the Netherlands: Transnational Institute.

Chhatre, A. and Agrawal, A. (2009). Trade-offs and synergies between carbon storage and livelihood benefits from forest commons. *Proceedings of the National Academy of Sciences*, *106*(42), 17667–17670.

Chomitz, K.M., Buys, P., De Luca, G., Thomas, T., and Wertz-Kanounnikoff, S. (2007). *At Loggerheads? Agricultural Expansion, Poverty Reduction, and Environment in the Tropical Forests*. A World Bank Policy Research Report. The World Bank, Washington, DC.

Clements, T. (2010). *Reduced Expectations: The Political and Institutional Challenges of REDD +*. UK: Flora and Fauna International.

Corbera, E., Kosoy, N., and Martínez, T.M.. (2007). Equity implications of marketing eco-system services in protected areas and rural communities: Case studies from Meso-America. *Global Environmental Change*, *17*(3–4), 365–380.

Dutschke, M., Wertz-Kanounnikoff, S., Peskett, L., Luttrell, C., Streck, C., and Brown, J. (2008). *Mapping Potential Sources of REDD Financing to Different Needs and National Circumstances*. CIFOR, Bogor, Indonesia, Amazon Environmental Research Institute, Brasilia, and Overseas Development Institute, London.

EC. (2008). *Communication from the Commission to the European Parliament, the Council, the European Economic and Social Committee and the Committee of the Regions. Addressing the Challenges of Deforestation and Forest Degradation to Tackle Climate Change and Biodiversity Loss*. Com(2008) 645/3. European Commission, Brussels.

Engel, S., Pagiola, S., and Wunder, S. (2008). Designing payments for environmental ser-vices in theory and practice: An overview of the issues. *Ecological Economics*, *65* (4), 663–674.

FAO. (2009). *Forest Tenure Assessment*, Rome, Italy: Food and Agriculture Organization of the United Nations. Available at: http://www.fao.org/forestry/tenure/en/ (Accessed on November 29, 2015).

_____. (2010). *State of the World's Forests 2009*, Rome, Italy: Food and Agriculture Organisation of the United Nations.

_____. (2015). *State of the World's Forests 2015*. Rome, Italy: Food and Agriculture Organisation of the United Nations.

Forest Trends. (2011). State of the Forest Carbon Markets 2011. http://www.forest-trends.org/publication_details.php?publicationID=2963.

Fry, I. (2008). Reducing emissions from deforestation and forest degradation: Opportunities and pitfalls in developing a new legal regime. *RECIEL*, *17*(2), 166–182.

Global Forest Coalition. (2008). *Life as Commerce, the Impact of Market-based Conservation on Indigenous Peoples, Local Communities and Women*. Amsterdam: Global Forest Coalition.

Global Forest Coalition, ICCA Consortium and IUCN Commission on Environmental, Economic and Social Policy. (2012). *The Do's and Don'ts of Supporting Forest conserva-tion and Restoration Initiatives by Local Communities and Indigenous Peoples*. Available at: http://globalforestcoalition.org/wp-content/uploads/2012/05/final-report-dos-and-donts.pdf. (Accessed on November 29, 2015).

Gupta, J., van der Grijp, N., and Kuik, O. (2013). *Climate Change, Forests and REDD: Lessons for Institutional Design*. London: Routledge Publishers.

Hall, R. (Ed.). (2010). *Getting to the Roots, Underlying Causes of Deforestation and forest Degradation and Drivers of Forest Restoration*. Amsterdam: Global Forest Coalition. Availableat:http://www.globalforestcoalition.org/wp-content/uploads/2010/11/Report-Getting-to-the-roots1.pdf (Accessed on November 29, 2015).

Humphrey, D. (2008). The politics of 'avoided deforestation': Historical context and contemporary issues. *International Forestry Review, 10*, 433–442.

ICCA Consortium. (2010). *Bio-cultural Diversity Conserved by Indigenous Peoples & Local Communities—Examples & Analysis, Companion Document to IUCN/CEESP.* Briefing Note No. 10. CENESTA, Tehran, 2010.

Intergovernmental Panel on Climate Change. (2007). IPCC Fourth Assessment Report: Climate Change 2007: Synthesis report Summary for Policymakers and Technical Summary of Working Group III. IPCC, Switzerland. Available at: http://www.ipcc.ch/publications_and_data/ar4/syr/en/spm.html (Accessed on November 30, 2015).

IPCC. (2007). *Climate Change 2007: Synthesis Report.* Cambridge: Cambridge University Press.

IPCCA. (2011). *Analytical Background Paper on the Legal Aspects of REDD+ and Recent REDD+ Policy Developments.* Indigenous Peoples Biocultural Climate Change Assessment, Cuzco, Peru.

Jonas, H., Kothari, A., and Schrumm, H. (2012). *Legal and Institutional Aspects of Recognizing and Supporting Conservation by Indigenous peoples and Local Communities. An Analysis of International Law, National Legislation, Judgements, and Institutions as They Interrelate with Territories and Areas Conserved by Indigenous Peoples and Local Communities.* Natural Justice, Bangalore and Kalpavriksh, Pune/Delhi.

Karsenty, A. (2008). The architecture of proposed REDD schemes after Bali: Facing critical choices. *International Forestry Review, 10*(3): 443–457.

———. (2012). *Financing Options to Support REDD+ Activities,* France, CIRAD.

Kuchli, C. (1997). *Forests of Hope, Stories of Regeneration.* London, UK: Earthscan Publications Ltd.

Landell-Mills, N. and Porras, I.T. (2002). *Silver Bullet or Fool's Gold? A Global Review of Markets for Forest Environmental Services and their Impacts on the Poor.* London, UK: International Institute for Environmental and Development.

Latacz-Lohmann, U. and Hodge, I. (2003). European agri-environmental policy for the 21st century. *The Australian Journal of Agricultural and Resource Economics, 47*(1), 123–139.

Lohmann, L. (2006). Carbon Trading: A Critical Conversation on Climate Change, Privatization and Power. What Next Development Dialogue No. 48, September 2006, Dag Hammerskjöld Centre, Uppsala, Sweden.

Lovera, S. (2008a). *Life as Commerce: The Risks of Market-based Conservation Mechanisms on Women.* Amsterdam: Global Forest Coalition. Available at: http://www.globalforestcoalition.org/wp-content/uploads/2010/12/Impacts-marketbasedconservationmechanisms-on-woman4.pdf (Accessed on November 30, 2015).

———. (2008b). *The Hottest REDD Issues: Rights, Equity, Development, Deforestation and Governance by Indigenous Peoples and Local Communities.* Commission on Environmental, Economic and Social Policies and Global Forest Coalition, Gland, Switzerland.

———. (2012). *Transcripts of Interviews with Key Governmental and Non-governmental Actors in the REDD+ Regime.* Amsterdam, the Netherlands: University of Amsterdam.

Milder, J., Scherr, S., and Bracer, C. (2010). Trends and future potential of payment for environmental services to alleviate rural poverty in developing countries. *Ecology and Society, 15*(2), 4.

Nagendra, H. (2008). Do parks work? Impact of protected areas on land cover clearing. *AMBIO: A Journal of the Human Environment, 37*(5), 330–337.

Nepstad, D., Schwartzman, S., Bamberger, B., Santilli, M., Ray, D., Schlesinger, P., Lefebvre, P., Alencar, A., Prinz, E., Fiske, G., and Rolla, A. (2006). Inhibition of Amazon deforestation and fire by parks and indigenous lands. *Conservation Biology, 20*(1), 65–73. Society for Conservation Biology. Available at: http://www.funai.gov.br/procuradoria/docs/Artigo%20Terras%20Ind%EDgenas.pdf (Accessed on November 27, 2015).

Ostrom, E. and Nagendra, H. (2006). Insights on linking forests, trees, and people from the air, on the ground, and in the laboratory. *Papers of the National Academy of Sciences, 103*(51), 19224–19231. Available at: http://www.pnas.org/content/103/51/19224.abstract. (Accessed on November 27, 2015).

Peskett, L., Huberman, D., Bowen-Jones, E., Edwards, G., and Brown, J. (2008). Making REDD work for the Poor. A Poverty Environment Partnership (PEP) Report. Available at: http://www.povertyenvironment.net/pep (Accessed on November 30, 2015).

Peskett, L. and Harkin, Z. (2007). *Risk and Responsibility in Reduced Emissions from Deforestation and Degradation.* London, UK: Overseas Development Institute.

Pfaff, A., Robalino, J., and Sanchez-Azofeifa, A. (2008). *Payments for Environmental Services: Empirical Analysis for Costa Rica.* Working Papers Series, Terry Sanford Institute of Public Policy, Duke University.

Pfaff, A., Sills, E., Amacher, G., Coren, M., Lawlor, K., and Streck, C. (2010). *Policy Impacts on Deforestation. Lessons Learned from Past Experiences to Inform New Initiatives.* Durnham, USA: Nicholas Institute Report, Duke University.

Porter-Bolland, L., Ellis, E., Guariguata, M., Ruiz-Mallén, I., Negrete-Yankelevich, S., and Reyes-Garcia, V. (2012). Community managed forests and forest protected areas: An assessment of their conservation effectiveness across the tropics. *Forest Ecology and Management, 268*, 6–17.Richards, M. and Jenkins, M. (2007). *Potential and Challenges of Payments for Ecosystem Services from Tropical Forests.* London, UK: Overseas Development Institute.

Rudel, T.K., Coomes, O.T., Moran, E., Achard, F., Angelsen, A., Xu, J., and Lambin, E. (2005). forest transitions: towards a global understanding of land use change. *Global Environmental Change, 15*(1), 23– 31.

Santilli, M., Moutinho, P., Schwartzman, S., Nepstad, D., Curran, L., and Nobre, C. (2005). Tropical deforestation and the Kyoto Protocol: An editorial essay. *Climatic Change, 71*(3), 267–276.

Stern, N. (2006). *The Stern Review: The Economics of Climate Change.* Cambridge, UK: Cambridge University Press.

TEEB. (2009). *TEEB: The Economics of Ecosystems and Biodiversity for National and International Policy Makers. Summary: Responding to the Value of Nature.* Nairobi, Kenya: UNEP.

The Munden Project. (2011). *REDD and Forest Carbon, Market Critique and Recommendations.* The Munden Project, USA.

UNICEF. (2007). *State of the World's Children, Women and Children, the Double Dividend of Gender Equality.* New York: UNICEF.

United Nations. (1987). *Our Common Future, Report of the World Commission on Environment and Development.* New York: United Nations.

Vatn, A., Barton, D., Lindhjem, H., Movik, S., Ring, S., and Santos, R. (2011). *Can Markets Protect Biodiversity? An Evaluation of Different Financial Mechanisms.* Noragric Report No. 60. University of Life Sciences, Norway.

World Bank. (2004). World Bank Atlas, Measuring Development, 2004. World Bank, Washington DC.

World Bank. (2008). *The Role of Indigenous Peoples in Biodiversity Conservation, The Natural but Often Forgotten Partners.* Washington, DC: World Bank.

World Commission on Forests and Sustainable Development. (1999) *Our Forests, Our Future*, Summary report, World Commission on Forests and Sustainable Development, WCFSD, Winnipeg, Canada. Available at: http://www.iisd.org/pdf/wcfsdsummary.pdf (Accessed on November 27, 2015).

Wunder, S. (2005). *Payments for Environmental Services: Some Nuts and Bolts.* Bogor, Indonesia: CIFOR.

_____. (2007). The efficiency of payments for environmental services in tropical conservation. *Conservation Biology, 21*(1), 48–58.

Wunder, S. and Vargas, M. (2005). *Beyond 'Markets' Why Terminology Matters* (guest editorial). *Ecosystem Market Place*, March 2005.

7

Selling Nature: Narratives of Coercion, Resistance, and Ecology

Soumitra Ghosh

Introduction

Selling nature is not new, although the neoliberal way of doing it might seem innovative and ingenuous, especially in the wake of the trade in virtual and intangible products such as carbon stored (or sequestered) in a tree. In the past, the sale had focussed more on tangible products that a particular natural system such as a forest could produce, usually at the cost of intrinsically disrupting the biodynamics that sustains the system, and more often than not destroying it altogether (Ramade, 1984). Loss of nature and natural systems on a colossal scale occurred in every colonial country as hordes of European colonialists invaded and then re-mapped almost every corner of the globe (Arnold and Guha, 1999; Cederlof and Sivaramakrishnan, 2005; Colchester, 2003; Colchester and Lohmann, 1993; CSD, 2004; Gadgil and Guha, 1992, 1995; NFFPFW, 2002; Rangarajan, 1996; Saberwal and Rangarajan, 2003; Sivaramakrishnan, 1999) in search of imagined and real bounties that nature might provide.

This included precious minerals, animal skins, timber, spices, land to colonize and rule, and, last but not the least, free human labor. The institution of slavery preyed upon indigenous communities of the newly colonized countries in today's global south and ensured that such labor remained available round-the-year. This often metamorphosed into bonded or indentured labor as more organized bouts of land-grab continued in later colonial days, as part of the state-making process, which was in turn influenced by the advent of industrialization and centralized production process in the industrially developed countries in the global north.

In a sense, this was self-contradictory. Industrialization and the resultant social changes in European countries such as Britain was driven and governed by capital and its dream of a laissez-faire world where human productivity would be unleashed (Locke, [1690] 1952). This meant human labor would be sold freely, under its own volition, in the new free market. The contradiction was inherent in the historical process that made this market possible in the first place: the process of building new enclosures around public pieces of nature that common people used (Marx, [1887]1954; Laveleye, 1878). Enclosures evicted whole bodies of people whose survival was linked to those commons. Many migrated to the rapidly growing urban spaces and were forced to sell their labor.

In India, this process continued through the colonial period, beginning from the mid-18th century when the British East India Company annexed Bengal. Thousands of new, fenced-off and government-owned reserved forests, huge plantation estates, and permanently settled agricultural tenures came up: forests and estates mostly as off-shore ventures by British capitalists, and agricultural areas leased or settled to private proprietors, Indians, and non-Indians alike (Ghosh, 2007; Sivaramkrishnan, 1999). In areas like North Bengal in eastern India, there was no need to buy labor. Like the forest, and the trees in it, forest labor had become either a state or private property. While this labor produced exchangeable, value-generating commodities like timber, cane, and honey—and ultimately capital—it itself had no visible monetary value.

For years, shipyards in Britain had devoured great bulks of Sal timber that came from the Sal forests of Sub-Himalayan Northern Bengal. New railway lines that crisscrossed the great forested plains of India and climbed up the mountains, used the same timber (Leeds, 1869). It was here that the process of converting forests to timber plantations had begun. Eventually, free, "valueless" human labor would transform entire forests into shippable, "valuable" commodities.[1]

On the one hand, feudalism created, reared and kept alive by capital. On the other, there was a commodification process that steadfastly refused to assign monetary value to human labor.[2] These dual yet connected dichotomies left indelible marks on the unrecorded saga of the forest villages of North Bengal. This short article looks at the historical process that changed the forest landscape of Northern Bengal in the 19th and 20th centuries, at great ecological, social, and economic costs. The first part briefly traces the largely unwritten history (Karlson, 2000)[3] of the ghettoized labor settlements that British foresters and later their Indian counterparts had set up so that they never ran short of forest labor. The second part deals with how popular resistance as well as policy changes ushered in an era of uncertainty and flux, which, by influencing and, to some extent, changing, the use and governance of forests, threatened to change the existing production relations in forests. The third and last part is a brief commentary on the political economy of "community control" in North Bengal forests—anticipating, mainly, probable responses that such a scenario might generate in the context of the latest wave of neoliberal commodification of forests in India, and elsewhere across the globe.

Part A: Forest/Taungya Villages in Sub-Himalayan West Bengal: A Brief Ecological History

North Bengal Forests: Changing Landscape

Like many other parts of Indian subcontinent, commercial land-use practices started in North Bengal during the colonial period. The present forest landscape in the region is an artefact that the British colonizers created within a time span of just 100 years. Fire protection measures adopted by colonial foresters allowed new vegetation to colonize extensive swathes of grasslands (Ghosh, 2000; Leeds, 1869). Old forests were logged and replaced with commercially valuable plantations, consisting mainly of monocultures of non-endemic species. Forested hill slopes were converted to tea gardens and terraced agricultural fields, and pastures were also replaced by with tea cultivation. Indigenous semi-nomadic shifting

cultivators and pastoral communities were evicted and forcibly seden-
tarized, to be soon overwhelmed by the vast population of migrant tea
garden workers, and settlers who occupied the newly established *khas-
mahals* (government estates) (Dash, 1947; O'Malley, 1907; Leeds, 1869).
The practice continued till the post-colonial period, up to the nineties of
the last century.

Ecological costs of this landscape reconstruction were enormous: the
process led to large-scale deforestation and change in the vegetational
structure of the remaining forests. Official "protected areas" in the area
(such as Mahananda and Senchal Wild Life Sanctuary) today have more
than 50 percent of their total areas under plantations of commercial species (Lama, 1999; NESPON, 2000). The surviving forests in Darjeeling
Hills as well as Dooars and Terai plains changed drastically in the 1974–
1990 period, when much of the forests were converted to *Cryptomeria
Japanica* (Dhupi) and *Tectona Grandis* (Teak) monocultures (FSI, 1987).

North Bengal forests were also "honeycombed" with forest villages,
taungyas and fixed demand holdings. These were settlements that the
colonial forest department brought into being to ensure uninterrupted
lumbering. The vegetational mosaic of the area's forests changed through
the agency of forest workers who lived in those settlements. The history
of forest landscapes in North Bengal is thus inseparable from the history
of these settlements.

What Is a Forest Village?

While forest villages are typical labor settlements that first came up in
late 19th century, the practice of establishing such villages continued
until 1980. Ghettoized labor colonies that served successive colonial and
post-colonial forest administrations, forest villages had to supply free or
begar[4] labor in lieu of land rights and other sundry rights (though all
these rights were called "privileges") over forest resources. This initially
included small timber, fuelwood, fodder/grazing, and later, the right to
agricultural land which could be tilled either under *taungya* or permanent types of tenures.

Earliest Settlements: 1890–1910

North Bengal was among the earliest areas in India to be extensively worked
under the colonial forest management system (Dutta, 1934; Homfray, 1931;
Lillingston, 1899; Osmaston, 1906; Skies Gamble, 1873; Sundar, 1895;

Waddell, 1899). Colonial forestry demanded that like everything else in the pre-colonial forest landscape, semi-nomadic forest communities would also change: forests and grasslands that had traditionally defined these societies would become part of an imposed and alien ecological order rooted in the utilitarian world view of the colonizers and homogenous and productive forests (every single working plan of forest department started with sort of a mission statement to make forests homogenous and productive[5]) would replace natural diversity and wilderness. Forest offices and forest villages set up by forest department would replace the makeshift settlements of swidden communities, and the slash-and-burn had to go. The new, ordered landscape that consisted of fire-protected forests, settled agriculture, and commercial plantations had no space for an incendiary civilization of fire-setters.

Up to the late 19th century, there were not too many settled or sedentary villages in the sparsely populated area being referred to in this paper (Gruning, 1911; Hooker, 1854; Hunter, 1876; Sundar, 1895; Waddell, 1899). Tall grass and dense Sal forests hid the few scattered landholdings (*jotes*). Broadleaved and montane (mountain) forests covered the hills, with breaks of alpine pastures. Semi-nomadic swiddener groups, such as Mech, Rava, Garo and Dhimal (in the swampy Terai and Dooars), and the Lepcha, Limbu, Rai and Dukpa (in the hills), inhabited the savannah and forests, and supplemented swidden with hunting and food-gathering (Hooker, 1854; Hunter, 1876).

By 1880, scientific forest management was well entrenched in India, and with the help of the 1865(78) Indian Forest Act, the colonial state had started taking absolute control of forest areas. It has been observed (Pyne, 1995) that fire—or its control—was the most effective tool that state had in this work. Because the forest-dwellers were all *jhumiyas* (or swiddeners), they burnt the savannah (in the plains), and forests (in the hills) for fresh agricultural lands. Grasslands and scrub were also burnt for creating new grazing areas and to increase availability of various food items such as tubers. A controlled fire regime spelled an ecological disaster for these people. It was ironic that these very people were the first settlers (along with people brought from the Chottonagpore area and neighboring Nepal) at the earliest forest villages in North Bengal. The villagers' sole task was to fire-protect forests; if any part of the forest caught fire, they had to somehow put it out. Old tribal settlements to survive the eviction drive sometimes remained within reserved forests (Sykes Gamble, 1873)—these were also later declared "forest" villages (Shebbeare, 1920a, 1920b). The labor the villagers gave was *begar*: the department paid no wages for it. Settlers seldom stayed for long in those early forest villages; living conditions were poor and the oppression severe (Shebbeare, 1920a, 1920b). Once people ran away, it was difficult to make them go back or to recruit new settlers. The practice of establishing forest villages had to be gradually abandoned (Shebbeare, 1920a, 1920b, 1945).

Forest villages started to play a really important role in the colonial forestry operations only after the introduction of *taungya*.

Advent of Taungya: Later Villages (1910–1947)

Taungya, a major ecological event for Indian forests, was based on swidden and had fire at its core. Without fire, *taungya* plantations could not grow. Skilled *taungya* workers were, almost without exception, people who understood the ecology of fire. Thus the *jhumiyas*, whom British foresters threw out of forests, staged a comeback as workers in the new *taungya* plantations.

Taungya called for clearfelling pre-marked forest coupes and burning the cleared areas, in order to let new forests generate. Sal forests had failed to regenerate naturally, despite the foresters' best efforts, which badly hurt the revenue-optimizing mechanism of colonial forestry. Anticipating this, some of the British civil servants in North Bengal had repeatedly warned forest department against expulsion of *jhumiyas* from Sal forests; it might irreparably damage the entire forest system, they contended. Col. J.C. Hutton, the Magistrate of Jalpaiguri in 1869, tried to stop the forest department from acquiring *jhumiya* areas and evicting tribals (Leeds, 1869). He also wrote to the Under-Secretary, Government of Bengal, in 1872. Quoting Mr. T. Anderson, the first Conservator of Forests, Bengal, he said that fire could actually benefit Sal forests, by facilitating natural regeneration. Overriding Hutton's, and later similar objections by Mr. Nolan, the Commissioner of Rajshahi Division, all *jhumiyas* were evicted from North Bengal forests. Fire-protection plans were introduced (Leeds, 1869).

The newly created *taungya* villages offered a "rehabilitation" space of sorts to the displaced *jhumiyas* and an opportunity to live "traditionally" by clearing forests and burning the cleared area before raising crops—a practice which was central to all swidden societies. Depending on soil conditions and factors such as the concerned forest officer's preferences

(Sheabbeare, 1920a, 1920b, 1945; Pyne, 1995), the cleared area could be used for cultivation for a period of two to four years, after which the cultivators had to plant the area with forest species. They had to weed and clean the plantations and save those from fire and grazing hazards for another four–five years, or until they were shifted to another plantation site.

In spite of the *begar* or wage-free labor, *taungyas* were an improvement on the earlier, pre-*taungya*, forest villages. In North Bengal, "permanent" forest villages started to come up from 1910 onwards, settlers of which had to enter into a written agreement with the department. The agreement listed the "privileges" due to a villager, like free timber for housebuilding and agricultural implements, free firewood and fodder, in addition to cultivable land. One can say that *taungyas* were simulacras of the *jhumiya* ecological order that was lost forever; they provided an ambience of social and economic security, at least for a while.

In Bengal, shortage of cultivable forest land and a fall in the numbers of skilled *taungya* workers forced the department to modify the system. Instead of leaving plantation areas entirely to the cultivators, it introduced intercropping—the practice of raising crops within two rows of trees, as long as possible. Permanent villagers were allotted a fixed plot as homestead and cultivable land (Shebbeare, 1945). The older variety of *taungya* was kept alive as "temporary forest village," and the modified system came to be known as "Bengal *taungya*" (Ghosh, 2001).

Forest Villages as "Service Jagirs": Evolution of Serf Labor

The bulk of forest villages in North Bengal came up within the last hundred years. Beginning in 1916–1917, the department started to maintain statistical records of forest villages, which were usually included in the annual progress reports and departmental working plans. Neither the reports nor the plans, however, offer information on the actual settlement process for particular villages.

The first "permanent" villages were set up between the years 1905 and 1911. It can be inferred that people living in these villages adapted well to the forest environment, without any exodus. This was perhaps natural, because the villagers were mostly from the indigenous forest communities. Records show that in 1916–1917, among 567 households in various villages of Jalpaiguri and Buxa Forest Division, 486 belonged to Rava, Mech, Oraon, and Munda communities (Government of Bengal, 1919).

However, forest villages had no real permanency or tenural stability. The worry that such villages could become fixed tenures to which Bengal Tenancy Act (BTA) of 1888 would apply, occupied colonial forest officers from the first. BTA provided for the *raiyot's* (original tiller, the farmer in possession) tenural rights over a piece of land he had been cultivating for 10 to 12 years (Ghosh, 2007; Sen, 1916). In 1904, A.L. McIntire, Conservator of Forests, Bengal, wrote to the Secretary to the Government of Bengal, Revenue (Forests) Department, seeking clarification on whether the forest department can form forest villages in reserved forests and allow the villagers to cultivate land free of rent, in return of supplying free labor. Also, whether in districts to which the Bengal Tenancy Act applies, inhabitants will acquire occupancy rights if they are allowed to cultivate land uninterruptedly for more than ten years (Proceedings of the Lt. Governer, 1905).

The letter further said that "intended improvements" in "management of forests" in North Bengal, in particular in Jalpaiguri, necessitated "the employment of increased supplies of labor" and such labor could only come from the labor-pools of "new forest villages" that the forest department had plans to establish. However, McIntire feared that "formation of such villages may give rise to rights of occupancy in reserved forests." The Bengal government took nearly a year to come up with a solution that would allow forest villages in reserved forests, after ensuring that the villagers thus settled would acquire no tenural rights over homestead and cultivable lands. The duration of their stay in the forest would depend upon their willingness to "supply labor" "whenever and wherever it was required of them" by forest officers. In short, a new form of tenure-sans-rights called *service jagir* came into being. A letter from A. Earle, Esq, Secretary to the Government of Bengal, in response to the Conservator of Forests' (Bengal) Memo 1276, dated March 8, 1905, explained what a *service jagir* was (Proceedings of the Lt. Governer, 1905):

What is a *service jagir*? The form that accompanied this letter explains:

I ... the party of the second part (villager) shall hold the land ... free of rent for(?) years and thereafter at a rent of annas 2 per *bigha* per annum as service jaigir only if he performs his duties and observes ... conditions ... prescribed. II. The land shall be held as service jaigir and shall not be alienable and shall be subject to resumption. *When the services of the grantee or his successor shall no longer be required or when such a course is otherwise found necessary by the Forest authorities, Government shall have the right to dispense with the services of the grantee ... [italics added]. VI. The party of the second part shall cultivate only such part or parts of his service jaigir ... as the Forest Officer shall permit [italics added]. VII. Any buildings erected by the party of the second part ... shall belong to Government and the Forest Officer may dispose of any such building on the ejectment of the party of the second part ... X. The Forest Officer shall have power at any time to declare this agreement terminated if in his opinion the party of the second part fails to comply with any or all of the preceding clauses of this agreement.*

The form, interestingly enough, mentioned daily wages (no figures) for a fixed number of days each year for work performed. This consisted of logging, cleaning, weeding, and fire-fighting, besides raising new plantations. The form said that no wage would be paid for fire-fighting. While this first agreement form underwent several later modifications, it nonetheless retained provisions of no tenural rights and ejection at will.

The *service jagir* was another simulacra. The concept offered an illusion of permanency in tenure, without providing any legal right. Though villagers settled in *service jagirs* for long (in permanent *taungyas*, the village remained in one place) started to feel that they were *ryots* of the department (direct subject of government, like other *ryoti* settlers in the Dooars and neighboring Darjeeling area), random, forceful, and often brutal "ejection" of tenants who failed to "supply labor" as desired by forest officers continued until the late 1960s. Naren Rava, from the Garo Basti Forest Village in Buxa Tiger Reserve, remembered:[6]

> At that time we had to give begar ... had to work for free for the department ... they didn't pay us any wages. We worked just like that ... and the department's beat officers and rangers and guards told us: "Go and work at the plantations ... for free! If you don't give *begar* at plantations or do the weeding for free, you can't stay in this village."

The forest village system, the earlier provisions for wages for the worker–settler in service *jagirs* notwithstanding, conveniently substituted "wages" with "privileges." Most of these "privileges" had no meaning for indigenous forest villagers, for whom a forest was home and activities like fishing, grazing, and collecting timber and firewood part of the everyday life, until the state threw them out.

Establishment of forest villages at random led to a brisk business in timber and also, rapid spread of plantations in erstwhile grasslands and natural forests. In the hills of Darjeeling district, this happened in the context of the fast disappearing original vegetation: from 1800 to 1865, broadleaved forests in the hills as well the famous Sal in Terai had been regularly harvested by contractors under a "permit" system. No figures exist for how much timber was harvested in this period, but it was observed that nearly all middle hill forests between altitudes 7,000 to 3,000 feet were lost (Leeds, 1869).

The Dooars area, along the foothills of the Bhutan Himalayas, contained some of the wealthiest timber-yielding forests. In 1916–1917, forests under Jalpaiguri Forest Division and Buxa Forest Division together produced nearly 4 million cubic feet of timber and firewood, and in another 10 years the yield jumped to about 6.5 million cubic feet (Government of Bengal, 1919; Directorate of Forests, Government of West Bengal, 2012). The yield in increase could be directly traced to the increase in the number of forest villages: whereas in 1916–1917 there were 28 villages in Jalpaiguri district, in 1928–1929 there were 48, with 971 families—in other words, 971 service *jagirs* and their ejection-at-will tenants-cum-free laborers.

Forest villages ensured that forests were felled regularly. At the same time, plantations raised by the villagers in clear-felled areas helped maintain both forest cover and timber content—these could be cleared and replanted later. That forests were losing in other values like biodiversity, food, and water was not an issue, mainly because those were not monetarily exchangeable products, and also because forest communities who recognized and used such values had no longer any rights in reserved government forests. It has been shown (Shankar and Lama, 1988) that plantations raised even in the best *taungya* tradition remains pathetically low in biodiversity, in comparison with neighboring natural forests.

Old forest villagers recall that not only the ground water level went down and perennial water sources gradually dried up, but also local agriculture was badly affected, in pine (mainly *Cryptomeria Japanica*, locally known as Dhupi) and teak (*Tectona Grandis*, locally known as Saygun/Segun) monoculture areas. Eighty-eight-year old Ram Gopal Tamang of Bamonpokhri Forest Village in the lower Kurseong foothills, Darjeeling said:[7]

> You call this a forest? I don't…. Before the plantations, these areas were the habitat of wild animals. Tiger, dear, bear etc. could be seen frequently. There were hardly any cases of man-animal conflict then. But the destruction of high forests has led to increasing elephant raids, and crop destruction.

Talking of crops, hardly anything grows here any more. Two of our best rice varieties, *kala timbure* (Black Timber) and *Sada Bacchi* (White Baby) were lost for ever because of this monster trees that drink all the water in the soil. And how can rice be grown without water?

Post-colonial Forest Villages

Forest villages did not change much in post-colonial India. The practice of *taungya* continued to the 1980s, even after the forest corporations appeared with their highly industrialized production forestry and mechanized logging operation. Though mechanization of forestry operations reduced the need for manual labor by forest villagers, temporary but large villages were being set up everywhere in North Bengal, with 30 to 50 families. The number of family units per village started to come down in permanent villages of Darjeeling and Jalpaiguri; from 1974 onwards, the department stopped showing villages as "permanent" or "temporary" and referred to them as simply "forest village" (Directorate of Forests, Government of West Bengal, 2002).

Temporary Taungyas: Villages That Did Not Exist

Though the department's policy was not to establish forest villages any more, new *taungya* sites had been opened in Darjeeling and Kalimpong Forest Divisions as late as 1985 (for instance, *Paintishe* (35-e: meaning that the village originally had 35 settler families) *permanen(t) taungya* in Dajeeling and *Daling* in Kalimpong—both villages were "permanently" settled in their present locations in 1985).[8] Increase in the number of *taungyas* was related to West Bengal Forest Development Corporation's policy of efficient and fast clearing of old-growth montane and broad-leaved forests and replacing those with monocultures of quick-growing Dhupi.[9] After converting most of Darjeeling Hill's natural vegetation to Dhupi plantations through aggressive "production forestry" and establishing a number of new *taungyas* and charcoal burners' settlements, the Forest Corporation handed over the forests of Darjeeling Forest Division to the Directorate of Forests, while retaining Kalimpong (West Bengal Forest Development Corporation, 1999). Seventy-eight-year old Pasang Dukpa,[10] of 9th mile Lamahata Forest Village, Darjeeling says:

The forest department did not care to inform the villagers about the ill effects of monoculture during plantation. They only told us about the good qualities of Dhupi. People did not bother too much about the future impacts of the monoculture. Now everyone understands that the Dhupi plantations are profitable only for the Forest department and not for the people. The plantations offer neither good fuelwood nor fodder, as the Dhupi tree stops other plants to come up in the surrounding areas.

Part B: Forest Villages in the Post-colonial Period (1947–2006)

Discontent and Popular Resistance

The torture by the department continued ... around 1969–70, the Forward Block party came first to Chilapata and then here to our village at Buxa ... they said you have toiled for so long and that too without money ... it's time to stop that. We stopped going to plantation duty, nobody worked until 1971.

—Tileswar Rava[11]

As we said, the ecology of forest villages was at best a simulacra; proximity to forests and the opportunity to practice a variant of *jhum* in *taungya* did not guarantee sustenance. Also, the wilderness space which had traditionally sustained forest communities was fast shrinking, with forests and grasslands being converted to tree plantations, tea gardens, settled agricultural areas, and new villages for migrant settlers.

Lack of lands suitable for *taungya* (and shifting cultivation) near villages forced indigenous communities of the area to take up permanent cultivation. With depletion of natural forests continuing unabated in post-colonial North Bengal, scope for traditional food-gathering and hunting also diminished (Ghosh, 2000).

In independent India, North Bengal was perhaps the only region where the people had no recorded or "declared" customary rights over forests. It has been observed (Karlson, 2000) that the political transition from the colonial to the post-colonial period did not influence the communities in forest villages. In the everyday world of the *taungya*, the "sahibs" continued to rule.

Considering the time-gap between the first "recorded" establishment of forest villages in North Bengal around 1910 and the first organized movement by forest villagers in 1966 (Jha forthcoming), it evidently took the villagers a long time to muster enough strength to challenge their "departmental" overlords. However, the movement ultimately had far-reaching impacts. Existing production relations in the forest villages changed, irretrievably changing the political economy of forestry, and led to a re-ordering of social hierarchies in the closed feudal society of service *jagirs* (Banerjee et al., 2010; Jha, forthcoming).

Although the system of forest village survived the turbulence of the movement, from an unvalued asset (Shebbeare, 1945), the villagers turned into a "liability" for the departments. Several reasons prompted the change, besides the movement in the 1960s. First, the 1988 National Forest Policy prescribed a ban on clear felling natural forests. Second, more than half of the region's total forest area was included in various wildlife conservation areas notified under the Wild Life Protection Act 1972. Both of these meant a net reduction in logging area, hence much less need of forest labor. As far as officialdom was concerned, forest villagers became persona non grata; most of them *faltus*, useless, or surplus[12]. By the turn of the century the forest department found out that labor outside was actually cheaper, if contracts were outsourced for logging and transport of timber.[13]

The First Struggle in North Bengal: Agitation against Begar, 1966–1974

In 1966, precisely a year before the famous land uprising in Naxalbari, perhaps for the first time in the history of the community, the Ravas, an otherwise peace-loving community and the ablest ally of the British Empire in North Bengal and Assam Dooars forests (Shebbeare, 1945), started an organized struggle against the forest department: en masse, forest villagers in Coochbehar, Jalpaiguri and Buxa forest divisions rose against the system of *begar*. The participation of other forest villager communities strengthened the anti-*begar* movement, which continued at least for another 8 years (Jha, forthcoming). Though this struggle remains unrecorded,[14] Ramesh Ray, a resident of Rajabhatkhawa (a settlement in Buxa Tiger Reserve) and the undisputed leader of the movement, recalled in a 2006 interview with the author:

> Agreements were signed through which the villagers were bound to work 90 days a year without any wages (Mainly, work at 1 acre each of old and new plantations).... The movement started at the end of 1966, initially with just a few Rava forest villages in places like Hashimara, Kodalbasty, Mendabari, Chilapata and Khayerbari, which gradually got bigger.... In

1967 a mass representation was given to Governor Dhramabira about the status of forest villagers.... The first demand was immediate discontinuance of the "free service system" (*begar* system) and introduction of the daily wage system.... Between 1966 and 1969 all plantation works had partially stopped in Coochbehar, Buxa, Baikunthapur and part of Jalpaiguri Forest Division, and gradually all types of forestry works stopped throughout the Dooars area stretching from Chalsa to Sankosh.... The Forest Department later agreed to pay ₹1.50 as daily wage to forest workers ... the villagers again started their movement to increase the wage to 2.50.... At least five Rava activists were killed by the police at Gosainhat of Moraghat Range in 1971.... The forest officials had to...invite the leaders of the movement to a meeting in Kolkata.... It was decided that no further encroachment of Forestland should be encouraged and the daily wage was increased to ₹2.50.

Simultaneously, forest villagers were also occupying new areas in government forests. This happened throughout Jalpaiguri district, and mostly in Buxa. As Tileswar Rava, the mondal(village chief) of South Poro forest village recalled:[15]

We occupied the cleared land at Bala ... to the north of our Poro village. The minister from Jalpaiguri arrived. I said: "Sir, we have grown in numbers ... but our lands do not grow. Therefore we have to occupy that fallow land near Bala river." "Oh, is that so, really? What's your name?" said the minister. Then I said: "X." "Your father?" "Y." "Hmmm. Then the more your numbers increase the more you will cut forests?," he said so. "Sir," said I, "We cannot clear forests as our numbers grow...but why didn't you tell us this when we were still in our mothers' womb: Do not come to this India. Do not come to this Earth. There's no room!... if you said so, we needn't have come and wouldn't have needed this argument."

Abolition of *service jagirs* (forest village system) challenged the very fundamentals of the timber economy. Labor procured from outside forest villages would no longer be free (or cheap) and readily available. At the same time, continuing the earlier system without either ejection-at-will or free labor made little sense to foresters. Contemporary records reflect forest department's vexation in the wake of forest villagers' movements.

"The forest village system, as previously described, worked fairly satisfactorily until the middle of the year 1969," said a 1974 note on the "Forest Village Problem" by the Northern Circle Conservator:

In the year 1969 the forest villagers raised plantations as per programme, but started agitation immediately ... under the leadership of various political parties and practically stopped tending of plantations in all the four plains

Forest Divisions of the Northern Circle. Though there was some agitation even in the hill divisions, the work continued as before. In the plains, in many places the forest villagers even turned hostile and many cases of assault of forest staffs were reported. Complete stoppage of tending work ruined plantations already raised and caused a huge loss to Government. The clear felling programme had to be drastically reduced particularly in Buxa and Cooch Behar Divisions.

In 1970, the forest department of West Bengal sent a directive to its divisional officers in North Bengal, asking them to stop all cultivation activities in permanent forest villages and employ forest villagers solely as day-laborers. Another directive called for wholesale eviction of villagers from forest villages and, if that was not possible, giving no work to noncompliant families (Directorate of Forests, Government of West Bengal, 1971).

Before the wages were finally negotiated in 1971, the Government of West Bengal issued a circular in September 1970,[16] prescribing a ceiling for landholdings of forest villagers. According to the new guideline, no family in a forest village could have more than 2.5 to 3 acres of agricultural land in the plains and 1.5 acres in the hills.

The department had to stop *begar*, and introduce a daily wage of ₹3 for all kind of forestry works by forest villagers. But it did so under duress, and never stopped resenting it. West Bengal Forestry Manual and revisions suggested to it by a committee in 1974 offers interesting insights to the government's perspectives on the status of forest villages. For instance, the suggested revisions sought to clarify

> [W]hether the privileges of free grazing of cattle, free collection of forest produce for personal consumption and free cultivation of forest land which forest villagers used to enjoy when they were not paid any wages for doing works in revised forests of Government should continue.

The Government Memo No. 4744-For/Con.-6/70, dated September 28, 1970, prescribed:

> [F]orest villagers who had been residing in forest villages within the forest areas on the hill areas up to 28-07-70 should be allowed forest lands at the rate of $1^1/_2$ acres. The forest villagers who had been residing inside forest areas on the plains up to 28-07-70 should be provided with $2^1/_2$ acres of land per each forest village family. All forest villagers who are occupying forest lands whether in hill forests or on plain forests whether inside such forests

or on their outskirts after 28-07-70 should be treated as trespassers and encroachers and they should be evicted from the lands which they are now occupying within forests on the hills or on the plains. The main purpose of this order was to fix a criterion for distinguishing between *bona fide* forest villagers from those forest villagers who should be deemed as *encroachers*. (emphasis added)

It was clear that the Bengal government was looking for a "permanent solution" to the forest village issue, and hence also mulled radical measures like de-reservation of forest villages and eviction of people not recognized by their books. The recommendation that "periphery" forest villages (the term "forest fringe" has evidently not been coined) should be de-reserved and handed over to the revenue department now appears to be an act of punishment. However, the decision to "de-reserve" forest villages was never implemented. This was perhaps due to the fear that once legal entitlement or "*patta*" was given to some, all villagers including those considered to be encroachers would also demand land ownership. At the same time, not implementing the decision meant that the department remained saddled with forest villages:

"*The decision regarding de-reservation of forest villages located on the periphery of the reserved forests and handing over to the Land Revenue Department for settlement with the forest villagers has, however, been kept in abeyance,*" said the aforementioned CF(NC)'s note (italics added). "*The forest villagers, therefore, continue to get all privileges ... and, in addition, they are getting daily wages of ₹3/- for every piece of work done,*" the note lamented, and went on to observe that, "*the forest villagers have also stopped signing agreements with the Department. Thus, we are virtually creating a specially privileged class of people.*"

In reality, though, the stagnant socio-economic fabric of forest villages was crumbling. In each village, agricultural holdings broke up as number of families increased. The department did not recognize most of the second-generation settlers as registered villagers. Thus, a new group of *faltu* (useless) villagers emerged in every settlement who had no official allotments of land. The per capita availability of departmental person-days decreased because these "unregistered" villagers seldom had other livelihood than the departmental work (Ghosh, 2000, 2001).

Fragmentation of agricultural lands also badly hit the basic subsistence economy of forest villages. Small landholdings could no longer meet the total food requirements of the forest villager who did not have money to buy food from the market. In addition, land ceiling in forest villages meant a complete reorganization of holdings, at the end of which many families were left with poor, uncultivable land. Agriculture ceased to be the mainstay of the forest villagers' lives, and a qualitative change occurred in their class status. From the bonded peasant and food gatherer of the past, a forest villager finally became a wage-laborer, a rural proletariat precariously hanging between incompatible dual identities: the social identity of a farmer and economic identity of a worker (Ghosh, 2000, 2001).

The identity crisis of the forest villager was rooted in the very nature of the timber economy created and celebrated by the forest department. As mentioned, this economy, despite being controlled by industrial capital, fostered and then later depended upon an essentially feudal system of captive labor—an inexhaustible and secure pool that would continue to supply generations of serf labor to the forestry operations of the department. The labor the forest villagers gave was officially invisible: as an intrinsic part of the service *jagir* tenure it was pre-assumed, hence unrecognized, unrecorded, and unvalued. The irony was that without this invisible labor, trees would neither be cut nor planted, and there would be no timber revenue.

The anti-*begar* movement of the 1960s and 1970s was the forest villagers' struggle to establish their identity as workers. Ending the unjust system of *begar*, it ensured that the invisible and unvalued labor became both visible and valued. Probably, if the timber economy of the yesteryears remained as robust today, the forest villagers' movements would have resembled other unionized workers' movements for enhanced wages and better working conditions.

Between 1974 and 2000, several unions affiliated to various political parties came up in forest villages.[17] Though the political legacy of the movement seemed to be lost, the elements of anarchy and chaos that the movement introduced to the closed world of forest villages lingered. Unofficially, defying the authority of departmental overlords, many forest villagers started using the forests as de facto open-access commons, as the Left Front government came to power in West Bengal in 1977 and continued to rule for the next 34 years. Involvement in unofficial logging did not, however, tilt the actual control of forests in the villagers' favor. Neither did the production process change much. It was just that a disorganized and unruly nexus between a section of the officialdom on the one hand and petty contractors, merchants, hooligans, and political leaders on the other gradually replaced the feudal rule of the forest officers. In the new system, as in the old, forest villagers kept on working as labor, albeit with better bargaining capacity.

Forest Villages Today: Continued Oppression, Emerging Struggles

Denial of Tenural Rights

From 1969 onwards, various governmental commissions, working groups, and agencies have observed that forest villagers did not have legal ownership or tenancy rights over their homestead and cultivable lands. This meant that forest villages did not have access to government welfare schemes. The denial of rights is in violation of the Indian constitution as it denies citizenship rights to forest villagers (Ghosh, 2001; Lochan, 1999; Prasad and Jahagirdar, 1993).

Though India's Panchayati Raj System now extends to the forest villages in North Bengal, its benefits have been limited. The panchayats (local self-governments) need "no objection certificates" (NOCs) from the forest department even for carrying out routine developmental activities in the village. There has been resistance on the part of the department to issue NOCs as land-based activities notionally (the activities normally do not cause deforestation) involve diversion of forest land for non-forest uses, such as the construction of a road, laying of pipelines for drinking water, and other such programs (NFFPFW-NBRC, 2005).

The legal status of forest villages appeared uncertain at different points of time. National Commission on Labour, in its 1969 Report, criticized the system of forest villages because the villagers had no tenancy rights on the lands cleared and cultivated by them, and could be evicted for refusing to work (Prasad and Jahagirdar, 1993). In 1978, a conference of State Forest Ministers recommended that forest villages should be converted into revenue villages and the villagers should be given tenancy rights over agricultural land (Prasad and Jahagirdar, 1993). In 1990, the Ministry of Environment and Forests (MoEF), Government of India, recommended that forest villagers and inhabitants of other types of settlements existing on forest lands should be conferred heritable, but inalienable rights over their lands. In February 2004, the MoEF issued a similar order (No.11-70/2002-FC (Pt) dated 3 February 2004), which was stayed by the Supreme Court of India.

Many forest officers have continued to consider these settlements as departmental fiefdoms and resented the idea of intrusion by panchayats. The terms *jagir* and *service jagir* remained in use in newer agreements signed even in the early 1980s. As a result, the development of more than 250 forest settlements in the state and their over 150,000 inhabitants has become a matter of choice of such officers (NESPON, 2000). The forest department, in a meeting with representatives of National Forum of Forest People and Forest Workers, North Bengal Regional Committee (June 2002 at Sukna, Darjeeling), agreed that,

> [T]here would be no difficulty in issuance of NoCs in favour of 'registered' forest villagers' huts under Indira Abas Yojna, construction of small rural road and other works of development including those related to intensification of agriculture.[18]

However, the NOC imbroglio continues to this day, and wherever forest villagers are not adequately aware of their legal rights and entitlements, forest officials keep on obstructing much-needed development projects— such as the laying of a water pipe, an approach road to the village, a small irrigation canal—on the ground that these would entail diversion of forests.[19]

Incidents of physical harassment, torture, and even murder of forest villagers were fairly common in North Bengal (NESPON et al., 2005). In Buxa Tiger Reserve, a public hearing conducted in April 2005 brought into light gruesome stories of torture and murder. The jury that was chaired by the sitting Chairperson of the State Legal Aid Authority observed that (NESPON et al., 2005):

> [C]riminal intimidation, sexual offences, grievous hurt and even cases of murders are being purportedly settled at the intervention of the police and officials of the forest department. The general rule for settling a case of murder and other heinous offences is that the offender/perpetrator is to pay some money to the victim or the members of family of the victim. In the Sub-Divisional Courts no case of civil or criminal are being filed by the forest dwellers. It is apparent that the BTR authorities are taking advantage of the situation, and denying the forest dwellers their just constitutional rights.

Lack of Employment

Beginning in 1990, the forest department stopped giving regular work to forest villagers. This, as explained, was partly due to discontinuance of clearfelling of natural forests (and raising new plantations in the cleared areas), following prescriptions of the National Forest Policy, 1988. The average annual availability of person-days in every forest division dwindled to a maximum of 10–40 days/family, later even less, and sometimes zero. Bringing extensive forest areas under notified protected areas (PA—denoting conservation areas constituted under Wild Life Protection Act, 1972) compounded this problem, because this reduced employment opportunities for forest workers yet further (NESPON et al., 2005). The forest villagers have pointed out that large-scale plantation activities in both reserved forests and PAs would generate a large number of person-days, and existing plantation areas—especially teak and dhupi monocultures—inside PAs can be clearfelled and utilized for this purpose. New plantations can also be raised in degraded natural forest areas (Ghosh, 1999, 2000, 2001).

Denial of Old "Privileges" and Re-introduction of Begar: Advent of JFM

By the turn of the century, the service *jagir* system, with its requirement of signing of annual agreements with the forest department, had become a thing of the past for the forest villager. The department neither renewed agreements nor provided jobs and other benefits. For villages inside PAs and reserved forests (approximately, 99 percent of North Bengal forest villages fall within either of these two categories), a villager had no "legal" access to any forest produce, irrespective of the earlier agreements.

Not surprisingly, villagers found little sense in forest department programs such as joint forest management (JFM), which formally came to North Bengal in 1992 (Karlson, 1999; NESPON, 2001). Some of them found in JFM a reintroduction of *begar*.[20]

A comparison between West Bengal's 1992/2008 JFM circulars and the service *jagir* agreement (a version from 1980) shows how JFM restricted, and also denied, forest villagers' privileges. To begin with, the individual villager was bypassed: JFM agreements were instead made with forest protection committees (FPC) that often included people also from the *bair bustee*s (villages outside the forest) and tea gardens. Second, while the later service *jagir* agreements provided for daily wages to individuals for a specified number of days, there was no provision for this in JFM. Further, service *jagirs* allowed individuals to "cut, collect and remove bamboo creepers, edible roots, fruits, poles not exceeding three feet, for their own use free of charge from the parts of the Reserved Forest adjacent to the village." There was no tenural security in the JFM system, while the earlier system allowed people to homestead as well as cultivable land on nominal rent.

For forest department however, JFM became a strategic imperative, especially in the wake of the Forest Rights Act (FRA). The department kept on using JFM, more specifically money from various government schemes that is routed through the JFM committees, to undermine and subvert the rights recognition process under FRA. We will come to this later.

Movement for Land and Forest Rights: The New Phase of Forest Villagers' Movements

Given this context of severely truncated forest access, no jobs, and not even the illusory security of service *jagirs*, land and forest rights expectedly became core issues in the new phase of forest villagers' movement in North Bengal that started around 1999–2000. Various forest workers' unions, which had been formed in the 1960s and 1970s as mass fronts of various political parties, never raised this demand, despite encouraging sporadic occupation of forest land. The Gorkhaland agitation of the 1980s in the Darjeeling hills led to the formation of Himalayan Forest Villagers Union (HFVU). It called itself a "forest villagers" union to differentiate from the "forest mazdoor union" affiliated to CPI(M) and also because the identity of the land-holding peasant seemed preferable than the "mazdoor" or worker identity.[21] Demands for comprehensive rights over forests and forest land distinguished the new movement formation called National Forum of Forest People and Forest Workers, North Bengal Regional Committee (NFFPFW–NBRC) that emerged in the region in 2000–2001. The new formation called itself a regional committee of a national platform for forest dwelling people, but in practice it was an autonomous and independent social movement that had typically local roots: it originated from a relatively small forum of forest dwellers called *Uttar Banga Banabasi Samittee* (UBBS—North Bengal Forest Dwellers' Committee) formed in early 1999. In 2001, the near defunct HFVU affiliated to Gorkha National Liberation Front, joined UBBS to form the NFFPFW–NBRC.

The growth of the new forest movement in North Bengal merits attention, not only because it organized big mobilizations (Jha, 2005). The forest villagers discovered in it something they could finally own. The movement overcame stiff opposition by forest department and all major political parties active in the region to become the most influential forest movement in the region. This author witnessed how in Jalpaiguri, villagers en masse left their party-affiliated unions, and in the hills, the Himalayan Forest Villagers Union reinvented itself as HFVU, a non-party process.

Forest Rights Act and the Struggle for Community Control of Forests

In 2005–2006, following countrywide resistance and mass protests by forest communities against ongoing eviction of forest dwellers from forests, the first UPA government brought in the Scheduled Tribes and Other Traditional Forest Dwellers (Recognition of Forest Rights) Act 2006, popularly known as FRA.

The political significance of FRA in the context of forest villages of North Bengal was not lost on the movement on the ground. Representatives of the movement (for instance, this author) had been involved in the campaign for the law from its very beginning in early 2005, and helped frame the clauses that deal with forest villages.[22] FRA guaranteed secure tenural right for the erstwhile departmental serfs, service *jagirdars* of yore, by making conversion of such villages to revenue villages a forest right, which in the long run connoted freedom from the stranglehold of the forest department. Finally, rid of the ever-present threat of eviction, the forest villager would no longer need a forest officer's permission to repair a leaking roof. The act covered all types of settlements on forest lands, including un-surveyed and unrecorded ones, and all forms of villages settled by government agencies from time to time to supply labor. This meant that temporary *taungyas*, charcoal burner's colonies, and fixed demand holdings—villages that forest department in North Bengal had so far refused to show in their records—turned into full-fledged forest villages.

The forest movement in North Bengal took note of all this and looked ahead: through the means of the FRA, in various gram sabhas that sprang up in more than 200 villages, it sought to reconstruct a notion of communities of forest dwelling people at peace with forests they would use and govern (Jha, 2010a, 2010b).

The movement anticipated the opposition that came from forest department to its call, *Gram Sabha banao, Adhikar dakhal karo* ("Form Gram Sabha, grab rights"). However, the manner in which the Government of West Bengal started implementing FRA in early 2008, took it by surprise. The "official" process and the resistance the forest villagers put up against that had been adequately documented elsewhere (Bannerjee and Ghosh, 2010; Jha, 2010a, 2010b).

Forest villagers saw the official process as a highly bureaucratic and politicized affair over which they had no control—they also regarded it as clearly violation of the FRA and therefore illegal. The conflict continues.

People's Implementation Begins (Mid–Late 2008)

Many villages in Jalpaiguri Forest Division and Coochbehar Forest Division in North Bengal did not yield to the official pressure. Instead, they demanded implementation strictly according to the law. Many villagers saw in the struggle for implementing FRA a last battle to establish community control over forests. Following a declaration from a meeting on community forest governance held in Takdah, Darjeeling, on June 2008, the movement gave an open call to resist commodification of forest resources and stop deforestation in community-controlled forests throughout North Bengal. In Coochbehar and Kurseong Forest Divisions, the gram sabhas acting together had brought departmental logging operations to a halt. In May and June 2008, the villagers at Chilapata forest area of Coochbehar Forest Division, and the lower villages of Kurseong Forest Division went as far as blockading departmental timber depots at various places, demanding proper implementation of FRA, and invoking powers under Section 5 of the Act. Later, the gram sabhas also resolved to enforce a ban on all such forestry activities by the department that had not been permitted by them (Bannerjee and Ghosh, 2010; Jha, 2010a, 2010b).

In October 2008, 12 gram sabhas in Coochbehar Forest Division adopted a joint resolution of protecting the forests that adjoin the forest villages and banned the extraction of forest resources by outsiders. Villagers with whom this author has been working for last twelve plus years usually had a very clear logic to justify their actions, besides the words of law:

> This is our forest: our ancestors gave *begar* to raise these plantations and we protected the trees for all these long years, though the department only exploited us. Why should they cut and sell these old tall trees without consulting us, the Gram Sabha? Why should contractors from outside carry away firewood and cane from our forests, and sand, gravel and stones from our rivers?

Official Retaliation: Gram Sabhas Targeted

The contest over control of forests in many forest areas further soured the relationship between forest villagers and forest department; repression against forest dwellers increased. In December 2008, the Government of West Bengal issued a new circular legitimizing JFM in the post-FRA situation. The circular violated the major provisions and principles of

FRA (particularly section 5, and nearly all forest rights mentioned under section 3.1, including community rights). The new JFM order reduced forest rights to "usufructs" provided by forest department and said that even those "usufructs" could not be collected from protected areas.

Joint Forest Management Committees (JFMCs) set up under the JFM program were being increasingly used to mobilize non-forest village populations against the forest village gram sabhas (Uttar Banga Van-Jan Shromojibi Manch, 2014). The department threatened to withhold the Government of India funds earmarked for forest village development and other government funds, until such time JFMCs were formed in forest villages and gram sabha's ban on clearfelling was revoked (Bannerjee and Ghosh, 2010). In Coochbehar forest division, the department actually suspended release of development funds under the forest village development scheme until the villagers withdrew the timber-felling ban in the contested forests (Bannerjee and Ghosh, 2010; Jha, 2010a, 2010b).

In Coochbehar and Kurseong forest divisions, actors other than the forest department also opposed gram sabhas' initiatives. These included timber merchants, local timber mafia, contractors and traders transporting and trading in forest produces, and political parties (Jha, 2010a, 2010b). In early 2010, several criminal cases were lodged against the leaders of the movement at Chilapata area in Coochbehar forest division and police raided forest villages of the area to arrest the alleged "criminals" who only tried to implement the FRA. While the arrests were averted, the legal cases still continue (NFFPFW–NBRC and UBVJSM, 2010–2014). More cases were started in 2011, and then again in 2013 and 2014, as the gram sabhas in Coochbehar forests refused to allow the departmental logging operations.

Part C: Whither Forest Villagers' Movement?

The Challenges in the New Scenario of Community-governed Forests

Establishing community control in North Bengal forests has not been a smooth process. Both the government administration and the political parties opposed it, and, despite great show of organizational strength in recent years and entrenched resistance, the new movement could not detoxify the collective psyche of forest villagers of its ingrained fear of authority. For thousands of villagers, more so those living in geographically isolated places, the FRA with its empowering provisions meant little, unless communicated explicitly by "officials," including those in forest department.

Also, there are issues of livelihood: a community conserved forest means voluntary withdrawal from all activities that might harm it, by every member of the concerned community. In many forest villages across North Bengal, this translates into starvation. Extraction of timber and firewood, and their subsequent sale, continues to be the main livelihood for a great number of forest villagers in the plains, as well as others living outside the forest area but accessing forest produce. There is a notion that because a community forest will make people the owners, trees can no longer be cut at will. In Nimati forest village in Buxa Tiger Reserve, for instance, successive gram sabha meeting had failed to have quorum in 2012 and early 2013; villagers thought that the gram sabha would stop them from cutting gutkhas (whole logs cut into smaller rounded pieces to make carrying easier). Inversely, a government forest belongs to nobody and, therefore, is free to be cut. There is also the fact that FRA is silent about community rights over timber—a situation that perpetually provokes conflict wherever gram sabhas exercise their powers and rights. A section of villagers still look toward the resumption of regular wage-work in forests as a pre-condition for withdrawing from unofficial logging. As Naren Rava puts it:[23]

> If the department doesn't employ us ... say begar ... say with wages ... how can we maintain our families? How can we feed our children? Or how can we give them ... education? And how shall we clothe them? Therefore ... in case of need, the trees our forefathers and we ourselves planted and nurtured have to be felled ... we have to steal if necessary! Why? Because we have to keep going ... and ... bring up our kids.... You give us work ... work in the plantations.

Tenural right over lands, which are badly fragmented and could at best support uncertain returns, that too only in cases where there are cash crops, is not seen as a substitute of cash wages. Communities living in forest villages have not been able to understand the future values that a community conserved forest may contain, let alone looking forward to monetary gains from those. What matters is that timber, the most economically valued species, cannot be harvested now. For a community hopelessly locked in the past, this is the overwhelmingly dominant issue.

Challenges of New Environmental Markets

The forest villagers' movement in North Bengal considers itself to be politically sensitive, implying that the social collective is aware of not only its own immediate political realities, but also the new neoliberal political economy of forests. This neoliberal environmental economy of natural capital and TEEB (the economy of environment and biodiversity)[24] has been unraveling for the last 10–15 years (MacDonald and Corson, 2012; Sukhdev et al., 2010), since multilateral agencies like the World Bank and its partners like ADB and others have begun promoting that tropical forests have to be preserved and not logged (Chomitz, 2000; Constanza et al., 1997; Ghosh, 2004; Landen-Mills and Porras, 2002; Pandey and Wheeler, 2001; Totten, 1999; World Bank, 2003). Ironically, this is inverse of the 1991 forest policy of the World Bank, which had emphasized logging (all forestry projects originating from the Bank and its allies, included those in India that helped institutionalize JFM, had logging at the core; World Bank, 2005). This is also a significant departure from the main and accepted use of forests in all industrial civilizations in the global North and emerging economies in the global South alike.

It is ironic that the movement, and the community conservation efforts in North Bengal (and in all such places where organized logging continuing for nearer two centuries had decimated original forests and also disrupted the synergy between forest communities and forests), has to be cognizant of this new discourse that discovers and values new environmental commodities in the old forests. Without an understanding of such values and linking the livelihood crisis with those, even a politically sincere and committed effort to establish a community regime over the already highly commodified and contested forests will not be possible.

Until the turn of the century, forests used to be seen either as reclaimable land, which could be put to other economically profitable use such as agriculture, industry, roads, townships, and so on, or, in the case of "good" forests, a bunch of trees waiting to be logged. Continued and large-scale depletion of forests, however, also meant the release of huge quantities of carbon dioxide into an atmosphere already oversaturated with it. This is better avoided in a scenario where global warming induced climate change is already happening, and yet the extraction and use of fossil fuels like coal and oil, the main agents behind global warming, cannot be scaled down or reduced without badly compromising the formula of uninterrupted economic growth, and thus in turn undermining the basis of capitalist economy (Gibertson and Reyes, 2009; Heynen et al., 2007; Lohmann, 2006).

Erecting new forest enclosures for logging and the official conservation process remained firm allies throughout the history of Indian forests. Conservation of forests was necessary for homogenizing them in the interests of enhanced productivity, in other words, logging. Rights and access of communities over forests were mapped and denied so that logging operations could continue. Workers' colonies such as forest villages were set up, once again for logging, and the notion of participatory management was invoked so that there is no dearth of free forest labor even in situations where either captive labor pools do not exist or labor costs were otherwise too high to make commercial logging unviable. JFM allowed for a community share of the timber revenue only in cases where the community has successfully conserved forests for at least five to ten years.

The neoliberal environmental market place conceptualized and invented new commodities where the "labor"—as in forest villages and JFM—no longer showed at all. According to the 2002 forest strategy of the World Bank, this new process of commodification was meant to benefit the forest-dependent communities, especially the poor. The commodities did not look like the old ones: for instance, carbon sequestered and stored in forest ecosystems (now known as "carbon sinks") were measured, priced, and sold. In real terms, however, what has been transacted is not carbon, but the guarantee that it would not "leak" into the atmosphere as CO_2, due to deforestation.

Apart from carbon sequestration, other marketable environmental services in forests include "hydrological services" like flow regulation (control of run-off water, streams, and rivers—to control flooding), maintenance of water quality (controlling pollutants and thus guiding/determining the uses of water—fisheries, drinking water, water for agricultural and industrial use) and water table regulation (maintaining the water table on a certain level). Then there are direct biodiversity services: medicines, plant derivatives and other non-timber forest produces; and indirect services: forests influencing agriculture, generating "social values" such as recreation and spiritual and cultural benefits—all providing space for development of tourism (Constanza et al., 1997; Landen-Mills and Porras, 2002; World Bank, 2003).

What Do the New Markets Mean for Forest Communities?

Who owns the services and values the forests contain? Who decides what, when, and where to market? Who collars the returns? In India, the answer is: the forest department. The process of valuing forests in terms of their environmental services has been in vogue since 2006, when the expert committee appointed by the Supreme Court of India to determine the net present value of Indian forests submitted its report, and the state forest departments are the end recipients of the huge money that has been accumulating in the CAMPA (compensatory afforestation management and planning authority) fund (Kohli et al., 2011). Besides this, a number of submissions made by the Government of India in various international forums, and to UNFCCC, also make it clear that the forest department will continue to "preserve and manage" forests. They will do so in a participatory manner, it is said, and in the interests of community. The submissions contained various contradictory estimates about monetary values of existing and nonexisting forest carbon and the projected sequestration potential of proposed new plantations. The pick of these has been the $20 billion claim India made to UNFCCC as compensation for preserving its forests (Ghosh, 2011).

India has also developed a Green India Mission (GIM), as part of its 2008 climate action plan. This mission states that community institutions like gram sabhas would play a pivotal role and the rights under the FRA will be a critical component of the mission. GIM is a ₹44,000 crore re-greening project that seeks to preserve forest carbon and enhance carbon sequestration, besides conserving other services/values of the forests in the interest of forest dependent communities.

A continued slump in global carbon market ensures that India's present position has moved away from carbon market-centric forest conservation that the global Reduction of Emission from Deforestation and Degradation (REDD) mechanism prescribes. India now lobbies for REDD+ model of compensated conservation, and REDD++ model of reduction of deforestation by enhancing environmental services the forests provide to communities (Ghosh, 2011).

This new found community-centrism in the Indian Government's policy approach in the forestry sector disguises a range of threats for the communities who are already in control of their forest resources or trying to gain control. All variants of REDD, carbon market-centric or not, mean absolute commodification of forests, and, in a market-friendly neoliberal policy regime, pose the biggest challenge today to communities owning and governing forests.

The main danger in any neoliberal marketplace is privatization. So far, Indian forests had failed to attract private investment mainly because of policy deterrents. Through a series of legislations such as Indian Forest Act 1927, Forest Conservation Act 1980, and Wild Life Protection Act 1972 and 2003, the state managed to retain its hegemonic control over all forest land. This did not allow for any business partnerships or alliances, other than those on a purely bilateral level, where the state continues to be the dominant partner. External funding to the forestry sector has so far been bilateral, and includes World Bank funding for projects under Joint Forest Management/Community Forest Management/Eco-development in Protected Areas. Though these projects continued to receive bank funds, the bank knew well that (World Bank, 2001, 2005) its projects did not change the prevailing forest governance mechanisms. The state (the forest department) remained the sole manager and governor of forests. Because communities gained no tangible benefits or greater access to forests, deforestation was neither slowed nor halted (Springate-Baginski and Blaikie, 2007; World Rainforest Movement et al., 2005).

This then called for radical departures from older models of bilateral funding. Here the state had to relinquish, or significantly reduce, its control over natural resources, if the existing forests in the country have any role to play in the global carbon/ecosystem services trade. Also, large quantity of land with forest humus has to be made available to the private sector investors to raise plantations or "new-growth forests" and, alternately, to conserve the existing forests (Baltodano, 2011; Ghosh, 2004, 2011; McAfee and Shapiro, 2010; McCarthy et al., 2012; Milne and Adams, 2012; World Bank, 2005).

Threat of Disempowerment and Disguised Coercion

Ground experiences from a number of countries, including India, suggest that the neoliberal environmentalism only marginalize and disempower forest communities further (Gibertson and Reyes, 2009; Ghosh, 2004;

McCarthy et al., 2012; Milne and Adams, 2012; Lohmann, 2006). It can be expected that in the days to come a consortium of forest/plantation companies, NGOs, certification agencies, local political leaders, and elites will replace the state as future governors and managers of the Indian forests. This is already happening in several parts of Andhra Pradesh where, even without proper legislative sanction, large tracts of community-tilled agricultural lands and commons were first reclaimed under the World Bank funded CFM project for raising new plantations with corporate funds (Lohmann, 2006; Samata, 2005a, 2005b), and later under carbon plantations raised under a forestry CDM project by Indian Corporate major ITC, and also a Bank funded "rural livelihoods" project in Andhra and neighboring Odisha (Mate and Ghosh, 2011).

From 2002 onwards, the forest department had started floating the concept of Forest Development Agencies (FDAs), which were projected as the highest federated form of JFM. The department said that these would be registered as autonomous societies or federations. Though these agencies have no real control over the forests, they receive central sector funds from all government and bilateral projects directly, and are also free to enter into all sorts of business alliances and partnerships. Because programmes such as JFM and CFM in India are essentially degraded forest regeneration programmes, FDAs offer an opportunity for direct forestry sector investments, especially in plantation projects. FDAs have been projected as nodal agencies in the GIM and the fund disbursal of the mission would be overseen by those.

This is not to say that gram sabhas can and will not enter into similar business arrangements in community-controlled situations. Unless gram sabhas are backed by strong social movements and are united and firm in their rejection of forestry projects that can eventually lead to privatization of forests, forest communities and their forests will continue to remain vulnerable.

In the context of North Bengal forests in the FRA implementation stage, FDAs, and the meagre funds they now control, have repeatedly been used by the forest department in dividing and sabotaging the forest villagers' movement. In Kodal Basti, new JFMCs had been formed in early 2012 and then again in 2015, despite the visible presence of a gram sabha. The reason was that money that flew through FDA: the department now makes signing of an agreement between the JFMC and the concerned FDA mandatory. The agreement spells out that noncompliance with the instructions of the FDA would result in the withdrawal of all development programmes; money earmarked for one village can be transferred to another in such instances.[25]

There are other, internal dangers as well. One reason why the department succeeded in forming the JFMC in Kodal Basti in 2012 was the alleged misappropriation of some money meant for the gram sabha by leaders of the Chilapata forest movement. The money raised through selling of firewood lots and allotted to the gram sabha by the local forest ranger (without any paperwork and without mentioning gram sabha anywhere) could not be accounted for. Villagers later alleged that this was apparently part of the department's strategy to weaken the gram sabha. Besides the firewood, the ranger also offered some of the leaders a piece of forest land and free timber to go with it, to start a restaurant in 2012. Although this was originally meant to be an initiative of the gram sabha, ownership had passed into the hands of three–four youths from the area, who had to leave the movement.

If this could happen at Kodal Basti, a stronghold of the Chilapata movement, there is enough reason to believe that other gram sabhas could face similar issues. The changed production relations in community controlled forests might not resist the process of commodification. The forest department can continue operating, with a judicious mix of bribes and coercion at one level, or the community leaders could themselves turn into traders and contractors.

We are still talking about small money here, in the present context of North Bengal forests. Given the already recorded experiences of Payment for Ecosystem Services (PES) and REDD programmes from a number of countries (Fletcher, 2012; McAfee and Shapiro, 2010; McCarthy et al., 2012; Milne and Adams, 2012). One can only guess the damage that GIM and REDD mechanisms might do (Ghosh, 2011; Kohli and Menon, 2011), or what can happen after the operationalization of TEEB.

Conclusion

The forest movement in North Bengal had been aware of the changed dynamics in the political economy of Indian forests, and the challenges related to that. The Takdah meeting of 2008 concluded:

> the only way to stop imminent privatization/commodification of forests and resources is to reclaim and reinvent forest/village commons, and establish social control over such areas.

The meeting pointed out that a range of new values have to be identified in the old "logging" forests, and for this new processes need to start. The political purpose/relevance of these processes were twofold and manifest, said the meeting: the forests first need to be enriched in usable values for the community for a meaningful community governance process to start, especially considering that the entire North Bengal forests had been badly mauled in the forestry practices continuing for about last two centuries, and that in many areas standing forests contain only timber-bearing monoculture plantations. Second, robust community processes can not only successfully resist local timber mafia and forest department's unsustainable operations, but also dubious international processes like REDD in the long run.

The movement in North Bengal has tried to develop an institutional mechanism which would consider the socio-ecological and economic needs of the forest communities according to their varied cultural profiles. The primary objective will be to resist the unequal social system of resource allocation and control hitherto used by the forest bureaucracy; this, the movement argues, will obstruct the systematic neoliberal commodification of forest resources (Jha, 2010a, 2010b).

It will be premature—and perhaps unwise also—to say whether and for how long the movement could continue to resist commodification. At the moment, one can only say that the movement has created a new space for political mobilization for some of the most marginalized and deprived people in the country. More importantly, it attempted to go beyond traditional political party lines, and their trade-union based struggles, which often get sucked into the mainstream, and later co-opted by state.

Notes

1. At least one British forester, E O Shebbeare recognized the yeomen's service that the forest workers provided to the "empire." He lamented that the government could not do anything for them. See Shebbeare (1945).
2. "A commodity is, in the first place, an object outside us, a thing that satisfies human wants of some sort or another," said Karl Marx, in the first volume of *Das Kapital*. A commodity has to be a product of labor, something abstract and not in sight, said Marx. Labor is embodied in commodities, as value, he showed, and went on to say that "all commodities are definite masses of congealed labor time."
3. The only notable exception is Karlsson (2000).
4. *Begar* was a system of compulsory free labor that was in vogue until as late as the 1970s.
5. See various *Working Plans*, of Buxa, Darjeeling and Jalpaiguri forest Divisions, 1920–1990.
6. Interview with the author, June 15, 2010.
7. Interview with the author, August 8, 2009.

8. Various interviews with villagers at *Paintishe Permanen* and Daling, 2006–2007
9. Directorate of Forests, Government of West Bengal (2002). People in Darjeeling Hills calls the forest corporation (WBFDC) a forest destruction corporation.
10. Interview with the author, August 10, 2009.
11. Interview with the author, August 10, 2009.
12. "Faltu" is a colloquial term coined by forest officers to segregate the villagers not registered with the department under "service *jaigir*" agreements.
13. Interviews with various forest staff and forest villagers: 1994–2014.
14. Jha (forthcoming) tells the history of the anti-*begar* movement.
15. Interview with the author, June 2010.
16. Memo No. 4744-For/Con.6/70, dated September 28, 1970 to The Chief Conservator of Forests, Northern Circle, from P K Rakshit, Deputy Secretary, Government of West Bengal.
17. Conversations with Ramesh Roy, 2004–2008 and other leaders of forest villagers, such as Prem Khawas, the founding Secretary of Himalayan Forest Villagers Union.
18. Minutes of the Meeting, signed by the PCCF, West Bengal, dated June 30, 2002.
19. Minutes of discussions, the inaugural conference of Uttar Banga Van-Jan Shromojibi Manch, 2014.
20. Interview with Prem Khawas, 2005.
21. Conversations with Prem Khawas, the founding Secretary of Himalayan Forest Villagers Union, 2000–2001.
22. In January 2005, this author's name was proposed as one of the nonofficial members of the drafting committee for FRA. Though this invitation could not be taken up because NFFPFW (the author was a member of the National Steering Committee) was not formally involved, the author kept in touch with various members of the committee, and was in a position to contribute substantially to the draft that came out from the first meetings. The draft underwent enormous changes in the subsequent two years, and yet, surprisingly, the formulation on forest villages was not disturbed.
23. Interview with the author, June 15, 2010.
24. See the Natural Capital Declaration (NCD) in www.naturalcapitaldeclaration.org. This was an initiative by large businesses, and the declaration came out just before the inaugural World Forum for Natural Capital in November 2013. See www.teebweb.org for TEEB studies on valuation of various environmental services. TEEB is currently being managed by United Nations Environment Programme (UNEP), after being officially adopted at CBD COP (Convention on Biological Diversity, 2010, Conference of Interested Parties).
25. Various interviews with villagers, Kurseong, Jalpaiguri and Coochbehar Forest Divisions, 2008–2013.

References

Arnold, D. and Guha, R. eds. (1999). *Nature, Culture, Imperialism: Essays on the Environmental History of South Asia*. New Delhi: Oxford University Press.

Baltodano, J. (2011). Plunging over the Climate Crisis Cliff. In *No REDD, A Reader*, Carbon Trade Watch and Indigenous Environmental Network, 2011. Available at: http://noredd. makenoise.org/ (Accessed on November 29, 2015).

Banerjee, A., Ghosh, S., and Springate-Baginski, O. (2010). *Obstructed Access to Forest Justice in West Bengal: State Violations in the Mis-Implementation of the Forest Rights Act 2006.* IPPG Discussion Papers. Available at: http://www.ippg.org.uk/papers/dp49.pdf (accessed on November 27, 2015).

CSD, Campaign for Survival and Dignity (2004). *Endangered Symbiosis: Evictions and India's Forest Communities.* Report of the Jan Sunwai (Public Hearing), Delhi.

Chomitz, K. (2000). *Arguments For and Against Forest Carbon Offsets: An Analytic Note,* Development Research Group, World Bank, 2000.

Cederlof, G. and Sivaramskrishnan, K. (Eds.). (2005). *Ecological Nationalisms.* Delhi: Permanent Black.

Costanza, R., D'arge, R., Groot, R.E., Stephen, F., Grasso, M., Hannon, B., Limburg, K., et al. (1997). The value of the world's ecosystem services and natural capital. *Nature, 387*(1), 253–260.

Colchester, M. (2003). *Salvaging Nature: Indigenous People, Protected Areas and Biodiversity Conservation.* World Rainforest Movement & Forest Peoples Programme, Montevideo, Uruguay and Moreton-in-Marsh, UK.

Colchester, M. and Lohmann, L. (Eds.). (1993). *The Struggle for Land and the Fate of the Forests.* Penang: The World Rainforest Movement, The Ecologist and Zed Books.

Colchester, M. and Lohmann, L. (Eds.). (2005). The struggle for land and the fate of the forests. In *The World Rainforest Movement.* Penang: The Ecologist and Zed Books.

Dash, A. J. (1947). *Bengal District Gazetteer, Darjeeling.* Calcutta: Bengal Secretariat Press.

Directorate of Forests, Government of West Bengal. (1971). *Working Plan for Jalpaiguri Forest Division, 1960–70,* Calcutta.

_____. (1983). *Working Plan for Jalpaiguri Forest Division, 1970–80,* Kolkata.

_____. (2002). *State Forest Report, West Bengal, 2001,* Kolkata.

_____. (1968–69 to 2003–4). *Annual Reports of Forest Administration and State of Forest Report for West Bengal,* Calcutta.

_____. (2012). *State of Forest Report, West Bengal, 2010–11,* Kolkata.

Dutta, S.K. (1934). *Second Working Plan, Kurseong Forest Division.* Calcutta: B. G. Press.

FSI, Forest Survey of India, Eastern Zone (1987). *Result of Plantation Inventory in Darjeeling and Kalimpong Divisions of West Bengal.* Calcutta: Forest Survey of India.

Fletcher, R. (2012). Using the master's tools? Neoliberal conservation and the evasion of inequality. *International Institute of Social Studies, Development and Change, 43*(1), 295–317.

Gadgil, M. and Guha, R. (1992). *This Fissured Land: An Ecological History of India.* New Delhi: Oxford University Press.

_____. (1995). *Ecology and Equity.* New Delhi: Oxford University Press.

Ghosh, S. (2000). *Uttarbanga Prakriti o Paribesh, in Bipanna Paribesh, An Anthology of Environmental Reports and Articles.* Kolkata.

_____. (2001). "Forest Villages: Struggle for Identity and Dignity" theme paper presented in the National Conference of Forest Villages, Sukna, Darjeeing, 2001.

_____. (2004). *Climate Change and the Market Politics of Environment.* Nagpur: NFFPFW.

_____. (2007). *Commons Lost and "Gained"? Forest Tenures in the Jungle Mahals of South West Bengal.* Overseas Development Group, University of East Anglia, Norwich, United Kingdom.

_____. (2011). REDD+ in India, and India's first REDD+ project: A critical examination. *Mausam, 3*(1): 6–11. Available at: http://www.thecornerhouse.org.uk/resource/mausam-0 (Accessed on November 30, 2015).

Ghosh, S., Yasmin, H., and Das, A. (2011). Imaginary sinks: India's REDD ambitions, in NFFPFW, NESPON and DISHA. In *Indian CDM, Subsidizing and Legitimizing Corporate Pollution*. DISHA, Kolkata. Available at: http://www.thecornerhouse.org.uk/sites/thecornerhouse.org.uk/files/The%20Indian%20CDM.pdf   (Accessed   on   November 30, 2015).

Gibertson, T. and Reyes, O. (2009). *Carbon Trading, Why It Works and Why It Fails*. Uppsala: Dag Hammarskjold Foundation.

Government of Bengal (1919). *Annual Progress Report of Forest Administration of Revenue Forest in Bengal, 1918*. Calcutta: Bengal Secretariat Press.

Gruning, J.F. (1911). *Eastern Bengal and Assam District Gazetteers, Jalpaiguri*. Allahabad: Pioneer Press.

Homfray, C.K. (1931). *4th Working Plan of the Reserved Forests of the Buxa Division: Vol. 1*. Calcutta: Bengal Secretariat Press.

Hooker, J. 1854. *Himalayan Journals*. London: John Murray.

Hunter, W.W. 1876. *A Statistical Account of Bengal, Volume 10, Darjeeling, Jalpaiguri and the State of Cooch Behar*. London: Trubner & Co.

Heynen, N., McCarthy, J., Prudham, S. and Robbins, P. (Eds.). (2007). *Neoliberal Environments*. London: Routlege.

Jha, S. (2005). *Forest Dwellers Movement in North Bengal: A Perspective on Citizen Action Against the State*. Draft paper for presentation in the 3rd International Conference on Citizenship and Governance, organized by Participatory Research in Asia, New Delhi, 8–10th Feb, 2005, Banaras Hindu University, U.P.

———. (2010a). Process betrays the spirit: Forest Rights Act in Bengal." *Economic and Political Weekly*, XLV (33), August 2010.

———. (2010b). The struggle for democratizing forests: The Forest Rights Movement in North Bengal, India." *Social Movement Studies*, 9 (4), 469–474, November 2010.

———. (forthcoming). Situating Resistance Below: Praxis and Empowerment in Movements."

Karlson, K.B. (1999). Ecodevelopment in practice, Buxa Tiger Reserve and Forest People." *Economic and Political Weekly*, 34(30), 2087–2094.

———. (2000). *The Contested Belongings*. London: Curzon Books..

Kohli, K. and Menon, M. (2011). *Banking on Forests: Assets for a Climate Cure?* New Delhi: Kalpavriksh and Heinrich Boll Foundation.

Kohli, K., Menon, M., Samdariya, V., and Guptabhaya, S. (2011). *Pocketful of Forests: Legal Debates on Valuating and Compensating Forest Loss in India*. New Delhi: Kalpavriksh & WWF–India.

Lama, S.D. (1999). Vegetation Survey in the Forests under Senchal Wild Life Sanctuary. Unpublished Paper, Darjeeling.

Landell-Mills, N. and Porras. I.T. (2002). *Silver Bullet or Fools' Gold? A Global Review of Markets for Forest Environmental Services and Their Impact on the Poor*. London: IIED.

Laveleye, E. de. 1878. *Primitive Property*. London: Macmillan and Co.

Lillingston, C.A.G. 1899. *First Working Plan for the Forest of Teesta Valley Range, Darjeeling Forest Division, Bengal, by DCF* (Revised by F B Manson, 1897). Calcutta: Bengal Secretariat Press..

Locke, J. ([1690] 1952). *The Second Treatise of Government*. New York: Macmillan

Lochan, K. (1999). *Under the Green Shadow*. Gorakhpur: Vikalp.

Lohmann, L. (2006). *Carbon Trading: A Critical Conversation on Climate Change, Privatisation and Power*. Development Dialogue: 48. Uppsala: Dag Hammarskjold Foundation.

Leeds, H. (1869). *Proceedings of the, Lt. Governor of Bengal* (Revenue Department Forests) 1869. Calcutta: Bengal Secretariat Press.

Marx, K. ([1887] 1954). *Capital Vol. I.* Moscow: Progress Publishers.

MacDonald, K. and Corson, C. (2012). TEEB Begins Now: A Virtual Moment in the Production of Natural Capital." *Development and Change, 43*(1), 159–184.

Mate, N. and Ghosh, S. (2011). *The Fraud by the Name of Carbon Forestry*, in NFFPFW, NESPON and DISHA, *Indian CDM, Subsidizing and Legitimizing Corporate Pollution.* DISHA, Kolkata, available at http://www.thecornerhouse.org.uk/sites/thecornerhouse. org.uk/files/The%20Indian%20CDM.pdf.

McAfee, K. and Shapiro, E.N. (2010). Payments for ecosystem services in Mexico: Nature, neoliberalism, social movements, and the state. *Annals of the Association of American Geographers, 100*(3), 577–599.

McCarthy, J.F., Jacqueline, V., and Suraya, A. (2012). Trajectories of land acquisition and enclosure: development schemes, virtual land grabs, and green acquisitions in Indonesia's outer islands. *Journal of Peasant Studies, 39*(2), 521–549.

Milne, S. and Adams, S. (2012). Market masquerades: Uncovering the politics of community-level payments for environmental services in Cambodia. *Development and Change (hereafter DAC), 43*(1), 133–158.

NFFPFW, National Forum of Forest People and Forest Workers (2001). *Status Report on Indian Forest Workers*, National Forum of Forest People and Forest Workers, Delhi.

_____. (2002). *The Struggle of Indian Forest Workers and Voices from the Forests*, National Forum of Forest People and Forest Workers, Nagpur.

NFFPFW–NBRC (2005). *Report of the 2nd Conference held at Rajabhatkhawa on March 31 and April 1, 2005.*

NFFPFW–NBRC and later Uttar Banga Van-Jan Shromijivi Mancha-UBVJSM (2010–2014 February). *Various Press Notes, Memorandums and Letters to Governmental Authorities Between 2010 April to 2014 February.*

NESPON (2000). *Combating Deforestation: A Note on North Bengal Forests*, Paper Presented in a Conference on Forest Protection and People's Rights on April 15, Siliguri.

_____. (2001). *A Study on JFM in North Bengal.* Siliguri: NESPON.

NESPON, DISHA and NFFPFW (2005). *Plight of the Forest People, Report of Public Hearing in Buxa Tiger Reserve*, Kolkata.

O'Malley, L.S.S. (1907). *Darjeeling District Gazetteer.* Calcutta: Bengal Secretariat Press.

Osmaston, D.B. (1906). *Working Plan for the Reserved Forests of Darjeeling Division* (Revised). Calcutta: Bengal Secretariat Press.

Pandey, K.D. and Wheeler, D. (2001). *Structural Adjustment and Forest Resources.* Policy Research Working Paper 2584. The World Bank Development Research Group.

Prasad, R.R. and Jahagirdar, M.P. (1993). *Tribal Situation in Forest Villages.* Delhi: Discovery Publication Houses.

Proceedings of the, Lt. Governor of Bengal (Revenue Department Forests). (1870–71 to 1910). Calcutta: Bengal Secretariat Press.

Pyne, S.J. (1995). *World Fire: The Culture of Fire on Earth.* Paperback ed. Washington, DC: University of Washington Press.

Ramade, F. (1984). *Ecology of Natural Resources.* Chicester and New York: John Wiley and Sons.

Rangarajan, M. (1996). *Fencing the Forest.* New Delhi: Oxford University Press.

Saberwal, V.K. and Rangarajan, M. (Eds.). (2003). *Battles over Nature: Science and the Politics of Conservation.* Delhi: Permanent Black.

Samata Social Organization (2005a). Joint Forest Management, A Critique Based on People's Perceptions, Hyderabad. Can be accessed at http://www.samataindia.org.in.

_____. (2005b). *Andhra Pradesh Community Forest Management Project: A preliminary independent evaluation of a World Bank forestry project.* Forest People's Programme, Moreton-in-Marsh, UK. Can be accessed at http://www.samataindia.org.in.

Sen, S. (1916). *The Bengal Tenancy Act, with Notes, Rules etc.* Calcutta: M.C. Sarkar and Sons.

Shankar, U., Lama, S.D., and Bawa, K.S. (1998). Ecosystem reconstruction through 'taungya' plantations following commercial logging of a dry, mixed deciduous forest in Darjeeling Himalaya. *Forest Ecology and Management, 102,* 131–142.

Shebbeare, E.O. (1920a). *Working Plan for the Reserved Forest in the Jalpaiguri Division.* Calcutta: Bengal Secretariat Press.

_____. (1920b). *Working Plan for the Reserved Forest in the Buxa Division of the Bengal Forest Circle.* Calcutta: Bengal Secretariat Press.

_____. (1945). Northern Bengal Taungyas. *Empire Forestry Review, 25*(1), 32–35.

Sivaramakrishnan, K. (1999). *Modern Forests: Statemaking and Environmental Change in Colonial Eastern India.* Indiana: Stanford University Press.

Springate-Baginski, O. and Blaikie, P. (Eds.). (2007). *Forests, People and Power: The Political Ecology of Reform in South Asia,* pp. 221–260, 366–383. London: Earthscan.

Sukhdev, P., Wittmer, H., Schröter-Schlaack, C., Nesshöver, C., Bishop, J., Brink, P.T., et al. (2010). The economics of ecosystems and biodiversity: Mainstreaming the economics of nature: A synthesis of the approach, conclusions and recommendations of TEEB. Available at teebweb.org.

Sundar, D.H.E. (1895). *Final Report on the Land Revenue Settlement of the Western Doors, Bengal.* Calcutta: Bengal Secretariat Press.

Sykes Gamble, J. (1873). *General Description of the Mahanuddy Terai and Sevoke Hill Forest Ranges in Annual Progress Report of Forest Administration of Revenue Forest in Bengal* (hereafter *Revenue Report*) 1872–1873. Calcutta: Bengal Secretariat Press.

Totten, M. (1999). *Emerging Markets for Storing Carbon in Forests.* Forest Trends and World Resources Institute, USA.

Uttar Banga Van-Jan Shromojibi Manch (2014). *Proceedings of the Inaugural Conference at Rajabhatkhawa,* February 5–6, 2014.

Waddell, L.A. ([1899] 1998). *Among the Himalayas.* Delhi: Pilgrims Book Pvt. Ltd.

West Bengal Forest Development Corporation Limited (1999). *24th Annual Report: 1998–1999.* Calcutta: West Bengal Forest Development Corporation Limited.

World Bank (2001). *India, Alleviating Poverty through Forest Development.* OED Evaluation Country Case Series, World Bank.

World Bank (2003). *Sustaining Forests: A World Bank Strategy.* Washington, DC: World Bank. http://documents.worldbank.org/curated/en/2003/01/7115219/sustaining-forests-world-bank-strategy

_____. (2005). *Unlocking Opportunities for Forest-Dependent People in India, Volume I: Main Report, 2005.* Washington, DC: World Bank.

World Rainforest Movement, CDM Watch, Forest People's Programme (2005). *Broken Promises: How World Bank Group Policies Fail to Protect Forests and Forest People's Rights.* Can be accessed at http://wrm.org.uy/wp-content/uploads/2013/04/Broken_Promises_How_World_Bank_Group_policies_and_practice_fail_to_protect_forests_and_forest_peoples_rights.pdf.

8

Putting Peoplehood at the Center of the Green Economy

Sanjay Kabir Bavikatte and Daniel F. Robinson

In the language of my people ... there is a word for land: Eloheh. This same word also means history, culture and religion. We cannot separate our place on earth from our lives on the earth nor from our vision nor our meaning as people. We are taught from childhood that the animals and even the trees and plants that we share a place with, are our brothers and sisters. So when we speak of land, we are not speaking of property, territory, or even a piece of ground upon which our houses sit and our crops are grown. We are speaking of something truly sacred.

—Peter Mathiessen quoting Jimmie Durham, a Cherokee litigant in a sacred sites case (Mathiessen, 1984)

Jimmie Durham viewed his personhood and the Cherokee peoplehood as integrally tied to the land. He was unable to conceive of the land as separate from whom he is as a person and who the Cherokee are as a people. He echoes the voices of some indigenous peoples and traditional communities who, when eclipsed by the market economy, articulate their alienation by asking, "how did land become property, trees become lumber, knowledge become intellectual property, life become genetic resources?" The questions posed by these communities make stark the central problem in the green economy paradigm,[1] which is one of universal commodification, that is, that everything can be valued in economic terms and can be bought and sold.

The problem of commodification in the context of the green economy is triggered when a monetary value is put on nature by categorizing it as "natural capital."

Commodification involves both valuation and the change in relationships between things and people into commercial relationships. It is just one of a number of processes that are commonly described as being part of a process of "neoliberalization," which is a trend toward adoption of neoclassical economic concepts (discussed later) by various societal and political actors. The valuing of nature in economic terms seeks to understand it as a "scarce good" in the wake of its unprecedented destruction. Economists argue that "open access" to nature's "resources" occurs because either property rights do not exist or are easily challenged (Turner et al., 1994). Others are critical of this depiction, and suggest that often these environments and resources have been regulated through customary laws and rules and may be seen as "communally owned" rather than privately or state-owned. The poor recognition of customary laws of indigenous peoples and local communities (IPLCs) has historical, colonial, and political underpinnings (which we will return to). It is important that when processes of valuation of nature occur, that they account for customary laws and other concepts of "property" (e.g., communal), and in recent years there have been many IPLCs involved in international and national-level negotiations to assert such resistances— some quietly, and some more vocal.

The green economy paradigm attempts to take nature out of the realm of "open access" and ensure that the services provided by nature are accounted for in every commercial transaction. The goal of the green economy is to put nature's services on the ledger and thereby limit its abuse, or (re)regulate its use, and generate finances for its conservation. In order to do this, the green economy model has spawned several new financing mechanisms for conservation such as the Nagoya Protocol on Access and Benefit Sharing (ABS)[2] and other emerging environmental regulatory frameworks like Reducing Emissions from Deforestation and Forest Degradation (REDD+)[3] and Payments for Environmental Services (PES).[4]

The valuing of nature might also be thought of as part of a "marketization" process. This valuation has been criticised for many reasons, one of which is that it may be seen to be a contributing part of broader neoliberal processes which will ultimately broaden the application of private property rights, impact the state regulation of the environment and resources, and have other impacts (described below). Castree (2008, pp. 142–143) provides an ideal-typical characterization of neoliberalization that provides a useful framing through which to understand the commodification of nature. He identifies the following things as constituting "neoliberalism" when one abstracts from the multiple "neoliberalizations" extant in the world:

- *Privatization* (that is, the assignment of clear private property rights to social or environmental phenomena that were previously state-owned, unowned, or communally owned. New owners of hitherto unprivatized phenomena can potentially come from *anywhere* across the globe).
- *Marketization* (that is, the assignment of prices to phenomena that were previously shielded from market exchange or for various reasons unpriced. These prices are set by markets that are potentially *global* in scale, which is why neoliberalism is often equated with geographically unbounded "free trade").
- *Deregulation* [that is, the "rollback" of state "interference" in numerous areas of social and environmental life so that (a) state regulation is "light touch" and (b) more and more actors become self-governing within centrally prescribed frameworks and rules].
- *Reregulation* (that is, the deployment of state policies to facilitate privatization and marketization of ever-wider spheres of social and environmental life).
- *Market proxies in the residual public sector* (that is, the state-led attempt to run remaining public services along private sector lines as "efficient" and "competitive" businesses).
- *The construction of flanking mechanisms in civil society* [that is, the state-led encouragement of civil society groups (charities, NGOs, "communities," and so on) to provide services that interventionist states did, or could potentially, provide for citizens; these civil society groups are also seen as being able to offer compensatory mechanisms that can tackle any problems citizens suffer as a result of the previous five things listed].

If we view the valuation of nature as part of this broader neoliberal process, questions inevitably arise about the potential for subsequent reregulation that diminishes local access/open access while creating new markets/ valuations that benefits other, more "powerful", actors. There is the potential for this to happen through REDD+ (e.g., through the assigning of protected areas which exclude people) and through ABS (e.g., where there is commonly patenting of genetic resources subsequent to R&D). However, the processes noted above are uneven and often partial, with competing actors and discourses resisting aspects of the deregulation, re-regulation, and marketization of nature that might deliver less typical "neoliberal" outcomes. For example, Bavikatte and Robinson (2011) explain the resistances made by IPLCs in the negotiation of the Nagoya Protocol on ABS, which, while restricted in its language and application, has asserted rights of IPLCs over traditional knowledge associated with genetic resources in ABS transactions. The Nagoya Protocol also encourages recognition and consideration of IPLC customary laws and community protocols and procedures in relation to traditional knowledge associated with genetic resources.[5] The outcomes are often messy, but we argue that subtle resistances can be made to the many "neoliberal" acts and discourses, and that often these resistances reflect a belief in the personhood of Nature, and even at times an embodied personification of its components.[6]

At the heart of the green economy approach to conservation is an assumption about human nature and its drivers, that is, the market (commodification) is the most reliable way to achieve social goals (conservation). This assumption, contrary to Jimmie's worldview, understands personhood as the *homo economicus* (the economic/self-interested man) delinked from the land and views communities (peoplehood) as a collection of commodity owners and consumers coming together for mutual self-interest.[7] The understanding goes all the way back to the foundations of the classical economics of Adam Smith who, in expounding on human nature, asserted in his work *The Wealth of Nations* that, "it is not from the benevolence of the butcher, the brewer, or the baker that we expect our dinner, but from their regard to their self-interest" (1986). Simply put, the advocates of the green economy argue that we have to sell nature in order to save it.[8]

Debates between the proponents and the detractors of the green economy paradigm circle around the question of the limits of commodification. While its proponents blithely argue that everything can be turned into property, its detractors are strident that putting an economic value on nature crowds out other ways of valuing it, such as that of Jimmie's. The detractors believe that it is the valuing and adopting the ways of people like Jimmie and his tribe which will conserve nature in the long run and not markets—in fact what got us here (the destruction of nature by self-interested actions) will not get us out of here (the conservation of nature through financial incentives). Both proponents and detractors, however, base their arguments on certain unqualified assumptions and caricature each other's positions, hence stymying the possibility of any clear resolution.

In this chapter we will endeavor to solve the central problem of the green economy by answering the question concerning the limits of commodification and the nature of property. In order to do this we will interrogate the dominant assumptions regarding personhood and the nature of markets. Through this we will propose a "better" approach to personhood and peoplehood that engages with the green economy without being made in its image. As a first step, the next section will attempt to historicize the *homo economicus* and make the claims of its naturalness suspect.

The Unnaturalness of the Market Values

> Homo economicus is not behind us, but before, like the moral man, the man of duty, the scientific man and the reasonable man. For a long time man was something quite different; and it is not so long now since he became a machine-a calculating machine.
>
> —Marcel Mauss, *The Gift: Forms and Functions of Exchange in Archaic Societies* (1967, p. 74)

Adam Smith's *The Wealth of Nations* (1986) was published in England in 1776. The impact of this text cannot be overestimated since it laid the foundations of the market economy, and its ramifications are felt to this day. The market economy is rooted in the idea of a self-regulating system or, in Adam Smith's terms, "the invisible hand of the market" (2000), which is the synergistic outcome of the interplay of individual self-interest. This person, or the *homo economicus*, is the philosophical cornerstone of the theory of the market economy; it is based on a two-fold assumption that human beings are fundamentally motivated by self-gain and that they behave in a manner to maximize this self-gain.

Adam Smith saw the market economy as a spontaneous and self-regulating manifestation of the self-interested activities of human beings. Based on this understanding of human nature, the only rational economic system of production and distribution we could envisage is one where all activities are motivated by private gain. As Smith says, it is the human being's natural propensity to "truck, barter, and exchange one thing for another"[9] that leads to the development of the market economy.

It was only in 1944 that the assumptions of the *homo economicus* and the "naturalness" of the market economy were fundamentally challenged by the economic historian Karl Polanyi (2000) in his ground breaking work *The Great Transformation*. While Polanyi did not challenge the existence of an economy in all societies, he disagreed with the assertion of a number of economists, that gain or profit-seeking made through commodity exchanges predominated in every society. Polanyi noted that, historically, the production and distribution of goods in societies was rooted in maintaining social relations and affirming community rather than in generating surplus for individual profit. He says:

> The outstanding discovery of recent historical and anthropological research is that man's economy, as a rule, is submerged in his social relationships. He does not act so as to safeguard his individual interest in the possession of material goods; he acts so as to safeguard his social standing, his social claims, his social assets. He values material goods only in so far as they serve this end. Neither the process of production nor that of distribution is linked to specific economic interests attached to the possession of goods; but every single step in that process is geared to a number of social interests which eventually ensure that the required step is taken ... the economic system will be run on noneconomic motives. (2000, p. 44)

Marshall Sahlins in his seminal work *Stone Age Economics* (1972) restates this point by noting that the notion of "economy" should not be understood as something separate from society but rather as:

> [T]he process of provisioning society (or the "socio-cultural system"). No social relation, institution, or set of institutions is of itself "economic." Any institution, say a family or a lineage order, if it has material consequence for provisioning society can be placed in an economic context and considered part of the economic process. The same institution may be equally or more involved in the political process, thus profitably considered as well in a political context. This way of looking at economics or politics—or for that matter, religion, education and any number of other cultural processes—is

dictated by the nature of primitive culture. Here we find no socially distinct "economy" or "government," merely social groups and relations with multiple functions, which we distinguish as economic, political and so forth. (1972, pp. 185–186)

The crucial point made by both Polanyi and Sahlins is that, until the 19th century, contrary to popular myth, the economy was embedded in social relations. The modern phenomena of social relations being embedded in or defined by the economy were strongly resisted by communities in the past (see Smith, 1986).

Production and distribution was not based on the need to create surplus for the purposes of trade and individual gain, but was designed to meet the needs of the community (see generally, Smith, 1986). Hence for Polanyi, the *homo economicus* is a fiction of relatively recent vintage. Ethnographic accounts of production and distribution in traditional societies show that the economy was not based on exchange, but on the principles of householding, reciprocity, and redistribution.

Householding was production for one's own use and was predominant in agricultural rather than hunter and gatherer societies. Householding meant that what one used was not procured through the exchange of surplus for goods that one needed to survive. On the contrary, one produced to meet one's essential needs first, and, only if there was any surplus was it exchanged. The primary motivation for householding was subsistence, not gain. Sufficiency and not profit or accumulation was the ethic (Smith, 1986, pp. 55–59).

Redistribution was based on the ethic of sharing, and was grounded in a pattern Polanyi calls "centricity." A portion of what was produced by the community members was given to a central political authority, such as the chief, who in turn ensured its redistribution, again belying the myth of trucking or haggling for self-gain (Smith, 1986, pp. 59–60). Reciprocity organized around the pattern of "symmetry" is based on the ethic of the caring in the "gift economy" where things were gifted away to the community, the giver secure in the knowledge that the community would at some point in the future reciprocate in equal measure (Balbus, 2009, e-book location, 1801–11).

The ethics of sufficiency, sharing, and caring are all interlinked. They reject avarice, self-interest, and opportunism, the values that undergird the *homo economicus*, as unnatural. On the contrary, these ethics indicate that the glorification of free markets disembodied from social relations is a reality peculiar to capitalist societies. Polanyi highlights the dangers of sacrificing the ethics of care at the altar of accumulation by noting:

> To allow the market mechanism to be sole director of the fate of human beings and their natural environment ... would result in the demolition of society.... Robbed of the protective covering of cultural institutions, human beings would perish from the effects of social exposure.... Nature would be reduced its elements neighbourhoods and landscapes defiled, rivers polluted ... no society could stand the effects of such a system of crude fictions even for the shortest stretch of time unless its human and natural substance as well as its business organization was protected against the ravages of this satanic mill. (Smith, 1986, p. 77)

The transformation of pre-capitalist cultures to cultures where the market economy predominates involves the transformation of the *homo socialis*[10] to the *homo economicus*. This has not been a universal or natural evolution, with obvious resistances and counter-actions. However, through dominant forces, much of it through colonization in recent centuries, pre-capitalist cultures have shifted toward market orientation. Of relevance to ABS for example, it was arguably economic rather than ornamental (and only sometimes purely scientific) imperatives that governed early European study of the rich and "undiscovered" fauna during plant hunting expeditions of the "New World" and much of Asia. During the 17th century, competition between Dutch and British trading companies intensified in the East Indies. These companies sought to establish not just trading posts, but monopolies that required colonies, laws, currency, courts—they were essentially states within states. These colonial impositions have had sustained impacts and have often quite firmly established institutions which support the market economy and ethos of *homo economicus* (see Aitken, 2006; Brierley, 1994; Robinson, 2010).

Furthermore the "gift economy" of communities has been highlighted by ethnographers as perhaps one of the most resounding arguments against the paradigm of the *homo economicus*. Amongst the most written about examples, are those that have been studied by Bronislaw Malinowski. He observes the Kula gift tradition of the Massim peoples of the South Sea Islands near the eastern tip of New Guinea, as embodying some of the most significant values of community (Malinowski, 1922). The continual movement of Kula gifts, as armbands or necklaces, around the Massim archipelago affirmed the leitmotif of the ethic of stewardship through the circle of gift exchange.

Malinowski makes a careful distinction between the Kula gift exchange and barter by arguing:

> The main principle underlying the regulations of actual exchange is that the Kula consists in bestowing of a ceremonial gift that must be repaid by an equivalent counter-gift.... The natives sharply distinguish it from barter which they practice extensively.... Often, when criticizing an incorrect, too hasty, or indecorous procedure of Kula, they will say—"He conducts his Kula as if it were *gimwali* (barter)" ... the equivalence of the counter-gift is left to the giver, and it cannot be enforced by any kind of coercion. (Malinowski, 1954, p. 373)

Making a sharp break from the myth of the *homo economicus*, Malinowski asks, what is it amongst the culture of the Massim people that ensured the counter-gift? To this question, he responds:

> The great misconception of attributing to the savage a pure economic nature, might lead us to reason incorrectly thus-The passion of acquiring, the loathing to lose or give away is the fundamental and most primitive element in man's attitude to wealth.... The fundamental error in this reasoning is that it assumes that "primitive man," as represented by the present day savage, lives, at least in economic matters untrammelled by conventions and social restrictions. Quite the reverse is the case. (1954, p. 374)

Malinowski concludes by emphasizing the strong social obligation to "give" that overrides the economic imperative to "take or keep":

> This (Kula) social code ... lays down that to possess is to be great, and that wealth is the indispensable appanage of social rank and attribute of personal virtue. But the important point is that with them (the Massim) *to possess is to give* (my emphasis)—here the natives differ from us notably. (1954, p. 374)

Every individual who receives a Kula gift is a recipient of an act of generosity and he is therefore a steward of this ethic and must bestow generosity in equal measure on another person. The gift cannot be used as capital nor is it based on a bargain. On the contrary, it is the vehicle through which the individual self-expands into the communal self.

Gift-giving processes can work in any number of ways: it often ties individuals to a group, it can engender certain commitments, it may align different individuals in certain ways politically, or it can be used to define a person's status in a group. For example, Strathern describes a process of gift-giving by Hagen men in Papua New Guinea as a political process through which "specific relations are created, and through relations that persons are defined in respect of one another." Gifts are given (she gives the examples of shells, pigs, or money), with the expectation of a return gift. The men receive valuables in the same way that they give them— they are transactable and therefore travel along relationships, shaping and defining people's status. They can be used as an aggressive political challenge to the recipient to make as good a return later. She goes on to explain that these objects or physical "property" conceal considerable social relations, and indeed the social relations are tied to the objects (Strathern, 1999, pp. 15–15, 36).

This is one example of how a specific cultural group employs gift-giving as a mechanism for asserting individual identity amongst the community. It is employed for hierarchical reasons and is somewhat different to an ethos of accumulation that we see in the way *homo economicus* is enacted, precisely because of the reciprocity entailed in every transaction.

Lewis Hyde in his beautifully written work, *The Gift: How the Creative Spirit Transforms the World* (1983), analyzes the ethos of stewardship that is developed through gift exchange between the Maori and nature. The Maori word *hau* is translated as "spirit," which is the "spirit" of the gift and of the forest that gives food. When hunters return with birds that they have hunted, they give some of the kill to the priests, who cook it over the sacred fire in a ceremony called *whangai hau*, which means nourishing the *hau* or feeding the spirit. They then eat some of it and prepare a talisman, which is called the *mauri*, the physical embodiment of *hau* of the forest. The *mauri* is then given back to the forest, which is believed to cause the birds to be abundant (Hyde, 1983, p. 19).

Hyde emphasizes the point that the movement of the gift has to go beyond the mutual reciprocity of two for it to become an ethic of giving. This ethic is born only when what is valued is shared or given without an immediate expectation of equivalent return. The value of the gift lies in its movement, and the movement of the gift from the forest to the hunters to the priests and back to the forest, expands the tribe to include Nature as a part of the widening, ethical circle. Hyde says:

> Every gift calls for a return gift, and so, by placing the gift back in the forest, the priests treat the birds as a gift of nature. We now understand this to be ecological.... Widening the study of ecology to include man means to look at ourselves as a part of nature again, not its lord.... So the circle is a sign of

an ecological insight as much as of gift exchange. We come to feel ourselves as one part of a large self-regulating system. The return gift, the "nourishing *hau*," is literally feedback, as they say in cybernetics. Without it, that is to say, with the exercise of any greed or arrogance of will, the cycle is broken.... The forest's abundance is in fact a consequence of man's treating its wealth as a gift. (1983, p. 19)

The gift economy is not restricted to the Massim, Hagen, or the Maori. Among the /Xam San of the Northern Cape, if three hunters tracked and killed a springbok, the division of the meat would be made by the other two hunters whose arrows did not make the kill. Lorna Marshall records that with the !Xun-speaking-San of the Nyae Nyae, the hunter was obliged to share the meat with the one who gave him the arrow that secured the kill, who in turn shared the meat with another from whom he received the arrow. She notes that the system of sharing meat and exchanging of arrows ensured that the hunter who made the kill received less meat than those further down the line of distribution, thus affirming the ethic of sharing and caring on which the clan depended. As was pointed out by the missionary Robert Moffat, amongst the /Xam, the one who received food gifts from the Dutch farmers, retained the least for himself and redistributed the rest (Hewitt, 2002, p. 44).

If history and ethnography point that the *homo economicus* is a fiction created by capitalism rather than the cornerstone of personhood, does this undermine the very basis of the green economy? Before we state in the affirmative, we would do well to remember Polaniyi's argument that while social relations eclipsed by market relations is a phenomenon of late capitalism, markets have always had their place in human societies. Nature in this sense has been valued in various ways, but it has also been valued as property, though this latter kind of valuing had its place and was driven by social and not economic goals (as, for example, in the Hagen case described by Strathern). We are surrounded by examples of indigenous peoples and traditional communities engaging with markets, buying and selling the bounties of nature, as has been occurring for centuries. If we think about the earlier description of colonial plant-hunting activities and the establishment of a global spice trade monopolized by European colonizers, clearly this was informed by existing local trade in the source regions of the East Indies (Indonesia) and Malacca (Malaysia), for example. A similar parallel occurs today in the R&D process, with traditional knowledge, practices, and local markets informing scientists about the utility of certain plants, animals, or genetic resources—the ABS process seeks to inter "fairness and equity" into the process and to create a *negotiation* where there formerly might have only been an "extraction."

If anything, these examples caution us against dismissing the green economy out of hand and thereby throwing the proverbial baby out with the bathwater. Instead, we must turn to the deeper question that asks, if we are not the *homo economicus* but have always engaged with markets and commoditized nature, then what is the real complaint of the detractors of the green economy? It is to answer this question that we shall turn to in the next section.

Understanding Personhood

> Most people possess certain objects they feel are almost part of themselves. These objects are closely bound up with personhood because they are part of the way we constitute ourselves as continuing personal entities in the world. They may be different as people are different, but some common examples might be a wedding ring, a portrait, an heirloom, or a house.... The opposite of holding an object that has become a part of oneself is holding an object that is perfectly replaceable with other goods of equal market value. One holds such an object for purely instrumental reasons. The archetype of such a good is, of course, money, which is almost always held to but other things.... Other examples are a wedding ring in the hands of the jeweller, the automobile in the hands of the dealer, the land in the hands of the developer ... I shall call these theoretical opposites-property that is bound up with a person and property that is held purely instrumentally-personal property and fungible property respectively.
>
> —Margaret Jane Radin, *Property and Personhood* (1982, pp. 959–960).

The above excerpt by Margaret Jane Radin, arguably one of the most significant contemporary property jurists, offers us an insight into the critical importance of examining the nature of personhood and developing an understanding of commodification on this basis. Radin works through Polanyi's arguments to their logical conclusion by asking the central question in the green economy debate: What are the moral limits of commodification, or rather, when is property personal and when is it fungible?

By asking this question, Radin was going to the heart of the matter: "human flourishing." Such a flourishing for Radin depended on our understanding of personhood, and thereby an understanding of the distinction between what should be commoditized (fungible property) and what should not be (personal property). From this basis, we could develop a coherent theory for engaging the green economy on what should be "market alienable," that is, freely bought and sold in the market to which an economic rationality can be applied, and what should be "market inalienable," that is, should not be viewed as purely fungible because they are so integral to personhood that a purely economic rationality cannot be applied. Radin makes this point with great clarity when she notes:

> In conceiving of all rights as property rights that can (at least theoretically) be alienated in markets, economic analysis has (at least in principle) invited markets to fill the social universe. It has invited us to view all (market) inalienabilities as problematic.... Indeed I try to show that the characteristic rhetoric of economic analysis is morally wrong when it is put forward as the sole discourse of human life.... I think we should evaluate inalienabilities in connection with our best current understanding of human flourishing. (1987, p. 1851)

The incisiveness of Radin's argument lies in the manner it brings any discourse on commodification back to personhood. Commodification or property for Radin must have a reason, and the only legitimate reason it could have is its contribution to human flourishing or well-being. By putting human flourishing and personhood at the centre of the property discourse, Radin provides us with an ethical compass with which to negotiate the green economy.

In essence, Radin's compass works by asking two questions, the answering of which provides us with an ethical solution to a green economy conundrum. They are: Is a "thing" (be it land, resources, culture and so on) absolutely integral to the flourishing of one's personhood? If so, would the loss of such a thing adversely affect one's personhood or curtail one's flourishing?

Even in circumstances where land or sea is commonly held by a community (as is often the case), it could be argued that personhood still exists in a common claim to that property (used in the broadest sense), its use, and its regulation. This is typified in many countries (e.g., in the Pacific) where customary title exists and there are customary laws and political structures through which the community regulates and manages the land and sea. Their personhood is reflected in the way customary laws are enacted. For example, in Vanuatu there is traditional marine tenure for nearshore reefs and fishing grounds accompanied with associated beliefs and practices that restrict natural resource use by individuals within (and from outside) the community. There are rules surrounding species-specific food avoidance because the species (e.g., a type of fish, turtle, shark, eel, or also other terrestrial species) has an ancestral totemic meaning for a specific family. The death of a chief or clan member can also result in the placing of a taboo on harvest in their family reef out of respect for the deceased (Hickey, 2006). These examples highlight the operation of personhood within the existence of communally regulated sea (and land areas). For people in these communities, the loss of land and species may result in an impact on one's personhood—especially if it is a totemic species, for example. The allocation of additional property rights (or the reification of existing customary rights for the understanding of external researchers), for example, a right to determine if a genetic resource can be used in research, does not necessarily guarantee the protection of that resource or the "fair and equitable" distribution of any benefits derived from it. What has occurred is a "re-regulation" through the Nagoya Protocol which seeks to impose a negotiation and transaction between users and providers through which issues of personhood can be discussed, consent can be granted or denied, and terms for benefit-sharing can be sought. The challenge will be determining who has the "established rights" to grant access to genetic resources (and associated knowledge), which we discuss later in the San–Hoodia ABS case.

Radin concludes that:

> Where we can ascertain that a given property right is personal, there is a prima facie case that that right should be protected to some extent against invasion by government and against cancellation by conflicting fungible property claims of other people. This case is strongest where without the claimed protection of *property as personal* (our emphasis), the claimants' opportunities to become fully developed persons in the context of our society would be destroyed or significantly lessened…. Where we can ascertain that a property right is fungible, there is a prima facie case that that right should yield to some extent in the face of conflicting recognized personhood interests, not embodied in property. This case is strongest where without the claimed *personhood interest* (our emphasis), the claimants opportunity to become fully developed persons in the context of our society would be destroyed or significantly lessened. (Malinowski, 1954, pp. 1014–1015)

Note that Radin makes two critical points here. Firstly, where property claims are personal, the claims should in general override fungible property claims. For example, an individual's property claim to her home should override a real estate developer's claim to the same piece of property. Secondly, even where the claimant may not have a legal property claim, but merely a strong personhood interest, such an interest should still override a fungible property claim. For example, a claim to a sacred site on state land that is to be leased to a golf resort.

Radin, of course, understands the difficulty of identifying objective criteria for human flourishing for the things that are essential for personhood. In an age of commodity fetishism, so much of people's sense of self is tied up with the acquiring or possessing of things. Well-being has been replaced by "well-having" and questions regarding what is essential for the good life, or what Aristotle termed as *eudaimonia*, are lost in the maelstrom of commodities. In such circumstances, it seems a formidable, if not impossible, task to delineate criteria for when personal property or personhood interests must be allowed to trump fungible property claims. Radin, in her seminal 1982 Stanford Law Review article "Property and Personhood," clearly outlines this problem when she says that:

> It intuitively appears that there is such a thing as property for personhood because people become bound up with "things." But this intuitive view does not compel the conclusion that property for personhood deserves moral recognition or legal protection, because arguably there is bad as well as good in being bound up with external objects. If there is a traditional understanding that a well-developed person must invest herself to some extent in external objects, there is no less a traditional understanding that one should not invest oneself *in the wrong way or to too great an extent* in external objects. Property is damnation as well as salvation, object-fetishism as well as moral groundwork. (Malinowski, 1954, p. 961)

Radin nevertheless concludes that, as with most things in life, there are no absolutes but rather a spectrum where, at the one end we have things that are absolutely fungible and at the other, things that are essentially personal. We then have things that fall somewhere along this continuum, some lying more to the fungible end and others to the personal end. Judges then have to engage in the task of identifying what is personal and what is fungible on a case-by-case basis. In any event, judges make this distinction unconsciously, be it in deciding the amount of damages to be paid for pain and suffering in tort law or in determining whether the state can expropriate a residential neighborhood for some public works.

Five years later, in 1987, Radin published her much-acclaimed article "Market-Inalienability" in the Harvard Law Review. This article
was a decisive response to advocates of universal commodification led
by Richard Posner of the Law and Economics school of jurisprudence
(see Malinowski, 1954, p. 374).[11] Here Radin had further developed her
argument regarding criteria for determining property for personhood
by attempting to distinguish between those goods and services that are
market alienable or can be commoditized and those that ought to be
market inalienable or should not be commoditized.

Radin's attempts brought her back to the same question that she had
posed in 1982 albeit from a different angle. If the question posed in
"Property and Personhood" was "how do we distinguish between personal property or personhood interest and fungible property?," then the
question that Radin posed in "Market-Inalienability" was "how do we
distinguish between those things that can be commoditized and those
that shouldn't?" Both these questions lie at the heart of the green economy debate and the answer to these questions lie in the most ancient
of all human quests: to understand what constitutes "well-being" or, in
Radin's terms, "human flourishing."

There is ultimately only one question here, which can be asked in
various different ways. The fact remains that, in whichever the fashion
we pose this question the answer will ultimately come down to a shared
understanding of human flourishing. One cannot answer the question
"what is property?" without answering the question of "what is personhood?"; and one cannot answer the latter question without answering
"what is wellbeing?" A shared understanding of wellbeing informs our
understanding of personhood and the rights that must be availed to
affirm such a personhood. A common conception of personhood would
then clarify what constitutes personhood interests or personal property
and what constitutes fungible or market alienable property.

Radin sets the framework for her thesis by identifying three inter-
related aspects or criteria for personhood: freedom, identity, and contextuality (see Malinowski, 1954, p. 1904). Rather than resting her
understanding of personhood on any one particular trait, Radin argues
that it involves a balance of all three traits. At the same time, she is pragmatic enough to note that we live in a non-ideal world with unequal
power relations that sometimes result in personal property being traded
as fungible property or being incompletely commoditized. Commercial
sex work is a typical example, where the lines are blurred between the

body as personal property and the body as fungible property. Another example is a community deciding to lease its ancestral lands to a logging company. These are cases of a moral "double bind" (see Malinowski, 1954, pp. 1915–1916) where it would be patronizing to tell the unemployed woman with children to feed or a desperately poor community that needs an income that the body or ancestral lands are personal property that should not be commoditized. In fact to force these people to do otherwise curtails their freedom to make choices, choices that are sometimes "desperate exchanges" (see Malinowski, 1954, pp. 1917–1918). For Radin, however, these situations should not be presented as examples of the possibility of universal commodification, but rather as situations of incomplete commodification, where the woman's body or the community's ancestral lands are still personal property that in certain non-ideal situations are commoditized. Much of this has occurred through colonial processes, as mentioned earlier, and through many different facets of the privatization, marketization, and other neoliberal actions affecting nature. While the personal is still vested in the "object," the body, or land, additional ownership claims overlie it and may be in conflict (hence Radin's use of incomplete commodification). Although it would appear that an array of neoliberal processes are driving a seemingly inevitable commoditization of everything, many resistances will continue to be made, either counter to commoditization or toward a commoditization on specific and explicit terms. Examples might include actions that are opposed to patents on life forms (e.g., submissions by the African Group and Bolivia in the WTO TRIPS Council), and those that engage in the negotiation of an ABS process to seek mutually agreed terms for the transaction of a genetic resource, respectively.

The above examples could represent the freedom or autonomous aspect of personhood, which highlights will or the ability to make one's own choices. Hence for example, one could argue in the context of ABS that it is the choice of the community whether or not they want to sell their traditional knowledge. Freedom is nevertheless not the only aspect of personhood. For Radin, personhood includes "identity" and "contextuality." The identity aspect involves the integrity or continuity of the self, which is necessary for individuation. Our personhood is based on an enduring self. This self of course goes through various transformations in an individual's lifetime, but it nevertheless is the manifestation of a memory that knits together the various events that this self-experiences.

Personhood in the context of identity is analogous to a node or a knot in a web of relations wherein it is clear that the knot is nothing if not the various strands of relations. It is also clear, however, that these relations can only become real if they are embodied through the knot or, so to speak, through the person. The identity aspect of personhood then contextualizes the freedom aspect. Identity constitutes the self that exercises the freedom to choose what is important to it; a self that is able to distinguish between what is personal and what is fungible. In the context of ABS then, the issue of identity poses the question of whether exercising the freedom to sell one's traditional knowledge is, in Radin's terms, a "desperate exchange" or something that affirms a strong identity.

Marx's notion of estrangement in capitalist societies is in essence one where the self or identity is slowly being cut off from the ensemble of social relations within which it is embedded. The *homo economicus* is an estranged being because it recognizes and affirms only one kind of relation, which is the market relation, thereby denying all other social relations that constitute the self. It is this idea of the self as an ensemble of social relations that Radin develops in attributing contextuality as the third aspect of personhood. Radin elaborates:

> The contextuality aspect of personhood focuses on the necessity of self-constitution in relation to the environment of things and other people. In order to be differentiated human persons, unique individuals, we must have relationships with the social and natural world.... I focus primarily on a certain view of contextuality and its consequences: the view that connections between the person and her environment are integral to personhood. (Malinowski, 1954, p. 1904)

Then again Radin adds:

> The relationship between personhood and context requires a positive commitment to act so as to create and maintain particular contexts of environment and community.... Universal commodification undermines personal identity by conceiving of personal attributes, relationships, and philosophical and moral commitments as monetizable and alienable from self. A better view of personhood should understand many kinds of particulars-one's politics, work, religion, family, love, sexuality, friendships, altruism, experiences, wisdom, moral commitments, character and personal attributes-as integral to the self. (Malinowski, 1954, pp. 1905–1906)

Radin makes three critical contributions to the debates around the green economy that greatly aids us in distinguishing different kinds of property and how they must be treated. The significance of the first contribution is the link between commodification and personhood thereby breaking free from the fetishism that is caused by discussing commodification, disassociated from its link to human flourishing. Radin's second contribution is her understanding of personhood from the perspective of human flourishing. Personhood is not merely an exercise of freedom and identity but also contextuality. The self therefore is not simply free but also relational, and this relationality is integral to human flourishing and positive liberty. Radin's third major contribution is to tie personal property or personhood interests to contextuality, arguing that the non-precedence of personal property or personhood interests over fungible property in capitalist societies is detrimental to contextuality and thereby to human flourishing and personhood itself.[12]

Property for Peoplehood

Radin made a meticulous case for personhood as the very raison d'être of property and, in our case, the green economy. She argued that the litmus test for any commodification is whether it positively contributes to human flourishing and thereby to personhood. In 2009, the *Yale Law Journal* published a pivotal article entitled "In Defense of Property" (Riley, 2009, pp. 1022–1125). The article was co-authored by three professors of law, Angela Riley, Kristen Carpenter and Sonia Katyal. These authors, 27 years after Radin's seminal arguments on the relationship between property and personhood, sought to adapt her ideas to argue for the rights of American Indians to their cultural property.

A year before, in 2008, Kristen Carpenter in her article titled "Real Property and Peoplehood" (Carpenter, 2008, p. 313) had reasoned that if, according to Radin, the protection of certain kinds of property was relevant for personhood, then equally the protection of some kinds of property interests was critical for "peoplehood." Carpenter explained:

> Much in the way that Radin's discussion of "personhood" invokes what is most essential to the individual human condition, "peoplehood" refers to the qualities that define a group and inspire individuals to participate in the

collective. In common parlance, peoplehood is the state of being a people or the sense of belonging to a people. (Carpenter, 2008, p. 313)

Carpenter in her article argued that American Indians as a people have rights to the use and management of sacred sites despite the fact that these sites were on public lands owned by the government. The rights of American Indians to their sacred sites were similar to Radin's notion of rights to personal property or personhood interests, which in most cases would trump fungible property rights. Carpenter argued that American Indians had rights to peoplehood interests in their sacred sites since their very existence as a people depended on the access, use, and management of these sites. Therefore, these peoplehood interests must override any state directive that determines the use of the public lands in ways that would profane sacred sites.

Carpenter's thesis made a strong case for the legal recognition of peoplehood interests in property despite the lack of formal ownership. The basis of her argument was that the flourishing, or sometimes the very survival of certain groups or peoples, depended on access and control of these properties. In 2009, Riley, Carpenter and Katyal further developed this argument into a fully fledged theory for the right to "cultural property" in order to secure peoplehood. They proposed that:

Peoplehood, we argue, dictates that certain lands, resources, and expressions are entitled to legal protection as cultural property because they are integral to the group identity and cultural survival of indigenous peoples ... some cultural resources are so sacred and intimately connected to a people's collective identity and experience that they deserve special consideration as a form of cultural property.... Classic ownership theory tends to overlook the possibility of non-owners exercising custodial duties over tangible and intangible goods in the absence of title or possession. Yet indigenous peoples have historically exercised such custodial duties.... Indigenous cultural property claims... thus reflect a fiduciary approach to cultural property and takes into account indigenous peoples' collective obligations toward land and resources.... To the extent that indigenous peoples' cultural property claims are premised on custodial duties toward specific properties, we argue that such claims are more appropriately characterized through the paradigm of stewardship rather than ownership ... cultural property law ... seeks to distribute entitlements along a spectrum so as to accommodate both the ownership and stewardship interests that attach to owners and non-owners. We contend that indigenous cultural property claims can be both explained and justified by this more expansive understanding of property, which we articulate through people-hood and stewardship. (see Malinowski, 1954, pp. 1028–1029)

Tracing the genealogy of a critical understanding of commodifica-tion, beginning with Polanyi, through Sahlins and Radin and leading to Riley, one can see a common theme emerging despite the different angles through which each of these theorists approached property. The theme is one that deconstructs the fetishism of property as a sacrosanct legal con-cept from which people derive certain rights. It argues that property has human origins, and that it is not human beings and communities who need to fit within the framework of property, but the discourse of prop-erty that must align itself with our collective understanding of flourishing of personhood and peoplehood.

In the context of the green economy, an approach like this breaks through the binary of should nature be commoditized or not and pro-vides a fresh lens to view the issue. This lens helps us see that the real issue is to ensure that green economy is implemented in a manner that foregrounds personhood and peoplehood and does not undermine it. It is to use the personhood and peoplehood test to evaluate green economy financing mechanisms that we shall now turn toward.

The Hoodia ABS Agreement: A Case Study on Commodification

One of the earliest ABS agreements in the world had to do with the traditional knowledge of the San relating to the hunger staving qualities of the Hoodia plant. Its specificities takes us beyond the abstract debate of whether or not to commoditize nature and instead ask the question what the impact of the ABS agreement was on the San's peoplehood.

The South African Council for Scientific and Industrial Research (CSIR) extracted a bioactive compound relating to the Hoodia's hunger staving properties based on San traditional knowledge. The process of extraction and the use of the bioactive compound for appetite suppres-sant purposes was patented by the CSIR. This patent was then licensed to a UK based company, Phytopharm, which, in turn, sublicensed it, first, to Pfizer and then later to Unilever to develop food supplements for the diet industry (Chennels, 2010, p. 413).

Recently, Phytopharm returned the patent to the CSIR, since both Pfizer and Unilever have for various reasons been unable to develop products based on the Hoodia patent. After initial concerns raised by the San that the CSIR had commercially used San traditional knowledge without their consent, the CSIR in 2003 negotiated a post facto ABS agreement with the San that involved payment to them of a percentage of royalties received by the CSIR from Phytopharm (Bouckley, 2013).

The significance of the San–Hoodia agreement cannot be overestimated. It was one of the world's first ABS agreements, and it was definitely the first such agreement in Africa between a historically marginalized indigenous community and a commercial entity. Nevertheless, it is critical to note that, despite the San receiving some milestone payments from the CSIR at specific stages of the clinical trials and product development, the commodification of the San traditional knowledge brought with it a unique set of problems (Bavikatte, 2013).

The South African San Council, which negotiated the ABS agreement with the CSIR, sought to represent the San of South Africa, Namibia, Angola, and Botswana, since it felt that all the San of the region collectively held the knowledge relating to the Hoodia. However, the urgency of responding to the fact that the CSIR had already registered a patent based on San traditional knowledge meant that the ABS agreement negotiations had to be hurried by the South African San Council without the necessary consultations with the larger San community (Vermeylen, 2008).

The negotiations between the San and the CSIR opened with the incontrovertibility of the CSIR patent on the Hoodia. The patent had already been registered and the San Council was informed that any commercial interest in the Hoodia and potential financial benefits for the San was possible only if the San did not challenge the patent. This meant that the San who had, until then, relied on their knowledge of the Hoodia as personal property were asked to engage in a negotiation, which regarded their traditional knowledge as fungible property. The moment this transformation of personal to fungible property occurred all other discussions around the context in which knowledge about the Hoodia had been historically developed, used, and shared by the San were abandoned. Negotiations from thereon focused on market potential, investment in research and development by the CSIR and its licensees, and share of benefits that the San could realistically expect from the ABS agreement.

This was the first step toward commodification, whereby the Hoodia traditional knowledge was approached in a manner that delinked it from the way of life of the San and their history of discrimination. The discussions became less about the real needs of the San, the breakdown of traditional leadership, and the limited representational mandate of the hurriedly constituted South African San Council, and more about traditional knowledge itself and its commercial potential. The time required for substantial consultation within the San community based on their customary values about the kind of benefits needed and how they would be collectively shared was unavailable (Vermeylen, 2007). Like all commercial negotiations, this too had to take place in "market time," with an emphasis on quick and efficient drawing up of an agreement to utilize the traditional knowledge and capitalizing on the "first mover advantage."

The second step toward commodification came when the Hoodia traditional knowledge became more real than the San themselves. The San were used as a part of a marketing campaign around the appetite suppressant qualities of the Hoodia to combat overeating. Pictures were beamed across the world of lithe San people, in their traditional clothes, hunting with bows and arrows, and set against the Kalahari landscape. This bore no semblance to the reality of San life, of a people who are chronic victims of discrimination and dispossession. The San's fast-disappearing way of life was no longer viewed on its own terms, with necessary attention to its insurmountable challenges, but merely as a means to an end—the end being profits from Hoodia diet supplements (see generally, Vermeylen, 2007).

The third step toward commodification was an alienation from nature itself. The growing demand for the Hoodia resulting from the extensive media coverage of the San–Hoodia case sparked off widespread illegal harvesting of the plant. This harvest put Hoodia on the endangered plants list in South Africa. At the same time, a number of commercial farmers began to cultivate Hoodia for the export market. Significant profits were made due to a spike in demand. Both the illegal harvesting and commercial cultivation of Hoodia viewed the San traditional knowledge as primarily fungible property.[13]

For the San, this unprecedented interest in Hoodia by the anti-obesity market obscured the way of life from which this traditional knowledge arose. The ethics of stewardship that underlies the San interactions with their ecosystem, and the context within which the Hoodia is used, was never mentioned in the market rhetoric around the traditional knowledge. The fetishism of Hoodia and the emergent market interest in it had the paradoxical effect of reinforcing an approach to nature as fungible property rather than an appreciation of the personal property relations that the San historically had with the Kalahari.

Finally, the ABS agreement resulted in the CSIR gaining exclusive use rights to traditional knowledge relating to Hoodia through the San acceptance of the CSIR's patent in exchange for benefits. This caused an estrangement between the San and the Nama (another indigenous group that shared with the San the knowledge about the Hoodia) (Wynberg and Roger, 2009, p. 115). When this knowledge functioned within the realm of use value, the San, the Nama, and other communities in the region all freely shared and exchanged it. However, the moment these social relations were overridden by market relations through the CSIR patent, the result was an estrangement between two communities that had lived in harmony for centuries.[14]

The Nama felt that the San did not have the authority to grant exclusive rights to the CSIR, and that they (the Nama) should also have been included as beneficiaries to the ABS agreement. The San, however, argued that they (the San) were "primary rights holders" since they were the original inhabitants of the region, the Nama having arrived later. The entire debate was ironic as both these communities had co-existed for several hundred years in South Africa and Namibia, and their ancient social relations were now precipitously punctuated with market terminology, such as "primary rights holders" and "profit percentages." The San and the Nama have since entered into an agreement amongst themselves to share in the benefits arising from the San-CSIR ABS agreement. Divorcing traditional knowledge from the cultural context in which it was communally used and shared, however, had the paradoxical effect of temporarily disrupting inter-community relations, which have played a crucial role in conserving the ecosystem of the region.

This analysis of the Hoodia agreement is not performed through the condescending gaze of posterity nor is it a tirade against the commodification of traditional knowledge. Roger Chennells, the lawyer representing the San did pioneering work in what is considered one of the earliest ABS agreements between an indigenous group and a commercial interest. It is also clear that the ABS agreement between the CSIR and the San was an important forerunner to the establishment of rights of communities to their traditional knowledge and the right to benefit from the commercial uses of such knowledge. During the negotiations, many San leaders held a considered view that the desperately poor community would clearly benefit from monies that would arise from the agreement. Moreover, the agreement also triggered a deep sense of pride and affirmation in a hitherto marginalized community.

Conclusion

The analysis of the Hoodia agreement takes us out of the theoretical debate about benefits and dangers of the green economy and its concomitant commodification of nature. Instead it highlights the implications for the peoplehood of a community when its personal property is turned into fungible property. In doing so, it also provides us with a realistic corrective to the green economy and ensures that its implementation should affirm peoplehood rather than undermine it.

The Hoodia agreement was to some extent, what Radin termed as, a "desperate exchange." It took place between a poor and historically marginalized community and a powerful research organization. While on the one hand, it was symbolic of the freedom of the San to assert their identity, on the other hand, this exercise in freedom was a desperate exchange and did not holistically represent the San identity nor did it affirm their contextuality—all aspects of their wellbeing.

For people like Jimmie and communities like the San whose ways of life are fast disappearing, notions of freedom, identity, and contextuality all become blurred when they confront a world where social relations are determined by market relations rather than the other way round. The green economy as in the case of the San clearly had the potential to bootstrap their impoverished community into financial security. As some of the San leaders argued, the ABS agreement would for the first time acknowledge their historically denied identity as a people and recognize their rights to determine how their resources and culture can be used as a free people. In fact, it is with this vision that the San leaders with their lawyer Roger Chennells continue to negotiate new ABS agreements. They are learning from the pitfalls of the Hoodia agreement, are organizing themselves better, negotiating strategically, and working closely with the other indigenous peoples that they share their knowledge with. In fact all the tumult caused by the

Hoodia agreement has paradoxically brought to fore with great urgency the questions of well-being and what it means to be San today.

The domestic and international legal frameworks that underpin green economy create a swathe of hitherto nonexistent property rights for communities, such as the rights to their genetic resources, traditional knowledge, carbon stocks, and so on. While the extent of these rights is an ongoing site of struggle, the real struggle for indigenous peoples and traditional communities is to effectively leverage on these new property rights to self-determine their personhood and peoplehood. As we have seen in the Hoodia agreement, it is quite possible that these rights become Trojan horses for further commodification of personal property and bring with it the cultural defoliation when market relations subsume all other kinds of relations. It is therefore critical that we approach the green economy with a sense of pragmatism that goes beyond the shrill ideological hand wringing and ask ourselves how can communities use and lobby the rights opportunities this economy brings to affirm their peoplehood. Along the lines of Larner's analyses of neoliberal processes and power (as a disjunctive assemblage of actors, actions, and discourses), the CBD, Nagoya Protocol and their terms relating to ABS, can be thought of as "a consequence of the contestation between dominant and oppositional claims, rather than being simply imposed from above" (Larner, 2000, p. 20; 2009, p. 1576). The fact that the US has not ratified the CBD points to the fact that the requirements for benefit-sharing have been controversial for some governments of the north and certainly for industries located there. The recent achievement of the Nagoya Protocol text also reflects considerable counter-lobbying and resistance by developing countries, biodiverse countries, indigenous organizations, and various NGO groups. The inclusion of requirements relating to "associated traditional knowledge" and references to customary laws and community protocols (Article 12) arguably reflect an effort to establish further rights and peoplehood claims.

Although, to date, ABS has only made some specific contributions to poverty reduction or biodiversity conservation (see for example, Robinson and Defrenne, 2011; Robinson, 2012), there may be other opportunities afforded by it. As we have seen in the growing number of examples of ABS and other similar PES agreements between communities and businesses, despite their limitations, there has also been a strategic use of rights to further peoplehood claims. Our analysis of the green economy and its implications for communities must begin to take on board what political scientist and anthropologist James Scott refers to as "infrapolitics" and the "hidden transcripts" that underlie such politics (Scott, 1990). In his work *Domination and the Arts of Resistance*, Scott (1990) shows how "each realm of open resistance to domination is shadowed by an infrapolitical twin sister who aims at the same strategic goals but whose low profile is better adapted to resisting an opponent who could probably win any open confrontation" (Scott, 2005, p. 66). It is time we start looking at the hidden transcripts of infrapolitics that underlie community engagements with the green economy. As Scott points out that the "hidden transcript is not just behind-the-scenes griping and grumbling; it is enacted in a host of down-to-earth, low profile stratagems designed to minimize appropriation"—or in this case to negotiate commoditization under explicit (beneficial) terms (Scott, 2005, p. 68). We therefore need to heed Scott's advice and appreciate that the implications of the green economy will "be inferred by practice—a quiet practice at that" (Scott, 2005, p. 69). It is time that we cultivate that quiet practice.

Notes

1. Effectively what a green economy does is put an economic value on biodiversity—specifically on the ecosystem services that nature provides humanity with in the form of public goods, such as clean air, water, carbon storage, pollination, rainfall, food, and so on. By doing so, a green economy approach seeks to understand Nature as "natural capital" and quantify in economic terms the monetary value of biodiversity. The Green Economy, as defined by the United Nations Environment Program (UNEP), is one that, "results in improved human well-being and social equity, while significantly reducing environmental risks and ecological scarcities" or, simply put, one that is low carbon, resource efficient and socially inclusive. According to UNEP, in a green economy "growth in income and employment should be driven by public and private investments that reduce carbon emissions and pollution, enhance energy and resource efficiency and prevent the loss of biodiversity and ecosystem services." UNEP launched the Green Economy Initiative in late 2008. The initiative consists of several components whose collective overall objective is to provide the analysis and policy support for investing in green sectors and in greening environmental unfriendly sectors. In July 2011, UNEP released the Green Economy Report titled Towards a Green Economy: Pathways Towards Sustainable Development and Poverty Eradication. The report, according to UNEP, seeks to demonstrate that the greening of economies is not generally a drag on growth, but rather a new engine of growth; that it is a net generator of decent jobs, and also a vital strategy for the elimination of persistent poverty. See http://www.unep.org/greeneconomy/Home/tabid/29770/Default.aspx (accessed on January 10, 2013). See also United Nations Environment Program Green Economy website at http://www.unep.org/greeneconomy/AboutGEI/WhatisGEI/tabid/29784/Default.aspx (accessed on January 10, 2013).

2. The Nagoya Protocol is an international treaty that was adopted in October 2010 by the 193 parties to the Convention on Biological Diversity (CBD). The protocol was intensely negotiated over six years under the framework of the CBD. The aim of the Nagoya Protocol on Access and Benefit Sharing is to give effect to the fair and equitable benefit-sharing provisions of the CBD. Specifically, Article 15 of the CBD that recognizes the rights of states to their genetic resources and Article 8(j) that recognizes the rights of communities to their traditional knowledge. The Nagoya Protocol seeks to ensure that commercial and research utilization of genetic resources and associated traditional knowledge shares the benefits of such utilization with the governments and communities that have conserved such resources and knowledge.

3. In 1992, the United Nations Framework Convention on Climate Change (UNFCCC) was adopted as the basis for a global response to the problem of climate change. With 194 parties, the ultimate objective of the convention is to stabilise greenhouse gas concentrations in the atmosphere at a level that will prevent dangerous human interference with the climate system. The convention is complemented by the 1997 Kyoto Protocol, which has 192 parties. Under this treaty, 37 industrialised countries and the European community have committed to reducing their emissions by an average of 5 percent by 2012 against 1990's levels. Industrialized countries must first and foremost take domestic action against climate change. But the protocol also allows them to meet their emission reduction commitments abroad through so-called "market-based mechanisms" (see UNFCCC, 2011).

4. A definition for payment for environmental services (PES) that has become fairly well accepted has been put forward by Sven Wunder, in which he explains, "A 'payment for environmental services scheme' is a voluntary transaction in which a well defined environmental service (ES), or a form of land use likely to secure that service is bought by at least one ES buyer from a minimum of one ES provider if and only if the provider continues to supply that service (conditionality)." See, Wunder (2005), quoted on CIFOR website: http://www.cifor.cgiar.org/pes/_ref/about/index.htm (accessed on March 23, 2012). The key characteristic of PES deals is that the focus is on maintaining a flow of a specified ecosystem "service"—such as clean water, biodiversity habitat, or carbon sequestration capabilities—in exchange for something of economic value. The critical, defining factor of what constitutes a PES transaction, however, is not just that money changes hands and an environmental service is either delivered or maintained. Rather, the key is that the payment causes the benefit to occur where it would not have otherwise. That is, the service is "additional" to "business as usual," or at the very least, the service can be quantified and tied to the payment. See, UNEP, Forest Trends and the Katoomba Group (2008, p. 3).

5. Article 12 of the Nagoya Protocol, but also see Articles 3, 6 and 7 relating to "scope" and "access" to genetic resources and associated traditional knowledge.

6. A good example of this is the "Hawai'i Taro case" in which the Taro plant is considered a sacred ancestor of the Hawai'ian people and when patented caused a considerable dispute. For a number of examples, see Robinson et al. (2014).

7. Regarding the origins of the homo economicus, see generally, Ng et al. (2008).

8. For a critique, see McAfee (1999).

9. See Smith (1986), Chapter 2, "Of the Principle which gives Occasion to the Division of Labour."

10. I use the term "homo socialis" to refer to the self in pre-capitalist societies that is construed as a locus of social relations where social obligations override self-interest.

11. For Posner's arguments on Law and Economics, see generally, Landes and Posner (1978, pp. 323–348).

12. There is growing research on well-being in the context of the CBD and ABS. Some researchers have applied the "capabilities framework" developed by Martha Nussbaum and Amartya Sen. The capabilities framework helps to describe the well-being of a social group (community) whose members have made decisions within the "freedoms given to them" and available "capabilities" (including natural endowments, skills, norms, values, and markets). It does not presuppose well-being based solely on "rational economic choice,|" but anchors well-being in both moral and economic choices. Other researchers such as Mathew Clarke have attempted to measure the well-being of nations by correlating it to the achievement of Maslow's "hierarchical framework of human needs," which include "basic needs," "safety," "belonging" "self-esteem," and "self-actualization." One of the most interesting tools to measure wellbeing is developed by M.S. Suneetha and Balakrishna Pisupati where Clarke's application of the Maslow framework is used in tandem with the Sen and Nussbaum "capabilities framework." The result is a framework of needs and related indicators to measure wellbeing where basic needs is captured by indicators related to food, health, and shelter; safety needs is captured by indicators related to settled lives and security from risks, including economic and natural risks; belonging needs is captured by indicators related to social groups and equity in transactions, including gender equity and non-discrimination; and self-esteem and self-actualization needs is captured by indicators related to autonomy, confidence and education. See generally, Nussbaum and Sen (1996); Clarke (2006); cited in Suneetha and Pisupati (2009, pp. 31–32).

13. Based on interviews conducted by the author with Robbie Gass, a Hoodia commercial farmer in South Africa.

14. The author was actively involved between 2007 and 2009 as a lawyer supporting the South African San Council and the Hoodia Trust in implementing the benefit-sharing aspects of the ABS agreement that had been entered into with the CSIR. The views expressed in this section are predominantly based on the author's personal experience in working with the San communities in South Africa in implementing their ABS agreement.

References

Aitken, R. (2006). *Botanical Riches: Stories of Botanical Exploration*. Melbourne: Miegunyah Press and State Library of Victoria.

Balbus, I. (2009). *Governing Subjects*. New York: Routledge.

Bavikatte, K.S. and Robinson, D.F. (2011). Towards a people's history of the law: Biocultural jurisprudence and the Nagoya Protocol on access and benefit sharing. *Law, Environment and Development Journal, 7*(1), 35.

Bavikatte, K., Jonas, H., and von Braun, J. (2013). Shifting Sands of ABS Best Practice. Available at: www.naturaljustice.org (Accessed on January 10, 2013).

Bouckley, B. (2013). Phytopharm CEO Insists Hoodia Still 'Interesting' Despite Patent Disposal. Available at: http://www.nutraingredients.com/Industry/Phytopharm-CEO-insists-Hoodia-still-interesting-despite-patent-disposal (accessed on November 25, 2015).

Brierley, J.H. (1994). *Spices: The Story of Indonesia's Spice Trade*. Kuala Lumpur: Oxford University Press.

Carpenter, K. (2008). Real property and peoplehood. *Stanford Environmental Law Journal, 27*(313).

Castree, N. (2008). Neoliberalising nature: The logics of deregulation and reregulation. *Environment and Planning A, 40*(1), 131–152.

Chennells, R. (2010). Ethics and practice in ethnobiology: The experience of the San peoples of Southern Africa. In Charles McManis (Ed.), *Biodiversity and the Law: Intellectual Property, Biotechnology and Traditional Knowledge*. London: Earthscan.

Clarke, M. (2006). Assessing well-being using hierarchical needs. In Mark McGillivray and Matthew Clarke (Eds.), *Understanding Human Well-being*. Tokyo: United Nations University Press.

Hewitt, R. (2002). An ethnographic sketch of the /Xam. In Miklos Szala (Ed.), *The Moon as Shoe: Drawings of the San*. Zurich: Scheidegger and Spiess.

Hickey, F. (2006). "Traditional Marine Resource Management in Vanuatu: Acknowledging, Supporting and Strengthening Indigenous Management Systems," SPC Traditional Marine Resource Management and Knowledge Information Bulletin #20, December 2006. See http://www.spc.int/DigitalLibrary/Doc/FAME/InfoBull/TRAD/20/TRAD20.pdf.

Hyde, L. (1983). *The Gift: How the Creative Spirit Transforms the World*. Edinburgh: Canongate.

Landes, E.M. and Posner, R.A. (1978). The economics of the baby shortage. *Journal of Legal Studies, 7*(2), 323–348.

Larner, W. (2000). Neo-liberalism: Policy, ideology, governmentality. *Studies in Political Economy, 63*(1), 20.

_____. (2009). Neoliberalism, Mike Moore, and the WTO. *Environment and Planning A, 41*(7), 1576.

Malinowski, B. (1922). *Argonauts of the Western Pacific*. London: Routledge and Sons.

_____. (1954). The Kula. In Margaret Mead and Nicolas Calas (Eds.), *Primitive Heritage: An Anthropological Anthology*. London: Victor Gollancz.

Mathiessen, P. (1984). *Indian Country*. New York: Penguin.

Mauss, M. (1967). *The Gift: Forms and Functions of Exchange in Archaic Societies*. New York: Norton Library.

McAfee, K. (1999). Selling Nature to Save It? Biodiversity and Green Developmentalism. *Environment and Planning D: Society and Space, 17*(2), 133–154.

Ng, Irene et al. (2008, April). Learning to be sociable: The evolution of homo economicus. *The American Journal of Economics and Sociology, 67*(2), 265–286.

Nussbaum, M.C. and Sen, A. (Eds.). (1996). *The Quality of Life*. Oxford: Clarendon Press.

Polanyi, K. (2001). *The Great Transformation: The Political and Economic Origins of Our Time*. Boston: Beacon Press.

Radin, M.J. (1982). Property and personhood. *Stanford Law Review, 34*(5), 957–1015.

_____. (1987). Market-Inalienability. *Harvard Law Review, 100*(8), 1849–1937.

Riley, A. Carpenter, K.A., Katyal, S.K., and Riley, A.R. (2009). In defense of property. *Yale Law Journal, 118*(2009), 1022–1125.

Robinson, D. (2012). *Towards Access and Benefit-Sharing Best Practice: Pacific Case Studies*. DSEWPAC, Canberra and GIZ, Eschborn, Germany. Available at; http://www.abs-initiative.info/uploads/media/ABS (accessed on November 25, 2015).

Robinson, D.F. (2010). *Confronting Biopiracy: Cases, Challenges and International Debates*. London: Earthscan/Routledge.

Robinson, D.F. and Defrenne, E. (2011). *"Argan: A Case study on ABS?"* Union for Ethical Biotrade, presented at the Beauty of Sourcing with Respect conference in Paris, May 6, 2011. Available at: http://www.ethicalbiotrade.org/dl/UEBT_D_ROBINSON_AND_E_DEFRENNE_final.pdf (accessed on November 25, 2015).

Robinson, D.F., Drozdzewski, D., and Kiddell, L. (2014). 'You Can't Change our Ancestors Without our Permission': Cultural Perspectives on Biopiracy. In M. Fredrikksson and J. Arvanitakis (Eds.), *Piracy: Leakages of Modernity* (pp. 55–75). Sacramento, CA: Litwin Books.

Sahlins, M. (1972). *Stone Age Economics*. London: Tavistock Publications.

Scott, J. (1990). *Domination and the Arts of Resistance: Hidden Transcripts*. New Haven: Yale University Press.

_____. (2005). The Infrapolitics of Subordinate Groups. In Louise Amoore (Ed.), *Global Resistance Reader*. London: Routledge.

Smith, A. (1986). On the division of labour. In *The Wealth of Nations*, Books I–III, 119. New York: Penguin Classics.

_____. (2000). *The Theory of Moral Sentiments*. New York: Prometheus Books.Strathern, M. (1999). *Property, Substance and Effect: Anthropological Essays on Persons and Things*. London: Athlone Press.

Suneetha, M.S. and Pisupati, B. (2009). *Learning from the Practitioners: Benefit Sharing Perspectives from Enterprising Communities*. Nairobi: UNEP/UNU-IAS.

Turner, R.K., Pearce, D. and Bateman, I. (1994). *Environmental Economics: An Elementary Introduction*. Hertfordshire: Prentice-Hall.

UNEP, Forest Trends and the Katoomba Group (2008). *Payment for Ecosystem Services–Getting Started: A Primer*. Nairobi: UNEP, Forest Trends and the Katoomba Group.

UNFCCC, United Nations Framework Convention on Climate Change (2011). *An Introduction to the United Nations Framework Convention on Climate Change and its Kyoto Protocol, Fact Sheet*. February 2011.

Vermeylen, S. (2008). From life force to slimming aid: Exploring views on the commodification of traditional medicinal knowledge. *Applied Geography*, 28(3), 224–235.

_____. (2007). Contextualizing 'fair' and 'equitable': The San's reflections on the Hoodia Benefit-Sharing Agreement. *Local Environment*, 12(4, August), 423–436.

Wunder, S. (2005). Payments for Environmental Services: Some Nuts and Bolts, Centre for International Forestry Research, Jakarta, p. 3. See http://www.cifor.org/publications/pdf_files/OccPapers/OP-42.pdf (accessed on December 28, 2015).

Wynberg, R. and Roger, C. (2009). Green diamonds of the South: An overview of the San Hoodia Case. In Rachel Wynberg, Doris Schroeder, and Roger Chennells (Eds.), *Indigenous Peoples, Consent and Benefit Sharing* (pp. 89–124). New York: Springer.

About the Editors and Contributors

Editors

Kanchi Kohli is a researcher and writer working on environment, forest, and biodiversity governance in India. Her work explores the links between law, industrialization, and environment justice. She works through the strength of different institutions and has authored several publications, individually and in teams. One of her current areas of research locates the concept of commodification of nature in real time environment policy and sustainability discourses.

Manju Menon is Senior Fellow, Centre for Policy Research, New Delhi. She has researched and written on environment, law, and development for over two decades. Her main areas of work are environmental law-making and implementation processes and regulatory decisions on siting of infrastructure projects. She collaborates with local, regional, and thematic networks working on decentralized resource governance and environmental compliance.

Contributors

Sanjay Kabir Bavikatte is the Executive Director of The Christensen Fund, a philanthropic foundation that backs stewards of biocultural diversity. Previously, he was the co-founder and co-director of Natural Justice, an international organization of environmental lawyers assisting indigenous peoples and local communities secure their rights to territories and cultures.

Shalini Bhutani is a legal researcher and policy analyst, who works independently in the Asia region. Her specialization is in intellectual property in agriculture and biodiversity. Her areas of interest range from global trade rules and their impact on peoples and the planet, to how science and technology policies deal with grassroots innovation. She is also guest faculty on law and regulatory affairs in different institutes.

Himanshu Burte is an architect, theorist, and faculty at Tata Institute of Social Sciences, Mumbai. His book, *Space for Engagement: The Indian Artplace and a Habitational Approach to Architecture* (2008) proposes an alternative conceptual framework for architecture centered on the act of dwelling. His current research interests include public space, urban infrastructure, housing policy, theatre architecture, and sustainable urbanism.

Shripad Dharmadhikary is an activist, researcher, and coordinator of the Manthan Adhyayan Kendra that studies water and energy policies. His interests include dams, rivers, environmental flows, water privatization, and coal-water nexus. A graduate engineer from IIT Bombay, he was earlier an activist for 12 years with the Narmada Bachao Andolan.

Soumitra Ghosh is an independent researcher, a social activist, and a maker of documentary films. Based in sub-Himalayan West Bengal, he works with the forest communities of the region, also elsewhere in India, and is associated with All India Forum of Forest Movements (AIFFM). Soumitra has written extensively on the political economy of climate change as well as forest communities and their struggles.

Vinuta Gopal is a chartered accountant by qualification and has been working with Greenpeace India for more than a decade. She currently heads the Indian operations of Greenpeace. She has worked on a range of environmental and social justice campaigns. She believes that systemic change is fundamental to addressing the environmental threats the planet faces today.

Simone Lovera is the Executive Director of the Global Forest Coalition. With a degree in international environment law, she has closely followed and participated as an expert in a range of international negotiation processes since 1990. She also is a guest researcher at the Centre of Sustainable Development Studies of the University of Amsterdam in the Netherlands.

Daniel Robinson is a Senior Lecturer and Program Director of the Masters of Environmental Management in the School of Biological, Earth and Environmental Sciences at the University of New South Wales (UNSW), Sydney, Australia. He has written two books on biodiversity, biopiracy, and traditional knowledge protection, as well as dozens of academic papers. He regularly works for/with organizations including UNDP–GEF, ICTSD, the GIZ-led ABS Capacity Development Initiative, Natural Justice, and others.

Jeremy Walker is a Lecturer in the Social and Political Sciences program at the University of Technology Sydney, where he works on the sociology, history, and philosophy of economics and ecology. His current interests include the renaissance of aboriginal pyro-technologies, the history of artificial biospheres, and the anticipatory politics of industrial microbiology.

Index